The Poetry of Cooking

The Poetry of Cooking

John Ross

Front cover painting: Sharron Russell
Back cover photo: Sharron Russell

Printed in the United States of America

ISBN 978-0-692-51072-8

ACKNOWLEDGMENTS

Most of the recipes in this book were adapted from my column "North Fork Chef," which has appeared in the Suffolk Times and Riverhead News Review for the past 8 years. I am grateful for their permission to use these recipes in my book. I am especially grateful to Lauren Sisson, my editor at the Suffolk Times, who has given me constant support for this project.

I would like to thank my editor and producer, Chris Fleck, of Overlook Books in Huntington, NY. He was responsible for organizing, editing, and formatting this book. He has provided much needed professional advice and encouragement, along with just plain hard work.

In testing my recipes for my column and for this book, I have had help from many friends and family. First, my wife Lois has suffered through many attempts at perfecting a recipe, sometimes having to eat the same thing over and over. She also had to get used to having almost all of our food photographed.

My son Stewart and his wife Heather have been constant supporters, along with their very food-conscious daughters, Madison and Sailor. My son Sanford and family and my daughter Sarah and family live far away, but still have enjoyed dining with us when possible. My amateur chef friends Jay and Sarah Miller have joined me in cooking many of these recipes at their kitchen and at mine. Their expertise has been very valuable. Many other friends and neighbors, too many to name, have been guests to help me test my recipes.

Cooking has been like therapy to me, and dining with others a constant joy. I am thankful to have people to enjoy my artistry, and it is my wish that this book will help them enjoy the art of cooking and dining with their friends and loved ones.

— *John Ross*

FOREWORD

For many people, cooking is just an everyday necessity, but it is much more. There is a growing realization that our lifestyle, including what we eat, is the most important factor in long-term health and happiness. Like never before, we want to know where our food comes from – and what goes into it – before it reaches our table.

Cooking from scratch, using local ingredients when possible, is the best way to enjoy healthy eating and to share in the artistry of the chef. It takes a commitment to freshness and some planning ahead, but when the thought process for preparing a meal begins, so does the imagination, and the ordinary dinner has a chance of becoming something special – maybe even a poem.

Each month of the year, the cycle of holidays, availability of ingredients, tradition, special events, and the weather all offer culinary opportunities and challenges. And especially when we dine with friends and loved ones, the food becomes part of the conversation.

Once you approach food this way and work it into your daily schedule, you will discover – as I did – that cooking can be a deeply satisfying experience.

TABLE OF CONTENTS

January

— What Will You Feed Them? —
By Anne Marie Macari

Scraping corn till its milk covers
my hands. Silky pile of husks. Tomato,
rosemary, chives from the garden.
Dreaming back far into the flesh of the plant.

How we are plants grown awkward and strange.

We saw the tail hanging from the hawk's
beak as it flew off, an apple protruding
from the mouth of the deer.

I whisked and pounded, sifted
and sliced. It was mortar
for their bones. It was what
we found in the woods.
the egg that fit so well in my palm
and what came out of it.

Fire. Blood. Fungus.
Muscle. Marrow. Greens.
Nuts and garlic, wild carrot.

It's the food inside the food,
the invisible heart of the berry,
how it goes on beating
in the hallways of the body.

When the Complete comes to find me
The one question will be, What did
you feed them? As if I could
remember the colors arranged

just so, the balance, a lifetime
of salt thrown into the pot
and whirling there. As if each
bite was language broken
down in the mouth, each word

tasting of its sour its bitter
its sweet, to stem the craving.
What we swallowed all those years –

Platter of distress, bowl
of hope. What I chewed – my own
fingers and life. What did you feed them?

I fed them love. What did you feed them?
Love and bones, gristle,
sermons, air, mercy,

rain, ice, terror and soup, anger and dandelion
and love. What did

You feed them? Go to sleep
in the straw and when you wake up
I will give you something warm in a cup,

I will mix it myself, and when the Complete
finally comes for me I'll have water
hot on the stove, the tea

just right, I'll say I've sucked
the bread of this life
but I'm never full, I'll go
with my mouth open –

Health and fitness are always the theme for January after we have just finished a long stretch of holiday celebrations. But what constitutes healthy eating has evolved in the minds of consumers as well as the scientific community, and it is difficult to change habits that we have had for years.

From 1956 until 1992 the USDA recommended its "Basic Four" food groups. These included vegetables and fruits; milk; meat; and cereals and breads. In 1992 the USDA introduced the food guide pyramid, which prioritized our eating by letting us have unlimited quantities of healthy foods at the bottom while showing foods to avoid at the top. In 2005 this pyramid was revised, and added daily exercise as part of a healthy diet.

In 2011, the USDA simplified its recommendations with a graphic called "My Plate." Currently, the most sophisticated advice comes from the Harvard School of Public Health. It is similar to the government version except that it limits dairy and emphasizes healthy oils, whole grains, and lean protein. It also says to stay active. The message to people who love food, but wish to stay healthy, is moderation and lots of variety. I also believe that fresh, unprocessed foods grown close to home are the best choice for a healthy lifestyle.

January is a time to use the fruits and vegetables from warmer climates while the North Fork is in hibernation. Our January menu and recipes are examples of a nice balance between what is good for you and what you can love.

Prime Meal

Guacamole and Pomegranate with Arugula

Asian-Style Roasted Haddock with Red Lentil Risotto and Stir-Fried Vegetables

Mango Pineapple Granita

Recommended wine: *Gruner Veltliner or Dry Riesling*

Selected recipes

1. *Mediterranean Chicken with Farfalle pasta*
2. *Southwestern Shrimp Enchiladas*
3. *Ragout of Black Beans, Quinoa, Corn, and Shrimp*
4. *Arctic Char with Avocado Remoulade Sauce*
5. *Oven-fried Seafood Platter with Sweet potato and Greens*
6. *Skirt Steak with Refried Black Beans and Avocado/Tomatillo/Tequila Sauce*
7. *Three-Bean Vegetarian Chili*
8. *Turkey Chili Con Carne*
9. *Vegetarian Stuffed Cabbage*

PRIME MEAL

– *First Course* –
Guacamole and Pomegranate with Arugula

4 to 6 portions

4 ripe avocados
2 limes, juice and zest

1 jalapeno pepper
¼ cup chopped cilantro
½ cup minced red onion
½ tsp kosher salt
¼ tsp ground pepper
Dash Tabasco sauce

Seeds of **1** pomegranate

1 pkg. baby arugula
Blue corn tortilla chips

1. Cut avocados in half lengthwise and twist to separate halves. Remove the seeds with the point of a knife. Score the flesh with a paring knife into ½" squares. Remove the flesh with a tablespoon, scooping between flesh and skin. Place diced avocado in a bowl and toss gently with the lime juice and zest.

2. Cut the jalapeno in half and scrape out the seeds. Rinse, mince finely, and add to the avocado mixture. Add the cilantro, red onion, salt, pepper, and Tabasco sauce.

3. Cut the pomegranate in half across the middle and scoop out the seeds and pulp into a large bowl of cold water. Separate the seeds from the pulp with your fingers, letting the pulp float to the top. Pick out and discard as much pulp as possible and strain the seeds. Fold the seeds into the avocado mixture.

4. Dip the arugula in cold water to wash and dry in a salad spinner. Portion out onto salad plates and place the guacamole on top. Garnish with the tortilla chips and a wedge of lime.

– *Entrée* –
Asian-Style Roasted Haddock
with Red Lentil Risotto and Stir-Fried Vegetables

4 portions

1½ lbs haddock fillet

Marinade
2 Tbsp soy sauce
1 tsp sugar
1 tbsp minced garlic
1 tsp grated ginger
1 Tbsp rice wine vinegar
1 Tbsp sesame oil
½ tsp ground pepper

Lentil Risotto
I cup red lentils
2 Tbsp canola oil
¼ cup minced shallots
1 cup chopped red pepper
1 cup white wine
1½ cups chicken stock
1 tsp kosher salt
½ tsp ground pepper

Cooking the Haddock
1 Tbsp Dijon mustard
½ cup panko crumbs

Stir-Fried Vegetables
1 Tbsp sesame oil
1 Tbsp canola oil
1 tsp minced ginger
2 tsp minced garlic
½ cup chopped green onions
1 cup thinly sliced carrots
1 cup snow peas
2 cups chopped baby bok choy
1 can (8oz) sliced water chestnuts
1 Tbsp soy sauce
2 Tbsp chopped cilantro
1 lemon, juice and zest

1. Cut the haddock into 4 equal portions and check for bones. Place the fish in a shallow casserole and refrigerate (you can substitute cod for this recipe).

2. Combine the soy sauce, sugar, garlic, ginger, vinegar, oil, and pepper to make a marinade. Pour this over the haddock and refrigerate 2 hours.

3. Rinse the lentils and drain. Heat a saucepan and add the canola oil. Stir in the shallots and red pepper, cook briefly, and add the lentils. Stir them to coat with oil. Add the wine and let it reduce until pan is almost dry.

4. Heat the chicken stock in a small pan and remove from the heat. Begin adding it to the lentil mixture one ladle at a time. Cook at medium heat and let each ladle of stock evaporate before adding more. Stir continuously with a wooden spoon until the lentils are tender, about 20 minutes. Add the salt and pepper and taste for seasoning.

5. Line a small sheet pan with foil and spray with no-stick. Heat the oven to 425 degrees. Remove the haddock from the marinade, dry with paper towels, and place on the sheet pan. Brush the top of each fillet with the mustard and sprinkle on the panko crumbs. Roast in the oven for 15 minutes, or until it turns opaque and just flakes apart.

6. Heat a large sauté pan and add the sesame and canola oil. When hot, add the garlic, ginger, onions, carrots, snow peas, bok choy and water chestnuts. Cook at high heat, tossing the vegetables to prevent burning. Add the soy sauce, cilantro, and lemon and remove from the heat.

7. To serve, place the risotto in the center of the plate and lay the haddock on top. Arrange the stir-fried vegetables around the fish and pour the sauce on top.

– Dessert –
Mango-Pineapple Granita

2 ripe mangos

2 cups fresh pineapple
1 cup orange juice
½ cup honey
2 limes, juice and zest

Mint leaves for garnish

1. Peel the mangos and slice off the flesh in large pieces. Chop coarsely and place in the bowl of a food processor.

2. Cut the top and bottom off of a fresh pineapple. Place on a cutting board and cut into quarters. Peel the outside skin and cut out the inside core. Dice the flesh and add 2 cups of it to the food processor. Add the orange juice, honey, and lime juice and zest to the processor also. Blend until smooth and transfer to a shallow glass casserole.

3. Put the mixture in the freezer for 1 hour. Remove and scrape into small crystals with a dinner fork and put back in the freezer. Repeat this procedure 2 more times, or until crystals are uniform and hard. Serve in stemmed glasses and garnish with mint leaves.

– Wine Notes –
This is a healthy meal with some citrus and Asian flavors, but not a lot of spice. A clean, crisp Gruner Veltliner or a dry Riesling would be my first choice. An off-dry Riesling would also work.

Mediterranean Chicken with Farfalle Pasta

4 portions

1½ lbs Boneless, skinless chicken breasts
2 tsp kosher salt
1 tsp ground pepper
1 cup flour

3 Tbsp olive oil

1 bunch green onions, sliced
4 cloves garlic, minced
1 pkg. baby bella mushrooms, quartered
1 pkg. frozen artichoke hearts
1 cup white wine

1 cup chicken stock

1 Tbsp cornstarch
2 Tbsp cold water
½ cup pitted Kalamata olives
1 cup grape tomatoes, halved
¼ cup chopped basil

1 bunch broccoli rabe, coarsely chopped
1 pkg. farfalle pasta
½ cup grated Parmigiano-Reggiano cheese

1. Cut the chicken breasts into uniform 2" chunks. Add the flour to a bowl along with the salt and pepper. Toss the chicken in the flour and set aside.

2. Heat the olive oil in a large sauté pan and add the chicken. Cook in batches at high heat to brown. Do not crowd the pan. Remove the chicken and set aside. It should be a little underdone.

3. Reduce the heat and add the green onions and garlic, adding a little more oil if necessary. Turn up the heat and add the mushrooms. When they have browned, add the artichoke hearts and the white wine.

4. Let the wine reduce for 3 minutes, turn down the heat, and add the chicken stock. Add back the chicken and continue cooking until chicken is fully cooked, about 5 minutes.

5. Dissolve the cornstarch in the water and add to the pan. Bring to a boil to slightly thicken and add the olives, grape tomatoes, and basil. Check for seasoning and remove from the heat.

6. Bring 3 quarts of water to a boil in a large pasta pot and add the farfalle. When it is almost cooked, add the chopped broccoli rabe to the same pot. Cook another 3 minutes and drain. Combine with the chicken mixture and serve. Garnish with Parmigiano-Reggiano cheese and basil.

*– **Wine Notes** –*
This is an everyday "go to" meal that is quick to prepare and very popular. An Italian Pinot Grigio would fit this profile. Also consider a Friulano from Northern Italy or from Long Island's South Fork.

Southwestern Shrimp Enchiladas

4 to 6 portions

Red Pepper Cilantro Sauce

2 red bell peppers
2 poblano peppers
1 jalapeno pepper
1 red onion

12 sundried tomatoes
½ cup pine nuts
1 cup chopped cilantro
1 Tbsp minced garlic
3 (jarred) chipotle peppers
 in adobo sauce
1 lemon, juice and zest
2 tsp kosher salt
1 tsp ground pepper

1. Line a sheet pan with foil and spray with no-stick. Place the whole red peppers, poblano peppers, and jalapeno pepper on the sheet pan. Peel the onion, slice into thick slices, and place on the sheet pan. Roast using the broiler setting on your oven. As the peppers blacken, turn them with tongs to blacken all sides.

2. Remove the peppers, wrap loosely in foil, and let rest for 15 minutes to cool. Cut the roasted onion into chunks and place them in the bowl of a food processor. Scrape the black skin off of the peppers, cut them open, and remove the seeds. Cut them into 2-inch pieces and add to the food processor.

3. Place the sundried tomatoes in a bowl of hot water to hydrate for 5 minutes, then add them to the food processor. Toast the pine nuts for 3 minutes in a dry sauté pan over medium heat before adding them to the processor. Add the cilantro, garlic, jarred chipotle peppers, and lemon juice and zest. Season with the salt and pepper, and pulse the food processor until all ingredients are blended together, but the chunky texture remains.

Shrimp and Corn Tortillas

1 lb jumbo shrimp,
 in the shell
2 tsp kosher salt

12 corn tortillas
2 Tbsp olive oil
4 oz Monterey Jack cheese
4 oz Cheddar cheese
¼ cup chopped cilantro
½ cup sour cream

1. Bring 2 quarts of water to a boil and add the salt. Add the shrimp and bring back to a boil. Drain the shrimp, cool under cold water, and peel and devein. Slice them into halves lengthwise and set aside.

2. Line a sheet pan with foil. Brush the tortillas with oil on both sides and lay out on the sheet pan. Place in a 400 degree oven for about 3 minutes to soften them up. Remove and stack on a plate.

3. Lay out 6 tortillas on a foil-lined sheet pan and spread ¾ of the red pepper cilantro sauce over them. Arrange the sliced shrimp on top of the sauce and lay the other tortilla over them. Spoon the rest of the sauce on the top.

4. Grate the Monterey Jack and cheddar cheese on the large holes of a box grater. Sprinkle the cheese on top of the tortillas. Cover the sheet pan loosely with foil and heat for 10 minutes in the 400 degree oven. Garnish with the chopped cilantro and sour cream.

– Wine Notes –
A German Kabinett Riesling or an off-dry Riesling from Long Island

Mediterranean Chicken with Farfalle

Southwestern Shrimp Enchiladas

Ragout of Black Beans, Quinoa, Corn, and Shrimp

4 to 6 portions

1 lb dried black beans

---

1 lb jumbo shrimp
2 Tbsp butter
1 Tbsp canola oil
2 Tbsp minced garlic
2 Tbsp minced shallots

---

1 cup uncooked white quinoa
1 cup chopped onion
2 cups chicken stock
2 tsp ground cumin
¼ tsp cayenne pepper
1 tsp black pepper
2 tsp kosher salt

---

1 pkg. frozen corn
1 lemon, juice and zest
½ cup chopped cilantro

1. Rinse the beans, cover with cold water, and soak overnight. Alternatively, place the beans in a soup pot and add 2 quarts of water. Bring to a boil, cover, remove from the heat, and let sit for 1 hour.

2. Drain the beans and put back in a soup pot with 6 cups of water. Simmer until just tender, about 45 minutes.
   Note: *substitute two 15oz. cans of black beans if desired.*

3. Peel and devein the shrimp, removing the tails. Place a large, shallow saucepan on low heat and add the butter and oil. Add the garlic, shallots, and shrimp and continue cooking at low heat until the shrimp turn opaque, about 10 minutes.

4. Remove the shrimp and set aside. Add the quinoa and the onions and turn up the heat to medium. Pour in the chicken stock, cumin, cayenne, salt, and pepper and bring to a boil. Lower the heat and simmer for 20 minutes.

5. Add the cooked quinoa mixture to the black beans. Stir in the frozen corn and simmer for 5 minutes. Add the reserved shrimp, lemon juice and zest, and cilantro. Check for seasoning and serve.

Arctic Char with Avocado Remoulade Sauce and Wilted Spinach

4 portions

1½ lbs arctic char fillets
1 tsp kosher salt
½ tsp ground pepper

Avocado Remoulade Sauce
2 ripe avocados
2 limes, juice plus **1 tsp** zest
¼ cup extra virgin olive oil
2 Tbsp minced shallots
2 Tbsp chopped cilantro
1 tsp Dijon mustard
1 tsp kosher salt
½ tsp ground pepper

Final cooking
1 pkg baby spinach
2 Tbsp olive oil

1. Cut arctic char into 4 equal portions. Leave the skin on if desired. Season the fillets with the salt and pepper and set aside.

2. Cut the avocados in half and remove the seeds with the tip of a knife. Score the flesh with a paring knife and scoop it out with a spoon. Put the avocado flesh in the bowl of a food processor along with the lime juice and zest.

3. Process until smooth and drizzle in the olive oil. Place this mixture in a bowl and fold in the shallots, cilantro, mustard, salt, and pepper.

4. Wash the spinach in cold water and drain. Heat a shallow saucepan and add the wet spinach. Cover and cook until wilted, about 3 minutes. Drain and place on 4 dinner plates.

5. Heat a large sauté pan and add the olive oil. When it shimmers, add the arctic char fillets, being careful not to crowd. Cook quickly, turning once with a total cooking time of about 5 minutes. Serve on top of the spinach with the avocado remoulade sauce on the side.

> *– Wine Notes –*
> *The delicate flavor and texture of Arctic Char and the light, flavorful sauce require a clean, crisp white wine. An Albarino from Spain or the North Fork, a Sauvignon Blanc, or a stainless steel Chardonnay would all work well.*

Oven-Fried Seafood Platter with Sweet Potato and Greens

4 to 6 portions

Breaded Seafood

12 jumbo shrimp,
    in the shell

¾ lb bay scallops
4 small flounder filets
½ pint shucked oysters
2 cups flour
1 Tbsp kosher salt
2 tsp ground pepper
1 tsp Old Bay seasoning
2 cups buttermilk
4 cups matzo meal

1. Peel and butterfly the shrimp by making a deep cut down the center and removing the vein. Remove the tails if desired.

2. Set up a breading station by placing the flour, salt, pepper, and Old Bay in a shallow pan. Put the buttermilk in a bowl and the matzo meal in another pan. Toss the shrimp in the seasoned flour. Dip each piece in the buttermilk, then flatten it into the matzo meal and set aside. Repeat with all the seafood, changing the breading if it becomes too chunky and moist.

3. Close to service time, line a sheet pan with foil and spray it with no-stick. Place the empty sheet pan in a 425 degree oven for 5 minutes. Remove the pan and quickly add the breaded seafood, spraying it with no-stick before putting it back in the hot oven. Cook about 15 minutes, or until seafood is lightly browned and cooked through.

Sweet Potato and Greens

4 medium-size sweet
    potatoes

1 head kale
1 head collard greens
1 head mustard greens
2 Tbsp canola oil
1 tsp kosher salt
1 tsp ground pepper
1 tsp minced garlic

1. Scrub the sweet potatoes, spray with no-stick and place on a small sheet pan. Roast in a 425 degree oven for 45 minutes to an hour, or until a skewer runs through them easily.

2. Slice the leaves from the stems of the kale, collard greens, and mustard greens. Do this by running a sharp paring knife along the stem from bottom to the top of the stem. Put all of the leaves in a sink of cold water and wash thoroughly. Lift them out of the water and cut into bite-sized pieces. Add the canola oil, salt, pepper, and garlic to a large bowl and toss the greens into it (the greens do not need to be dry).

3. Close to service time, line a sheet pan with foil and spray it with no-stick. Place in a 425 degree oven for 5 minutes. Remove and quickly place all of the greens on the hot pan (if crowded, use two pans or do two batches). Plavce back in the oven and bake about 15 minutes. The greens will be brown on the edges and a little crisp.

Accompanying Sauces

Tartar Sauce

1½ cups mayonnaise
2 Tbsp chopped dill pickle
2 Tbsp minced shallots
2 minced anchovies
1 Tbsp capers
1 tsp dry mustard
1 Lemon, juice and zest
½ tsp pepper
½ tsp sugar
2 Tbsp chopped parsley
1 Tbsp chopped fresh tarragon

Place the mayonnaise in a bowl. Stir in the dill pickle, minced shallot, minced anchovies, capers, and dry mustard. Remove the zest and juice from the lemon and add to the bowl. Season with the pepper and sugar. Stir in the chopped parsley and chopped fresh tarragon (makes 2 cups).

Red Pepper Aioli Sauce

4 cloves garlic
1 tbsp bread crumbs
1 tbsp red wine vinegar
2 egg yolks
¾ cup extra virgin olive oil
½ tsp salt
pinch of cayenne pepper
1 small jar roasted red peppers
1 Tbsp lemon juice

Mince garlic as fine as possible and combine with bread crumbs and red wine vinegar in a food processor. Add egg yolks and pulse while drizzling in the olive oil. Season with the salt and cayenne pepper. Drain the roasted red peppers, chop coarsely, and add to the processor. Add the lemon juice, pulse until blended, and remove (makes 1 cup).

Avocado Sauce

½ cup chopped shallots
1 Tbsp minced garlic
1 Tbsp olive oil
¼ cup chopped parsley
1 lemon, juice and zest
1 diced avocado

Coarsely chop the shallots and garlic and place them in a food processor. Pulse until finely chopped, and add the olive oil. Add the parsley and continue processing. Remove the zest and juice from the lemon and add. Cut the avocado in half, remove the pit, score the flesh with a paring knife, and remove with a spoon. Add the avocado to the processor and pulse until combined. Pulse in the salt and cayenne pepper, and taste for seasoning (makes 1 cup).

– Wine Notes –
Breaded seafood, even though it is not deep-fried, requires a full bodied white wine. A barrel fermented Chardonnay from Long Island would be my first choice.

Skirt Steak with Refried Black Beans and Avocado/Tomatillo/Tequila Sauce

4 portions

1½ lbs skirt steak
1 tsp kosher salt
½ tsp ground pepper

Refried Beans
2 cans (15 oz) black beans
    with juice
2 cloves garlic, minced
¼ tsp dried oregano
⅛ tsp ground cumin
3 minced green onions
1 tsp chili powder
1 tsp kosher salt
½ tsp ground pepper

¼ cup chopped cilantro
2 Tbsp minced red onion

Avocado/Tomatillo/Tequila Sauce
2 cups water
3 tomatillos
1 avocado
1 lime, zest and juice
2 Tbsp tequila
1 jalapeno pepper, seeds
    removed, minced
¼ cup chopped cilantro
1 tsp kosher salt

1. Sprinkle steaks with salt and pepper and refrigerate.

2. Place the black beans along with their juice in a large saucepan. Add the garlic, oregano, cumin, green onions, chili powder, salt, and pepper to the pan and mash them by hand with a potato masher.

3. Place the saucepan on the stove and bring to a boil. Reduce the heat to low and cook, stirring, until the mixture thickens, about 15 minutes. Stir in the cilantro and red onions and keep warm.

4. For the sauce, bring the water to a boil in a saucepan. Remove the husks from the tomatillos and plunge them into the boiling water for 2 minutes. Remove, drain, and run under cold water. Remove the cores, cut into quarters, and place in the bowl of a food processor.

5. Cut the avocado in half, remove the seed, and scoop the flesh into the food processor. Add the tomatillos, the lime zest and juice, tequila, jalapeno pepper, cilantro, and salt. Process until smooth and transfer to a bowl.

6. At service time, heat a grill pan to very hot, spray the steaks with no-stick, and cook at high heat until rare, about 3 minutes per side. Remove and let rest in a warm place for 10 minutes. Carve the steak across the grain into thin strips and serve over the black beans with the sauce on the side.

– Wine Notes –
A Spanish Rioja Crianza would be a good choice for an inexpensive red wine with enough structure to match this meal. A little more tannic Malbec would also be a good choice.

— If This Be Heaven, Pass The Chili —
By F. Jackrabbit McMurry

I reckon time's about to run out –
Time to think what life's about,
Lookin' back on where I've rode
And all the wild oats I've done sowed.

I've been stomped and I've been throwed
By the meanest horses ever knowed.
I swam the river when it flowed,
I heard the rooster when he crowed.

I tasted dust along life's road,
And felt the cold wind when it blowed.
Thru eatin', drinkin', actin' silly,
This cowboy found the taste of chili.

No other food can bring the bliss
Of rapture like a lover's kiss;
But most folks fear the mighty pepper,
Which ain't no hill for a manly stepper.

The best durned chili I ever knowed
Was thick and red, so that it glowed.
For all the charms that chili's got,
It still ain't nuthin' if it ain't hot.

You want a bowl? Well, now you got'er:
You're healthier, happier, and hot-to-trotter;
The fire in your belly'll change your heart,
And make you smile and sing and smart.

And when we get to rainbow's end,
That pot ain't gold, it's chili, friend –
That's where we'll find eternal pleasure,
So I'm gone to claim the cowboy's treasure.

But I ain't leavin' till I've been fed
A final bowl of Texas red.
It's no use now to gild the lily –
If this be heaven, then pass the chili.

Three-Bean Vegetarian Chili

8 to 10 portions

1 lb dried black beans
1 lb dried pinto beans
1 lb dried kidney beans

---

3 cups water
1 cup coarse cornmeal
  or grits

---

2 Tbsp canola oil
1 large onion, chopped
1 green pepper, seeded and
  chopped
1 red pepper, seeded and
  chopped
1 jalapeno pepper, seeded
  and minced
2 Tbsp minced garlic
4 cups vegetable stock
1 can crushed San Marzano
  tomatoes

---

1 cup sundried tomatoes,
  chopped
½ cup chopped cilantro
2 Tbsp honey
¼ cup red wine vinegar
1 Tbsp ground cumin
¼ cup chili powder
¼ tsp hot red pepper flakes
1 Tbsp kosher salt

1. Rinse all the beans in cold water and combine in a large soup pot. Cover with cold water 4" over the beans and refrigerate overnight.

2. Drain the beans in a colander and place in a large soup pot. Cover with water 2" above the beans and bring to a boil. Simmer, uncovered, until tender, about 1 hour.

3. Bring 3 cups of water to a boil in a small saucepan and add the cornmeal. Cook, stirring, for 5 minutes, cover, and remove from the heat.

4. Heat a large soup pot and add the oil. Stir in the onions, green and red peppers, the jalapeno, and the garlic. Cook at low heat for 10 minutes and turn up the heat to medium. Add the vegetable stock and the crushed tomatoes and continue cooking.

5. Stir in the sundried tomatoes, cilantro, honey, vinegar, cumin, chili powder, red pepper flakes, and salt. Bring to a simmer and add the cooked beans. Continue cooking at low heat for 30 minutes to blend the flavors. Stir in the cooked cornmeal and check for seasoning.

Optional Chili Garnishes

Sliced avocado, chopped red onion, chopped cilantro, sour cream, and shredded cheddar cheese are traditional garnishes for chili.

– Beverage Notes –
A local craft beer is my first choice for chili. For a wine, a Cabernet Franc from Long Island would be very good.

Turkey Chili Con Carne

4 to 6 portions

1 lb dried kidney beans

---

2 Tbsp olive oil
1 large onion, chopped
1 red bell pepper, seeded and chopped
1 green bell pepper, seeded and chopped
1 jalapeno pepper, seeded and minced
2 Tbsp minced garlic

---

2 Tbsp chili powder
1 Tbsp ground cumin
¼ tsp hot red pepper flakes
1 Tbsp dried oregano
1 Tbsp kosher salt
½ tsp Tabasco sauce

1½ lbs ground turkey
1 can crushed San Marzano tomatoes
2 Tbsp tomato paste
2 Tbsp red wine vinegar

1. Soak the beans overnight in cold water to cover.

2. Drain the beans and place in a soup pot. Cover with water 2" over the beans and bring to a boil. Simmer until tender, about 45 minutes, and drain.

3. Heat a Dutch oven and add the olive oil. Add the onion, red and green peppers, the jalapeno pepper, and the garlic. Cook at low heat for 5 minutes.

4. Combine the chili powder, cumin, red pepper flakes, oregano, salt, and Tabasco in a small bowl. Stir them into the chili mixture and continue to cook at low heat.

5. Raise the heat and add the ground turkey, breaking it up with a wooden spoon as it cooks. When the turkey turns brown, add the tomatoes and the tomato paste. Fold in the cooked kidney beans and let the chili simmer at low heat for 30 minutes. Add the vinegar and check for seasoning.

Oven-fried Seafood Platter

Turky Chili con Carne

Vegetarian Stuffed Cabbage

6 to 8 portions

1 head green cabbage

1 cup brown rice
3 cups water
1 cup red lentils
3 cups water

2 Tbsp canola oil
1 onion, chopped
1 leek, white part, sliced
1 Tbsp minced garlic
1 red pepper, seeded and chopped

1 cup dry roasted peanuts
1 cup dried apricots, diced
2 eggs, lightly beaten
¼ cup chopped cilantro
1 tsp turmeric
1 tsp ground cumin
¼ tsp hot red pepper flakes
1 Tbsp kosher salt
1 tsp ground pepper

1 Tbsp ground cinnamon
2 cups tomato puree
1 cup vegetable stock

1. Remove the outside leaves of the cabbage and cut the core out with a sharp knife. Bring 4 quarts of water to a boil in a large stock pot. Put the cabbage in the boiling water, cover, and cook for 5 minutes.

2. Remove the cabbage with a big fork and place it in a colander. Remove the outer leaves and place the cabbage back in the boiling water. Cook another 3 minutes and remove. Take more leaves off and repeat if necessary. Reserve the inner core for the stuffing.

3. Cook the brown rice in a small saucepan in 3 cups of water for 45 minutes and drain. Cook the red lentils in 3 cups of water in another small saucepan for 20 minutes and drain.

4. Heat a large sauté pan and add the canola oil. Add the onion, leek, garlic, and chopped red pepper.

5. Chop the peanuts coarsely and add to the vegetables. Chop the apricots and add to the vegetables. Combine the cooked rice and lentils with the vegetable mixture. Stir in the lightly beaten eggs and season with the cilantro, turmeric, cumin, red pepper flakes, salt, and pepper.

6. Place a cabbage leaf on a cutting board and cut out the hard area around the core. Place about ¼ cup of filling in the center of the cabbage leaf and fold over the edges. Roll it up tight to make a sealed envelope. Repeat until all the filling is used.

7. Chop 2 cups of leftover cabbage from the inner core and place it in the bottom of a casserole. Place the stuffed cabbage rolls on top. Add the ground cinnamon to the tomato puree and vegetable stock and pour over the cabbage in the casserole. Cover with foil and bake in a 350 degree oven for 45 minutes. Garnish with sour cream or Greek yogurt if desired.

February

— Linguini —
By Diane Lockward

It was always linguini between us.
Linguini with white sauce, or
red sauce, sauce with basil snatched
from the garden, oregano rubbed between
our palms, a single bay leaf adrift amidst
plum tomatoes. Linguini with meatballs,
sausage, a side of brascioli. Like lovers
trying positions, we enjoyed it every way
we could – artichokes, mushrooms, little
neck clams, mussels, and calamari – linguini
twining and braiding us each to each.
Linguini knew of the kisses, the smooches,
the molti baci. It was never spaghetti
between us, not cappellini, nor farfalle,
vermicelli, pappardelle, fettucini, perciatelli,
or even tagliarini. Linguini we stabbed, pitched,
and twirled on forks, spun round and round
on silver spoons. Long, smooth, and always
al dente.
 In dark trattorias, we broke crusty panera,
toasted each other – La dolce vita! – and sipped
Amarone, wrapped ourselves in linguini,
briskly boiled, lightly oiled, salted, and lavished
with sauce. Bellissimo, paradisio, belle gente!
Linguini witnessed our slurping, pulling, and
sucking, our unraveling and raveling, chins
glistening, napkins tucked like bibs in collars,
linguini stuck to lips, hips, and bellies, cheeks
flecked with formaggio – parmesan, romano,
and shaved pecorino – strands of linguini flung
around our necks like two fine silk scarves.

February begins with Super Bowl Sunday. This NFL game has outgrown normal sports events and has emerged as an unofficial American holiday. The pregame shows, the parties, the half time show, and the commercials all contribute to a full day of festivities. What began with chicken wings and chips has now evolved into game-time food that is better than the game itself.

February is also when we celebrate Valentine's Day. Valentine's is a time to celebrate love, either as a romantic couple, or as a group of friends. Food is always at the heart of it. If you go out to one of our fine restaurants, it is often for a special dinner – and if you stay in to cook, it is time for something elegant. Our Prime Meal for this month requires a little work ahead of time cutting the meat and preparing the stock, but the end product of veal tournedos with demi-glace is a culinary masterpiece that will give you and your loved ones a deep sense of satisfaction and pride.

Prime Meal

"Russian" Shrimp Cocktail

Tournedos of Veal with Roasted Fingerling Potatoes and Green Beans

---

Chocolate Fondue

Recommended wine: *Vodka or Champagne first, then a Bordeaux or Bordeaux blend*

Selected Recipes

1. *Super Bowl Food:*
   - *Homemade Soft Pretzels*
   - *Pickled Vegetables with Hummus*
   - *Gravlax with Deviled Eggs and Caviar*
   - *Swedish Meatballs*
2. *Linguine with Clam Sauce*
3. *Seafood Fra Diavolo with Linguine*
4. *Veal Saltimbocca with Linguine*
5. *Seafood Pot Pie*
6. *Chocolate Ganache Cupcakes*
7. *White Veal Stew (Blanquette de Veau)*

PRIME MEAL

– First Course –
"Russian" Shrimp Cocktail

8 portions

1½ lbs jumbo shrimp, in the shell
1½ cups vodka
1 lemon
1 tsp kosher salt
¼ tsp red pepper flakes

Beet Salad
2 lbs large winter beets
2 Tbsp balsamic vinegar
2 Tbsp fresh grated horse-radish
1 red onion, peeled and thinly sliced
1 tsp kosher salt
½ tsp ground pepper

Horseradish Sauce
½ cup sour cream
1 Tbsp mayonnaise
2 Tbsp fresh grated horse-radish
1 Tbsp Dijon mustard
Few drops Tabasco sauce
2 Tbsp chopped dill

1 head Boston lettuce

1. Place a saucepan on the stove and add the vodka. Cut the lemon in half, squeeze the juice into the pan, and add the rind. Add the salt and red pepper flakes along with the shrimp. If necessary, add a little water to just cover the shrimp.

2. Bring to a boil and remove from the heat. Cover and let the shrimp steep in the vodka for 5 minutes. Remove the shrimp and refrigerate. Boil the cooking liquid for another 5 minutes, strain, and cool. Peel and devein the shrimp, leaving the tails on.

3. Wash and dry the beets, spray them with no-stick, and wrap loosely in foil. Place on a sheet pan and roast in a 400 degree oven until a skewer goes through them easily, about 1 hour.

4. Remove the beets from the oven, cool slightly, and slip the skins off. Cut the beets into ¼" thick rounds. Using a heart-shaped cookie cutter, cut out 8 hearts from the largest slices. Cut the remaining beets into ¼" thick "matchsticks."

5. Combine the balsamic vinegar, horseradish, onion, salt, and pepper in a large bowl. Add the beets, toss gently, and refrigerate.

6. Make a sauce by combining the sour cream, mayonnaise, horseradish, mustard, Tabasco, and dill. Stir in 2 Tbsp. of the reserved poaching liquid.

7. Wash the Boston lettuce, separating the leaves, and dry in a salad spinner. Line 8 small plates with the lettuce and place the beet salad in the center. Arrange the shrimp around the beets and put a beet heart on top. Spoon a little sauce on the side and pass the rest.

"Russian" Shrimp Cocktail

Brown veal stock

– Entrée –
Tournedos of Veal with Bordelaise Sauce, Roasted Fingerling Potatoes and Green Beans

8 portions

Preparing the meat

1 split rack of nature veal
8 sage leaves
2oz thinly sliced pancetta
2 tsp kosher salt
1 tsp ground pepper

Making the stock

1 onion, peeled and
    chopped
2 carrots, peeled and
    chopped
1 stalk celery, chopped

4 sprigs fresh thyme
6 parsley stems
1 bay leaf
1 leek, white part, split
2 Tbsp tomato paste
6 whole peppercorns

Making the sauce

1 cup red wine
½ cup minced shallots
4 whole peppercorns
1 bay leaf
2 Tbsp cold butter

1. Using a stiff, sharp, boning knife, cut the meat from the rib bones by cutting parallel to the bone. After trimming the excess fat and silverskin it will resemble a small beef tenderloin. Cut the meat crosswise into 8 small filets about 2" thick (ask your butcher to do this if desired).

2. Place a sage leaf on the side of each veal filet and wrap a piece of pancetta around it. Secure by tying with a piece of string. Sprinkle the salt and pepper on the meat and refrigerate.

3. Cut the reserved rib bones apart and place them in a roasting pan along with any scraps of meat left from trimming. Brown in a 425 degree oven for 30 minutes. Add the onion, carrots, and celery and continue cooking for another 30 minutes.

4. Remove the bones, put them into a stock pot, and barely cover with cold water. Place the roasting pan on the stove and add 1 cup of water. Turn up the heat and deglaze the pan by scraping up all the drippings with a wooden spoon. Pour all of this liquid into the stock pot with the bones and bring it to a boil. Skim the surface for impurities, and reduce the heat to a simmer.

5. Tie the thyme, parsley stems, bay leaf, and leek together with string to make a bouquet garni. Place this in the stock pot along with the tomato paste and the peppercorns. Simmer for 6 hours and strain, then refrigerate overnight. The next day, remove the solid fat from the surface and bring the stock to a boil. Let it boil gently until reduced by half.

6. To finish the sauce, place the red wine in a saucepan with the shallots, peppercorns, and bay leaf. Let it boil until the wine is almost evaporated, then add to the reduced stock. Cook briefly and strain into a clean saucepan. Close to service time, swirl in the cold butter and serve.

7. Remove the veal from the refrigerator and bring to room temperature. Spray with no-stick and brown on a hot grill pan to make crosshatch marks on both sides. At service time, put the veal on a small sheet pan and place in a 425 degree oven for about 10 minutes, or until a meat thermometer reads 120 degrees internal temperature. Serve the meat with the Bordelaise sauce drizzled over it.

Note: *This stock and sauce preparation may seem like a lot of trouble to make, but it is well worth it. There is no commercial substitute for this kind of stock.*

<u>Roasted Fingerling Potatoes and Green Beans</u>

2 lbs fingerling potatoes
1½ lbs fresh green beans

¼ cup olive oil
2 Tbsp chopped rosemary
1 lemon, juice and zest
1 Tbsp kosher salt
2 tsp ground pepper

8 large white mushrooms
2 Tbsp butter

1. Rinse potatoes and cut large ones in half. Rinse the green beans and trim off the ends.

2. Combine in a large bowl the olive oil, rosemary, lemon juice and zest, salt, and pepper. Toss the potatoes in the oil mixture and transfer to a foil-lined sheet pan. Toss the beans in the oil mixture and place them on another foil-lined sheet pan.

3. Put the potatoes in a 400 degree oven until tender, about 45 minutes. Put the beans in the same oven in a single layer until brown and beginning to shrivel, about 25 minutes.

4. Trim the stems off the mushrooms and wipe off any dirt with a damp paper towel. Heat a sauté pan and add the butter. Place the mushroom caps top side down and cook until lightly browned, about 5 minutes. Turn and cook until fully cooked, about 5 minutes more. Serve on top of the veal filets.

Note: *For a fancy professional look, flute the mushrooms before cooking.*

– *Dessert* –
Chocolate Fondue

8 portions

1 cup heavy cream
24 oz bittersweet chocolate
2 Tbsp Amaretto liqueur
Assorted fresh and dried
   fruit – Fresh pineapple,
   strawberries, pears, mango,
   kiwi, dried apricots, candied
   ginger, etc.

1. Place the cream in a double boiler or heavy enamel-lined saucepan and heat until simmering. Stir in the chocolate until it melts, then stir in the Amaretto liqueur.

2. Transfer this mixture to a fondue pot (or just a warm bowl) and place the fruits around it. Using fondue forks, dip the fruits in the chocolate and enjoy.

– *Wine Notes* –
For this Valentine's celebration, begin with Champagne or other sparkling wine or with a Russian vodka. The entrée should be accompanied by a Bordeaux or a good quality Bordeaux blend.

Veal Tournedos

Seafood Fra Diavolo

SUPER BOWL FOOD

Homemade Soft Pretzels

8 pretzels

1½ cups warm water
   (110 degrees)
1 Tbsp sugar
1 pkg. active dry yeast
1 tsp salt
4 cups bread flour
4 Tbsp butter, melted

1 tsp canola oil

3 quarts water
½ cup baking soda

1 egg yolk
1 Tbsp water
1 Tbsp dry onion flakes
1 Tbsp kosher salt

1. Combine the warm water, sugar, yeast, and salt in the bowl of an electric mixer with a dough hook. With the mixer on low speed, add most of the flour and all of the melted butter. As the dough forms, gradually add the rest of the flour (add a little more flour if the dough doesn't come clean from the bowl). Continue mixing at medium speed for 10 minutes.

2. Remove the dough and place it in a clean bowl along with the oil. Cover with a towel and let the dough rise until double in bulk, about 1 hour.

3. Bring 3 quarts of water to a boil and set the oven for 450 degrees. Turn the dough out on a lightly floured surface and divide into 8 equal pieces. Roll each piece into a long rope about ¾" thick. Form the rope into a U shape, cross the ends over each other, and wrap them around to form a pretzel shape.

4. Add the baking soda to the boiling water. Plunge each pretzel into the water and let it cook for about 1 minute before removing with a slotted spoon. Place the pretzels on a parchment-lined sheet pan.

5. Make an egg wash with the yolk and water and brush it on the pretzels. Sprinkle the onion flakes and salt over the pretzels and bake at 450 degrees for 15 minutes. They should be golden brown and firm.

Soft Pretzels

Pickled Vegetables with Hummus

3 cups cider vinegar
3 cups water
1 cup sugar
¼ cup kosher salt
1 tsp crushed mustard seeds
½ tsp hot red pepper flakes

Assorted Vegetables:
  cauliflower, carrots, red and
  yellow bell peppers, celery,
  and broccoli
12 small beets
1 red onion, thinly sliced
1 Tbsp prepared horseradish

1. Heat the vinegar, water, sugar, salt, mustard seeds, and red pepper flakes in a saucepan. Bring to a boil and simmer for 15 minutes. Set aside.

2. Trim and cut the assorted vegetables into bite-sized pieces, but not too small. Bring 4 quarts of water to a boil in a large pasta pot and cook each vegetable separately, removing it with a slotted spoon when just cooked. Cook the beets with their skins on last, in the same water.

3. Place all the vegetables except the beets in a large stainless steel or glass bowl. Peel the beets, cut them into wedges, and place them in a separate bowl. Pour the pickling liquid over all the vegetables. Add the sliced onion and the horseradish to the beets. Marinate all the vegetables overnight in the refrigerator.
   Note: *add jarred pepperoncini and and whole sweet piquante peppers to the vegetables at serving time for extra flavor.*

Hummus

1 can (15 oz.) chick peas
¾ cup tahini
1 lemon, juice and zest
1 Tbsp minced garlic
¼ cup chicken stock
½ tsp kosher salt
Few drops Tabasco

Rinse the chick peas and place in the bowl of a food processor. Add the tahini, lemon juice and zest, garlic, chicken stock, salt, and Tabasco. Process until smooth and serve with pickled or raw vegetables.

Pickled Vegetables

Gravlax

1 boneless, skinless side of
   fresh salmon (2-3 lbs)
1 Tbsp whole black peppercorns
1 Tbsp coriander seeds
½ cup kosher salt
¾ cup sugar

2 bunches fresh dill
¼ cup vodka

Honey mustard
Capers

1. Purchase the fresh salmon 3 days before you plan to use it.

2. Crush the peppercorns and coriander seeds in a mortar and pestle (or with the flat blade of your chefs knife on a cutting board). Combine the peppercorns and coriander with the salt and sugar. Line a sheet pan with plastic film and place ⅓ of the salt mixture on the bottom.

3. Place the salmon on the salt mixture and spread the rest on top. Put the fresh dill on the salmon and moisten it with the vodka. Cover with more plastic film and weigh it down with a heavy pan or cans of food. Refrigerate 48 hours, turning the salmon over once and draining off excess liquid.

4. At service time, scrape off the brine and slice thinly on the bias. Garnish with honey mustard on the side and sprinkle capers over the salmon. Garnish with sprigs of dill.

Devilled Eggs and Salmon Caviar

1 dozen eggs

1 tsp Dijon mustard
1 tsp Worcestershire sauce
2 Tbsp mayonnaise
1 tsp kosher salt
Dash cayenne pepper

2 oz salmon caviar
Fresh dill

1. Add the eggs to a saucepan and cover with cold water. Bring to a boil, cover, and remove from the heat. Allow to rest for 15 minutes. Lift them out of the water and plunge them into ice water.

2. Peel the eggs and cut them in half lengthwise. Remove the yolks with the point of a small knife and place them in a bowl. Mash them with a dinner fork and stir in the mustard, Worcestershire, mayonnaise, salt, and cayenne.

3. Stuff the filling back into the egg whites and garnish them with the salmon caviar and a sprig of dill.

Devilled Eggs and Salmon Caviar

Swedish Meatballs

1 large onion, peeled
1 Tbsp butter

6 slices white bread
½ cup milk

1 lb ground beef
1 lb ground pork
2 eggs, beaten
1 tsp ground allspice
½ tsp ground cardamom
½ tsp ground nutmeg
1 Tbsp honey
1 Tbsp kosher salt
1 tsp ground pepper

Sauce
2 Tbsp butter
¼ cup flour
3 cups beef stock
1 cup sour cream
½ cup chopped dill

1. Grate the onion using the large holes of a box grater. Place the grated onion in a colander to drain excess juice. Heat a sauté pan and add the butter. Sauté the onion at medium heat until soft, about 3 minutes.

2. Remove the crusts from the bread and cut into small dice. Place the bread cubes in a bowl with the milk.

3. Combine the beef and pork in a large bowl. Add the sautéed onions and the soaked bread along with the beaten eggs, allspice, cardamom, nutmeg, honey, salt, and pepper. Mash the meatball mixture together with your hands.

4. Line a sheet pan with foil and spray with no-stick. Roll the meatballs into the size of a golf ball and place them on the sheet pan in tight rows. Roast in a 350 degree oven for about 40 minutes, or until fully cooked in the center. Remove to a clean sheet pan with a slotted spoon.

5. For the sauce, melt the butter in a saucepan and stir in the flour. Cook for 3 minutes to make a roux. Whisk in the beef stock and bring to a boil. Lower the heat and fold in the sour cream. Pour the sauce over the meatballs and garnish with chopped dill.

Linguine with Clam Sauce

4 to 6 portions

2 dozen littleneck clams

2 Tbsp olive oil
4 cloves garlic, peeled and sliced
4 oz fresh chorizo sausage, diced

1 bunch green onions, trimmed and chopped
¼ tsp hot red pepper flakes
½ cup sundried tomatoes, sliced
4 fresh plum tomatoes, diced
1 cup white wine

1 Tbsp cornstarch

1 lb linguine
1 tsp kosher salt
1 bunch broccoli rabe
2 oz Parmigiano-Reggiano cheese

1. Scrub the clams under cold water and set aside.

2. Heat a large, shallow saucepan and add the olive oil. Add the sliced garlic and cook until it turns golden, about 2 minutes, and remove with a slotted spoon. Add the sausage and cook at medium heat for 10 minutes. Remove and set aside.

3. Add the green onions and the red pepper flakes and continue cooking. Stir in the sundried tomatoes, the diced fresh tomatoes, and the white wine.

4. Bring the mixture to a boil and add the clams. Cover and continue cooking at high heat until clams begin to open. As each clam opens, remove it with tongs and set aside. Dissolve the cornstarch in cold water and add to the sauce. Bring to a boil and reduce the heat to a simmer.

5. Bring 4 quarts of water to a boil in a pasta pot. Add the salt and the linguine. While the pasta cooks, wash the broccoli rabe, trim off the stems, and chop coarsely. Add it to the pasta just before the linguine is fully cooked. Boil another 2 minutes and drain.

6. To serve, portion out the pasta/broccoli mixture into 4-6 large pasta bowls. Ladle sauce over the pasta and arrange the clams around the edge of the bowl. Sprinkle the cooked garlic slices on top along with shaved parmesan cheese.

– Wine Notes –

A Muscadet from France's Loire Valley will add a briny, mineral feeling to complement the clams. An Albarino or a Sauvignon Blanc would also be good.

Seafood Fra Diavolo with Linguine

6 portions

1 lb jumbo shrimp,
  in the shell
½ lb fresh sea scallops
½ lb cleaned calamari,
  cut into rings
1 dozen littleneck clams
1 lb mussels

Seasoning mix
2 tsp kosher salt
1 tsp ground pepper
¼ tsp cayenne pepper
1 tsp garlic powder
1 tsp onion powder
1 tsp dried thyme
1 tsp dried oregano

Fra Diavolo Sauce
3 Tbsp olive oil
1 onion, peeled and chopped
1 red pepper, seeds removed,
  chopped
3 cloves minced garlic
1 cup white wine
1 can San Marzano tomatoes,
  chopped, with puree
¼ tsp hot red pepper flakes
½ cup chopped fresh basil

1 lb linguine
1 Tbsp kosher salt

1. Peel and devein the shrimp, removing the tails. Scrub the clams and mussels under cold water and set aside.

2. Combine the salt, pepper, cayenne pepper, garlic powder, onion powder, thyme, and oregano in a large bowl. Toss the shrimp, scallops, and calamari in this seasoning and set aside.

3. Heat a large, shallow saucepan and add the olive oil. Cooking at high heat, quickly brown the shrimp, scallops, and calamari in small batches, adding more olive oil if necessary. Do not crowd the seafood and be careful not to burn the drippings. Remove the seafood and set aside.

4. Lower the heat and add the onions, peppers, and garlic to the pan. Cook briefly and pour in the wine. Bring to a boil and add the clams and mussels. Cover and cook at high heat until they begin to open. Remove them as they open with tongs to avoid overcooking.

5. When all shellfish are removed, turn down the heat and add the chopped tomatoes, red pepper flakes, and basil. Add back the shrimp, scallops, and calamari and simmer at low heat for 3 minutes and add the clams and mussels.

6. Bring 4 quarts of water to a boil in a pasta pot and add the salt. Stir in the linguine and cook until al dente, about 10 minutes, and drain. Portion out the pasta in large pasta bowls and arrange the clams and mussels around the side of the bowl. Ladle the sauce over the top and serve.

– Wine Notes –
Gavi, the elegant white wine from the Piedmont region of Northern Italy or a less expensive Soave from the Veneto. A local Pinot Blanc would also work well.

Veal Saltimbocca with Linguine

4 portions

1½ lb veal cutlets
¼ lb thinly sliced
   prosciutto ham
12 sage leaves

1 cup flour
1 tsp kosher salt
½ tsp ground pepper

2 Tbsp butter
2 Tbsp olive oil
4 cloves garlic, peeled and
   sliced
4 sage leaves

1 pkg. baby bella mushrooms
½ cup marsala wine
1 lb whole grain linguine
1 Tbsp kosher salt
¼ cup chopped parsley

1. Cut the veal into 8 pieces, matching 4 pairs of fairly equal size. Put the cutlets on a cutting board between sheets of plastic film. Pound them as thin as possible with a meat hammer or frying pan. Line a sheet pan with foil and lay out the 4 bottom cutlets. Place a slice of prosciutto on each cutlet along with 2 sage leaves. Lay the matching veal cutlet on top and press firmly together.

2. Mix the flour with the salt and pepper and place in a sheet pan. Dust the cutlets in the seasoned flour on both sides. Fold a small piece of prosciutto on top of the cutlet along with a sage leaf. Secure with a toothpick pushed through at an angle.

3. Heat a large sauté pan and add the butter and olive oil. Add the sliced garlic and the sage leaves. When the garlic turns golden and the sage crisp, remove them with a slotted spoon. Immediately add the cutlets to the hot pan and brown on each side, about 5 minutes total. Place back on the sheet pan and keep warm.

4. Slice the mushrooms and add them to the sauté pan. Cook at medium heat until brown and add the marsala wine. Continue cooking at low heat and add back the veal.

5. Bring 4 quarts of water to a boil in a pasta pot and add the salt. Stir in the linguine and cook until al dente, about 10 minutes, and drain. Portion out the linguine on 4 large plates and put the cutlets on top. Spoon the mushrooms and sauce over all and garnish with the toasted garlic and sage leaves. Sprinkle with the chopped parsley and serve.

– Wine Notes –

An Italian red wine from Tuscany or the Piedmont would complement the earthy aromas of sage, prosciutto, and mushrooms. A Chianti Classico or a Barbera d'Alba would be a good choice.

Seafood Pot Pie

4 portions

1 pkg. frozen puff pastry
sheets
1 lobster tail (6 oz.)
½ lb jumbo shrimp,
in the shell
½ lb fresh sea scallops
1 dozen littleneck clams
1 lb fresh mussels

1 Tbsp butter
¼ cup minced shallots
1 cup white wine
1 cup water

3 Tbsp butter
1 cup diced onion
½ cup diced celery
1 cup diced carrots
1 Tbsp chopped tarragon
1 tsp kosher salt
1 tsp ground pepper

¼ cup flour
2 cups seafood broth
1 cup heavy cream

2 Tbsp dry sherry
1 pkg. frozen peas
1 pkg. frozen pearl onions

1 egg yolk
1 Tbsp water

1. Let the puff pastry sheets thaw at room temperature for 30 minutes. Thaw out the lobster tail and scrub the clams under cold water. Rinse the mussels.

2. Heat a large, shallow saucepan and melt the butter. Stir in the shallots, cook for 2 minutes, and add the wine and water. Add the clams and mussels and bring to a boil. Remove the clams and mussels as they open with a pair of tongs.

3. Add the shrimp (in their shells) to the broth, bring back to a boil, then remove the shrimp. Add the scallops (they will cook fast), bring to a boil, then remove the scallops.

4. Add the lobster tail and cook until the meat turns opaque and the shell bright red. Remove the lobster and strain the broth into a bowl. Peel and devein the shrimp, cut the lobster into bite-sized pieces, and take the clams and mussels out of their shells.

5. Clean the saucepan and place it back on the stove. Add the butter and stir in the onion, celery, and carrots. Cook at medium heat for 5 minutes, and season with the tarragon, salt, and pepper.

6. Stir in the flour to make a roux. Continue cooking and stir in the seafood broth and the cream. Bring to a boil and cook until it thickens (if too thick, add some more broth).

7. Turn down the heat and add the sherry, peas, and pearl onions. Add back all the seafood and simmer for 10 minutes. Check for seasoning and transfer to a large, shallow casserole.

8. Trim the puff pastry sheet to fit the casserole, tucking it inside the rim. Combine the egg yolk and water and brush the top of the crust. If desired, decorate with puff pastry trimmings. Bake in a 400 degree oven for 30 minutes.

Note: *You can also ladle this mixture into individual crocks and cut rounds of puff pastry to fit.*

Chocolate Ganache Cupcakes

12 cupcakes

For the Ganache

2 oz chopped bittersweet chocolate
¼ cup heavy cream
1 Tbsp confectioners sugar
1 Tbsp Amaretto liqueur

For the cupcakes

3 oz bittersweet chocolate
⅓ cup cocoa powder
¾ cup hot coffee

1 cup flour
¾ cup sugar
½ tsp salt
½ tsp baking soda
6 Tbsp canola oil
2 eggs
2 tsp vinegar
1 tsp vanilla extract

For the frosting

6 oz semi-sweet chocolate
½ cup heavy cream
8 oz butter
2½ cups confectioner's sugar, sifted

1. Prepare the ganache by placing the bittersweet chocolate, cream, confectioners sugar and Amaretto in the top of a double boiler. Cook, stirring, until melted and combined. Remove and refrigerate.

2. Place the bittersweet chocolate and the cocoa in a bowl. Pour the hot coffee over them, cover, and let sit for 5 minutes. Whisk until combined and refrigerate.

3. Whisk together the flour, sugar, salt, and baking soda in a clean bowl. Remove the cocoa mixture from the refrigerator and whisk the canola oil, eggs, vinegar, and vanilla into it.

4. Stir the flour mixture into the cocoa mixture and divide equally between 12 cupcake liners set in a muffin tin.

5. Remove the ganache from the refrigerator. Place a heaping teaspoon of it on the top of each cupcake, and bake in a 350 degree oven for 20 minutes. They will be just firm with a liquid center. Remove and cool on a rack for 1 hour.

6. In a saucepan, combine the chocolate, cream and butter. Cook over medium heat until melted and smooth. Remove from the heat and whisk in the sifted confectioner's sugar.

7. Cool in the refrigerator, stirring occasionally until frosting holds its shape. Spread generously over the cooled cupcakes, chill, and serve.

Note: the ganache and cake parts of this recipe were adapted from the America's Test Kitchen Cooking School Cookbook. *The frosting is my own recipe.*

Chocolate Ganache Cupcakes

White Veal Stew (Blanquette de Veau)

4 to 6 portions

1½ lbs veal stew meat
18 small white onions
2 cups chicken stock
1 leek, white part, sliced
6 parsley stems
1 small celery stalk
3 sprigs thyme
1 bay leaf

2 Tbsp butter
1 cup chicken stock
Reserved onions
1 bunch young carrots, peeled, cut in 2" pieces
1 celery root, peeled, cut in 2" pieces
2 turnips, peeled, cut in 2" pieces
12 white mushroom caps
1 tsp kosher salt
1 tsp ground pepper
2 sprigs thyme

2 Tbsp butter
3 Tbsp flour

½ cup heavy cream
¼ cup chopped parsley

1. Bring 2 quarts of water to a boil in a soup pot. Place the unpeeled white onions in the boiling water for 2 minutes and remove with a slotted spoon. Add the veal stew meat to the same water and bring back to a boil. Simmer for 3 minutes and remove. Discard the water. Peel the onions and set aside.

2. Place the blanched veal in a casserole on the stove. Add the chicken stock. Tie the leek, parsley stems, celery, thyme, and bay leaf together with a string to form a bouquet garni. Add this to the veal and bring to a boil. Reduce the heat and simmer, covered, for 1 hour, or until veal is very tender.

3. Heat a large saucepan and add the butter and chicken stock. Add the peeled onions, carrots, celery root, turnip, and mushroom caps. Season with the salt, pepper, and thyme and simmer, covered, until all the vegetables are tender, about 30 minutes. Drain the vegetables and set aside.

4. Remove the veal from the casserole and discard the bouquet garni. Strain the liquid into a bowl. Clean the casserole, place it back on the stove, and add the butter. When it melts, stir in the flour to make a roux.

5. After 2 minutes, whisk in the reserved veal cooking broth and bring it back to a boil. Stir in the heavy cream and reduce the heat. Add back the veal and the vegetables. Fold in the chopped parsley and check for seasoning. Serve with boiled new potatoes or rice.

– Wine Notes –

A Pouilly-Fuisse or a St. Veran from the Maconnais region of Burgundy or a red Beaujolais would be good French choices. A barrel fermented Chardonnay from Long Island would also be very good.

March

— Corned Beef and Cabbage —
By George Bilgere

I can see her in the kitchen,
Cooking up, for the hundredth time,
A little something from her
Limited Midwestern repertoire.
Cigarette going in the ashtray,
The red wine pulsing in its glass,
A warning light meaning
Everything was simmering
Just below the steel lid
Of her smile, as she boiled
The beef into submission,
Chopped her way
Through the vegetable kingdom
With the broken-handled knife
I use tonight, feeling her
Anger rising from the dark
Chambers of the head
Of cabbage I slice through,
Missing her, wanting
To chew things over
With my mother again.

Like Valentine's in February, we look forward to Saint Paddy's in the middle of March.

St. Patrick's Day is a Catholic feast day celebrated on March 17th. Saint Patrick lived during the fifth century, converting Irish pagans to an Irish style of Catholicism. Irish families celebrate this holiday during lent by attending church in the morning and celebrating in the afternoon.

Lenten prohibitions against the consumption of meat are waived for the day and people sometimes dance, drink, and feast on the traditional Irish bacon and cabbage. But since 1762, the St. Patrick's Day parade in New York has become an international success, inspiring parades across the country, and giving Americans a day to celebrate all things Irish. And the food that is served on this day in America is corned beef and cabbage. This is our featured meal for March, with all the trimmings, and through our cooking we all become Irish for a day.

Prime Meal
Mussels in Green Sauce

---

*House-made Corned beef and Cabbage with Colcannon,
Roasted Beets, Carrots, and Horseradish Sauce*

Lemon Sponge Pudding

Recommended beverage: *A full-bodied craft beer*

Selected Recipes
1. *Shepherd's Pie with Lamb*
2. *Braised Shoulder Lamb Chops with Potatoes and Whiskey*
3. *Slow-Roasted Pork Loin with Horseradish Crust*
4. *Horseradish-Crusted Salmon with Dill Sauce*
5. *Rainbow Trout with Crabmeat Stuffing*
6. *Sautéed Shad Roe with Bacon and Shallots*
7. *Ale Batter Shrimp with Horseradish Marmalade Sauce*

PRIME MEAL

– *First Course* –
Mussels in Green Sauce

4 portions

2 lbs fresh mussels
1 cup white wine
2 Tbsp minced shallots
1 Tbsp sliced garlic
2 bay leaves
2 sprigs fresh thyme
½ tsp ground pepper
¼ tsp hot red pepper flakes

For the sauce
1 egg
1 tsp minced garlic
1 tsp Dijon mustard
1 Tbsp lemon juice
4 cups chopped spinach leaves
¼ cup chopped parsley
½ cup chopped green onion
½ cup extra virgin olive oil
¼ cup chopped parsley
lemon wedges

1. Rinse the mussels and place them in a large, shallow, saucepan. Add the wine, shallots, garlic, bay leaves, thyme, pepper, and red pepper flakes.

2. Cover, bring to a boil, and cook until mussels begin to open. As they open, remove them with a pair of tongs and set aside. Discard those that don't open. Strain the broth into a bowl and let the sediment settle. Pour the clear liquid into a small saucepan, reduce by half, and cool.

3. Add the egg, garlic, mustard, lemon juice, and the reduced broth to the bowl of a food processor. Process until smooth, then add the spinach, parsley, and green onion. Pulse until chopped (but do not puree) and drizzle in the olive oil while processing to make a thick sauce.

4. Transfer the sauce to a saucepan and place on low heat. Put the cooked mussels in a casserole (or individual bowls) and pour the sauce over them. Garnish with chopped parsley and lemon wedges.

– Entrée –
House-made Corned Beef with Colcannon, Cabbage, Roasted Beets, and Horseradish Sauce

4 to 6 portions

For corned beef

Fresh beef brisket – flat piece only – or fresh beef eye of round. **Note:** *the brisket is traditional but the eye of round will be much leaner and maybe a little less tender.*

¼ cup kosher salt

---

2 quarts water
1 cup kosher salt
¼ cup sugar
2 bay leaves
6 whole black peppercorns
1 Tbsp pickling spice
2 cloves sliced garlic

cooking liquid
2 quarts water
2 bay leaves
6 whole black peppercorns
1 Tbsp pickling spice
2 cloves sliced garlic

Horseradish sauce
½ cup sour cream
2 Tbsp mayonnaise
1 tsp. Dijon mustard
2 Tbsp grated fresh horse-
        radish
1 Tbsp lemon juice

1. Rub the beef with the salt and set aside.

2. Make a brine by placing 2 quarts of cold water in a saucepan. Add the salt, sugar, bay leaves, peppercorns, pickling spice, and garlic. Bring to a boil, stirring to dissolve the sugar and salt. Place the beef in a large stainless steel or glass bowl and pour the hot liquid over it. Cool to room temperature, cover, and refrigerate for 3 days.

3. Remove the meat from the brine and rinse under cold water. Place in a clean soup pot and add the water to cover. Season with the bay leaves, peppercorns, pickling spice, and garlic.

4. Bring to a boil, turn down the heat, and simmer, uncovered, for 2½ hours. Check for tenderness by running a fork into the meat – it should go in easily. Remove and let rest for 20 minutes. Carve into very thin slices, cutting across the grain.

5. Make the horseradish sauce by combining in a small bowl the sour cream, mayonnaise, mustard, horseradish, and lemon juice. Serve on the side with the corned beef.

For colcannon

2 lbs russet potatoes
1 head celery root
2 tsp kosher salt
1 head kale
1 bunch green onions
2 Tbsp butter
½ cup milk
1 Tbsp kosher salt
1 tsp ground pepper
¼ tsp ground nutmeg

1. Peel and cut the potatoes into large pieces. Peel the celery root and cut into smaller, 1" pieces. Bring 2 quarts of water to a boil, add the salt, and put the potatoes and celery root in the pan together. Simmer until tender, about 25 minutes and drain.

2. Rinse the kale and cut off the stems. Remove the leaves from the stems by running a paring knife along the stem from bottom to top. Chop the leaves coarsely. Trim the green onions, peel off the outer layer, and chop.

3. Heat a large sauté pan and add the butter. Add the chopped kale and green onions to the pan, cover, and cook for 5 minutes. Add the milk and remove from the heat.

4. Place the cooked potatoes and celery root in a large bowl and mash by hand with a potato masher. Add the kale and green onion mixture and the salt, pepper, and nutmeg. Mash it all together and transfer to a casserole. Cover with foil and keep warm.

For cabbage, carrots and onions

1 head green cabbage
4 large carrots
12 white boiling onions

1. Remove the outer leaves of the cabbage and cut it into 8 wedges, leaving the core intact. Peel the carrots and cut into 2" pieces. Peel the white onions.

2. When the corned beef finishes cooking, place the broth back on the stove and add the cabbage, carrots, and onions. Bring to a boil and simmer until tender, about 20 minutes. Remove and keep warm, reserving the broth.

For beets

6 medium size winter beets
1 Tbsp butter
1 red onion, peeled and sliced
1 Tbsp grated horseradish
1 Tbsp balsamic vinegar
1 tsp kosher salt
½ tsp ground pepper

1. Rinse the beets and trim off the stems and roots. Spray with no-stick and wrap loosely in foil. Place on a sheet pan and roast in a 400 degree oven for 1 hour, or until tender. Remove from the oven, slip the skins off, and cut into bite-sized wedges.

2. Heat a saucepan and add the butter. Add the sliced onion and cook for 3 minutes before adding the beets, horseradish, vinegar, salt, and pepper. Transfer to a casserole and keep warm.

Horseradish sauce

Combine ½ cup sour cream with 2 Tbsp mayonnaise, 2 Tbsp prepared horseradish (or fresh grated), 1 tsp Dijon mustard, and 1 Tbsp lemon juice.

Serving the beef and vegetables

At service time, slice the corned beef and place it on a platter. Ladle some of the hot broth over it to moisten. Arrange the vegetables and colcannon around the beef and serve the horseradish sauce on the side.

– *Dessert* –
Lemon Sponge Pudding

6 Tbsp butter
1 cup sugar
4 egg yolks
2 lemons, juice and zest

²/₃ **cup** flour
¼ tsp salt
1¾ **cups** milk

4 egg whites
¼ tsp cream of tartar
Dash of salt

¼ cup confectioners sugar

1. In an electric mixer with a paddle attachment, cream the butter and sugar until light and fluffy. Add the egg yolks one at a time on medium speed, then drizzle in the lemon juice and zest.

2. Scrape down the bowl and lower the speed before adding the flour and salt. Continue mixing on low speed and drizzle in the milk. Transfer the batter to a large bowl and clean the mixing bowl.

3. Using the whisk attachment, beat the egg whites, cream of tartar, and salt in the electric mixer until stiff peaks form. Using a rubber spatula, fold the whites into the batter, being careful not to overmix.

4. Place six 12 oz. soufflé dishes in the bottom of a shallow baking pan and spray them with no-stick. Divide the batter equally between them. Set the oven for 350 degrees and bring 1 quart of water to a boil.

5. Place the pan with the soufflé dishes in the oven and pour the boiling water into the pan to make a water bath. Bake for 45 minutes, or until the tops are light brown and the filling is firm. Remove and cool. Sprinkle with confectioners sugar and serve.
Note: *if desired, the pudding can be removed from the soufflé dishes and served on a plate.*

Shepherd's Pie with Lamb

4 portions

2 lbs lamb stew meat
½ cup flour
1 tsp ground allspice
1 tsp kosher salt
1 tsp ground pepper

2 Tbsp canola oil
½ cup minced shallots
2 Tbsp minced garlic
1 pkg. baby bella mushrooms, quartered
2 carrots, peeled and diced
1 parsnip, peeled and diced

1 Tbsp tomato paste
1½ cups beef stock
2 bay leaves
3 sprigs thyme

Potato crust
1½ lbs russet potatoes
1 celery root
2 tsp kosher salt
1 Tbsp butter
¼ cup milk
1 tsp kosher salt
½ tsp ground pepper
¼ tsp ground nutmeg
3 green onions, minced
1 Tbsp butter, melted

1. Cut the stew meat into ½" pieces, trimming any fat and gristle away. Combine the flour, allspice, salt and pepper in a large bowl. Toss the meat in the flour mixture until evenly coated.

2. Heat a Dutch oven and add the oil. Brown the lamb at high heat, being careful not to crowd. Remove the lamb and lower the heat.

3. If the pan is dry, add a little more oil. Stir in the shallots and garlic and cook for 2 minutes. Add the mushrooms and raise the heat to medium. When the mushrooms release their liquid and begin to brown, add the carrots and parsnip.

4. Add the browned meat back along with the tomato paste. Stir the whole mixture together and cook for 5 minutes before adding the beef stock. Season with the bay leaves and thyme, bring to a boil, cover, and simmer for 30 minutes, or until the meat is tender.

5. Peel the potatoes and cut into large pieces. Peel the celery root and cut into smaller, 1" pieces. Bring 2 quarts of water to a boil and add the salt. Add the potatoes and celery root and simmer until tender, about 25 minutes. Drain and mash, adding the butter, milk, salt, pepper, and nutmeg. Fold the green onions into the mixture and taste for seasoning.

6. Transfer the lamb mixture to a shallow casserole (or to individual ramekins) and spoon the potato mixture over the top. Brush the potato crust with melted butter and place in a 400 degree oven for 20 minutes.

– Wine Notes –

This meat and potatoes dish would be excellent with one of the fine Merlot wines from Long Island. A modest-priced Malbec from Argentina would also be good.

Braised Shoulder Lamb Chops with Potatoes and Whiskey

4 portions

4 shoulder lamb chops
4 strips bacon, diced
2 tsp kosher salt
1 tsp ground pepper
1 onion, peeled and
    chopped
2 carrots, peeled and diced
¼ cup flour
2 Tbsp tomato paste
½ tsp sugar
1½ cups beef stock
¼ cup Irish whiskey
Bouquet garni (*sliced leek, bay
leaf, 6 parsley stems, 3 sprigs thyme
tied together*)
2 lbs russet potatoes
1 head of kale

1. Trim the tails and as much fat as possible from the chops. Season the meat with the salt and pepper. Heat a Dutch oven and add the bacon. When it renders its fat, remove, and turn up the heat. Brown the lamb chops on both sides and remove.

2. Reduce the heat to low and add the onions and carrots. Cook for 3 minutes and add the flour. Let the flour begin to brown before adding the tomato paste and sugar. Turn up the heat to medium and stir in the beef stock and the whiskey. Add the bouquet garni and let the sauce simmer for 30 minutes, adding a little more stock if the sauce becomes too thick. Remove the bouquet garni.

3. Peel and slice the potatoes into ⅛" slices. Wash the kale and trim the leaves from the stems. Chop the leaves coarsely to make 4 cups.

4. Spray the bottom of a large casserole with no-stick and line the bottom with half the potatoes. Place a layer of kale on top of the potatoes and then the browned lamb chops. Cover the chops with more kale and then finish with a layer of potatoes.

5. Pour the sauce over the potatoes and sprinkle the bacon on top. Cover with foil and place in a 300 degree oven for 1 hour.

I go dig up the horseradish
its long bitter spear of harshness
reminds me of the taste of spring
always a slight aftertaste from the year before
the resentful winter and the cold
if you mix it in, just so –

it is zippy and bright
but relentless
too much
and it drags you
to the depths of regret
not enough?
you forget what was there ...

— from "Horseradish" by Odarka Polanskyj Stockert

Horseradish root is a winter vegetable that emerges in March from winter storage. We don't give much thought to it or buy it in any quantity, if at all. But it is a harbinger of spring and has an unmistakable flavor that is easily recognized by all and enjoyed by many people. There are great rewards for making horseradish sauces from scratch rather than relying on processed versions. When the horseradish root, a member of the mustard family, is peeled and shredded, the root cells are crushed, releasing powerful volatile oils known as isothiocyanates. These are what "clears your sinuses" and brings tears to your eyes. Adding vinegar stabilizes the reaction and preserves the horseradish. But over time the flavor is weakened and the 'zing' is lost. Making your own horseradish for use in many sauces and recipes is very easy. Just purchase one root, peel it, and cut it into ½" chunks. Pulse these in your food processor until they are finely chopped and add ¼ to ½ cup of white vinegar or a combination of vinegar and lemon juice. Cover tightly and keep refrigerated for up to 3 weeks without losing much flavor.

Slow-Roasted Pork Loin with Horseradish Crust

6 to 8 portions

1 3 lb pork loin, boneless, center cut
2 tsp kosher salt
1 tsp ground pepper
1 Tbsp chopped fresh thyme
1 Tbsp chopped fresh rosemary
1 Tbsp chopped fresh sage
1 Tbsp chopped fresh parsley

Horseradish crust
2 heads of garlic
¼ cup olive oil
½ cup grated fresh horse-radish
½ cup panko crumbs
1 tsp smoked paprika

Gravy for pork
1 onion, peeled and chopped
1 carrot, peeled and chopped
1 stalk celery, chopped
¼ cup flour
2 cups chicken stock

1. Trim any fat and silverskin from the pork loin. Make a deep cut down the middle along the length of the roast and open it up like a book. Sprinkle the inside and outside with the salt and pepper. Place the herbs down the center of the pork and fold it back up. Tie securely with string and set aside.

2. Cut the tops off the heads of garlic and place them in a small baking dish. Pour the olive oil over them, cover with foil, and bake in a 350 degree oven for 30 minutes. When cool enough to handle, squeeze the cloves of garlic into the oil and discard the skins. Place the garlic, oil, and grated horseradish in the bowl of a food processor and puree. You will end up with a smooth paste.

3. Rub this paste over the pork loin and coat with the panko crumbs. Sprinkle the smoked paprika over the panko and set aside.

4. Place the chopped onion, carrot, and celery in the bottom of a small roasting pan. Put the pork roast on top of the vegetables and roast in a 300 degree oven until the internal temperature reaches 145 degrees, about 1½ hours. Remove the meat and tent with foil.

5. Add the flour to the drippings and place on the stove at medium heat for 5 minutes. Add the chicken stock to the roasting pan and bring it to a boil, scraping the bottom with a wooden spoon. Strain the sauce into a small saucepan and bring to a simmer. Skim any fat off the top and check for seasoning. Serve on the side with the pork roast.

– Wine Notes –
A Cabernet Franc from Long Island, a Pinot Noir from Oregon, or a St. Emilion from Bordeaux would be good choices to complement the mild flavor of the pork and the spicy crust.

Horseradish-Crusted Salmon with Dill Sauce

4 portions

1½ lbs boneless, skinless salmon fillets
1 cup flour
1 tsp kosher salt
½ tsp ground pepper
2 Tbsp prepared horseradish
1 egg, beaten
2 Tbsp heavy cream
1 cup panko crumbs
¼ cup canola oil

Mustard cream sauce
⅔ cup heavy cream
1 tsp Dijon mustard
1 Tbsp prepared horseradish
1 tsp lemon juice
½ tsp kosher salt
Dash cayenne pepper
2 Tbsp chopped fresh dill

1. Cut the salmon into 4 equal portions. Combine the flour with the salt and pepper in a shallow bowl. Mix the horseradish with the egg and the cream in another bowl and place the panko crumbs in a pie tin.

2. Dredge the salmon fillets in the seasoned flour, then in the horseradish mixture, and then in the panko crumbs. Bread both sides of the fish and set it on a foil-lined sheet pan. At service time, heat a large sauté pan and add the oil. Cook the salmon at medium heat until golden on both sides, about 5 minutes total time.

3. For the sauce, bring the heavy cream to a boil in a small, heavy saucepan. Let it reduce to about ½ cup. Remove from the heat and stir in the mustard, horseradish, lemon juice, salt, pepper, and dill. Serve on the side with the salmon.

– Wine Notes –

The rich texture of salmon and the cream, mustard, and horseradish need a full-bodied white wine such as a chardonnay from the Sonoma Valley in California, or a Reserve Chardonnay from Long Island.

Whole Rainbow Trout Stuffed with Crabmeat

4 portions

4 whole trout, boned, and butterflied
1 cup lump crabmeat
1 Tbsp chopped fresh tarragon
2 Tbsp minced green onion
1 Tbsp mayonnaise
1 lemon, juice and zest
½ tsp kosher salt
¼ tsp ground pepper
2 Tbsp olive oil

1. Purchase the boned and butterflied trout from your fish dealer or bone out whole fresh trout yourself, being careful to not separate the 2 halves of the fish. Lay out 4 sheets of heavy foil measuring 12 by 18 inches. Spray them with no-stick and place the fish skin side down on the foil.

2. For the stuffing, empty the crab into a bowl and pick out any cartilage. Add the tarragon, green onion, mayonnaise, lemon juice and zest, salt, and pepper. Carefully fold the ingredients in so as not to mash the crabmeat.

3. Place the crabmeat in the cavity of each fish and pull the fillets together to form a whole fish. Brush the outside of the fish with olive oil and wrap loosely in the foil. Seal the edges and place all 4 fish on a sheet pan.

4. At service time, roast the fish in the oven at 425 degrees for about 20 minutes. Check one for doneness, being careful not to overcook.

   Note: *This recipe goes well with brown rice and green beans almondine. It can also be cooked in a covered chargrill.*

Sautéed Shad Roe with Bacon and Shallots

4 portions

4 small pairs shad roe
1 cup flour
1 tsp kosher salt
½ tsp ground pepper

8 strips thick-cut bacon
1 Tbsp butter

1 cup chopped shallots
2 Tbsp lemon juice
2 Tbsp chopped parsley

1. Purchase shad roe as fresh as possible. If the pairs available are large, two pairs will suffice for four people. Combine the flour with the salt and pepper in a pie tin. Dredge the shad roe in the flour and set aside.

2. Heat a heavy skillet and cook the bacon at medium heat until crisp. Remove and pour off most of the bacon fat. Place the skillet back on the stove and add the butter.

3. Add 2 pairs of the shad roe and cook at medium heat (do not use high heat as the membrane around the roe will burst). Turn the shad roe after about 5 minutes and sprinkle half the shallots and half the cooked bacon into the pan.

4. Cook another 5 minutes at low heat and sprinkle with lemon juice and chopped parsley. Remove to a warm oven while cooking the rest.

Note: *Serve with boiled red potatoes and a green vegetable.*

– *Wine Notes* –

I would choose a Pinot Noir from Oregon, California, or the North Fork. A Bourgogne Rouge from a good producer in France would also be delicious with this meal.

Ale Batter Shrimp with Horseradish Marmalade Sauce

4 portions

16 very large shrimp (U-12), in the shell
1 cup flour
1 tsp kosher salt
½ tsp ground pepper

1 egg
1 bottle pale ale
1¼ cups flour
1 Tbsp smoked paprika
2 tsp kosher salt
1 tsp ground pepper
3 cups canola oil

Horseradish Marmalade Sauce
1 cup orange marmalade
1 navel orange, juice and zest
1 lemon, juice and zest
¼ cup grated fresh horse-radish
1 Tbsp grated fresh ginger

1. Peel the shrimp, leaving the tails on. Butterfly them by making a deep cut down the middle and removing the vein. Combine the flour, salt, and pepper in a pie tin and coat the shrimp all over with the seasoned flour.

2. Break the egg into a stainless bowl and whisk in the ale. Gradually whisk in the flour to make a batter about the consistency of pancake batter (quantity of flour will vary). Season the batter with the paprika, salt, and pepper.

3. Add the canola oil to a heavy Dutch oven (or deep fryer) and heat to 350 degrees. At service time, dip each floured shrimp into the ale batter and swirl it around until it is well coated. Holding each piece by the tail, dip it into the hot oil and hold it for a couple of seconds to prevent sticking to the bottom, then drop into the oil. Repeat with the other shrimp, working quickly. As the cooked shrimp rise to the surface, remove them with tongs and place on a sheet pan lined with paper towels.

4. For the sauce, place the marmalade, orange juice and zest, lemon juice and zest, horseradish, and ginger in the bowl of a food processor and pulse until smooth, but not pureed. Serve as a dipping sauce with the shrimp.

– Wine Notes –
Deep-fried seafood is best with a barrel-fermented Chardonnay from Long Island. A good quality Pinot Grigio from Italy would also match this dish.

APRIL

— Perhaps the World Ends Here —
By Joy Harjo

The world begins at a kitchen table. No matter what, we must eat to live.

The gifts of earth are brought and prepared, set on the table. So it has been since creation, and it will go on.

We chase chickens or dogs away from it. Babies teethe at the corners. They scrape their knees under it.

It is here that children are given instructions on what it means to be human. We make men at it, we make women.

At this table we gossip, recall enemies and the ghosts of lovers.

Our dreams drink coffee with us as they put their arms around our children. They laugh with us at our poor falling-down selves and as we put ourselves back together once again at the table.

This table has been a house in the rain, an umbrella in the sun.

Wars have begun and ended at this table. It is a place to hide in the shadow of terror. A place to celebrate the terrible victory.

We have given birth on this table, and have prepared our parents for burial here.

At this table we sing with joy, with sorrow. We pray of suffering and remorse. We give thanks.

Perhaps the world will end at the kitchen table, while we are laughing and crying, eating of the last sweet bite.

The month of April marks the beginning of spring. It often comes to the North Fork in fits and starts, with a few beautiful days surrounded by some miserable reminders of winter. The local produce is pretty limited as the farm stands and markets begin to open with an array of plants and flowers. Spinach, horseradish, and green onions are available first, with the promise of asparagus, rhubarb, and peas to follow.

April is also the month when we celebrate Easter, Passover, and other religious traditions, often featuring spring lamb as a symbol of renewal. Our Prime Meal features roasted spring vegetables with jumbo shrimp and we have included an Easter dinner with a menu of foods from antiquity.

Prime Meal
Asiago Spinach and Swiss Chard Cakes

Jumbo Shrimp with Roasted Spring Vegetables and Polenta

Rhubarb, Strawberry, and Blackberry Pie

Recommended wine: *Sauvignon Blanc*

Selected Recipes
1. *Pan-Seared Sea Scallops over Spring Mirepoix*
2. *Spinach Quiche with Goat Cheese*
3. *Moroccan Lamb Tagine*
4. *Moroccan Carrot and Orange Salad*
5. *Edgar Allen's Tossed Salad*
6. *Easter Dinner –*
   Potato, Leek, Wild Leek (Ramps) Soup
   Deviled Eggs with Smoked Salmon and Mache
   Braised Lamb Shanks in Merlot with Whole Farro
   Sautéed Kale, Asparagus, Radishes, and Peas
   Arborio Rice Pudding
7. *Greek-Style Lamb Steaks with Barley Pilaf*
8. *Sesame-Crusted Salmon with French Lentils*

PRIME MEAL

– *First Course* –
Asiago Spinach and Swiss Chard Cakes

4 portions

1 bag field spinach
(about 8 oz)
1 bunch swiss chard

2 eggs, beaten
1 cup ricotta cheese
1 cup shredded asiago
cheese
1 Tbsp minced garlic
1 tsp ground nutmeg
2 tsp kosher salt
1 tsp ground pepper
1 Tbsp olive oil

1. Remove the stems from the spinach and swiss chard. Cut the swiss chard stems in pieces and set aside. Wash the greens in a sink of cold water, lifting the leaves out of the water so the sand settles to the bottom. Drain, chop coarsely, and dry in a salad spinner. Place in the bowl of a food processor and pulse to chop fine. Work in batches if necessary and place the chopped greens in a large bowl.

2. In a separate bowl, combine the eggs, ricotta, shredded asiago, garlic, nutmeg, salt, and pepper. Fold into the chopped greens.

3. Spray 4 souffle dishes (12 oz.) with no-stick and divide the spinach mixture between them, pressing down with a spoon to compact them. Place the filled soufflé dishes in a 400 degree oven and cook for 25 minutes. Remove and cool on a rack for a few minutes before cutting around the edges with a paring knife and turning them out on a plate.

4. Heat the olive oil in a sauté pan and add the reserved swiss chard stems. Cook, uncovered, for 3 minutes and serve alongside the spinach cakes.

– *Entrée* –
Jumbo Shrimp with Roasted Spring Vegetables and Polenta

4 portions

Polenta
6 cups water
1 tsp kosher salt
2 cups polenta (coarse cornmeal)
½ cup Pecorino Romano cheese
2 Tbsp cold butter

Flavored olive oil
½ cup extra virgin olive oil
2 heads of garlic, tops trimmed off
6 sprigs fresh thyme
2 sprigs rosemary
1 lemon, juice and zest

Shrimp and Vegetables
24 jumbo shrimp (16-20 per lb)
2 Tbsp kosher salt
1 Tbsp ground pepper
1 bunch local asparagus, trimmed
2 leeks, trimmed, split in half
2 large artichokes, split in half, outer leaves and choke removed
1 bunch young carrots, stems on
1 head fennel, trimmed, bulb sliced
½ lb sugar snap peas, trimmed
1 bunch green onions, trimmed

1. For the polenta, bring the water to a boil in a saucepan and add the salt. Stir in the polenta gradually with a wooden spoon and reduce the heat. Cook until very thick bubbles form, about 15 minutes. Remove from the heat and add the cheese and the butter. Spray a shallow casserole with no-stick and scrape the polenta into it with a rubber spatula. Chill for 1 hour.

2. For the flavored oil, put the heads of garlic, the thyme, and the rosemary into a small casserole and pour the olive oil over them. Cover tightly with foil and roast in a 350 degree oven for 45 minutes. Remove and cool, discarding the thyme and rosemary. Squeeze the garlic cloves back into the oil and discard the skins. Add the lemon juice and zest to the oil.

3. Peel the shrimp and remove the tails. Butterfly the shrimp by making a deep cut down the center. Remove the vein and stand them up in a shallow casserole. Place the roasted garlic in with the shrimp and brush them with the flavored oil.

4. Combine the salt and pepper in a small bowl to use on the shrimp and vegetables. Sprinkle some of this mixture on the shrimp.

5. Line a sheet pan with heavy foil and spray with no-stick. Place the asparagus, leeks, artichokes, carrots, and fennel on the pan. Brush all the vegetables with the oil and sprinkle with the salt mixture.

6. Close to service time, cut the polenta into squares, place on a small foil-lined sheet pan, and brush with the flavored oil.

7. Set the oven to 425 degrees and put the shrimp, polenta, and vegetables in the oven at once. The shrimp will cook quickly, about 15 minutes along with the polenta. The vegetables will take about 25 minutes until brown and tender. When serving, put the polenta in the center of the plate with the shrimp on top. Surround them with the roasted vegetables.

Jumbo Shrimp with Roasted Vegetables

– Wine Notes –
A Sauvignon Blanc from New Zealand or a reserve Sauvignon Blanc from Long Island. French Sancerre or Pouilly Fume would also be delicious.

– Dessert –
Rhubarb, Strawberry, and Blackberry Pie

8 portions

Crust
2½ cups flour
½ tsp salt
1 cup chilled shortening
½ cup ice water

Filling
6 cups rhubarb, ½" dice
½ cup sugar
1 pint strawberries
½ pint blackberries

---

1 cup sugar
½ cup cornstarch
1 orange, zest and juice

---

1 Tbsp cold butter
1 egg
1 tsp water
1 tsp sugar

1. Add the flour and salt to the bowl of a food processor. Pulse to combine and add the chilled shortening. Pulse a few times until it resembles coarse cornmeal.

2. Transfer to a bowl and gently stir in the ice water with a dinner fork. Empty onto a floured board and divide into 2 equal balls of dough. Flatten these into discs and wrap in plastic film. Refrigerate for 30 minutes.

3. Add the sugar to the diced rhubarb and let rest at room temperature for 20 minutes. Trim and slice the strawberries and combine them with the blackberries in a bowl. Drain the rhubarb mixture and add it to the berries.

4. Whisk together the sugar and cornstarch and add to the rhubarb mixture along with 2 Tbsp. of orange juice and the zest.

5. Roll out the pie crust and fit into a 10" pie pan. Add the filling and dot with the butter. Roll out the other pie crust and cut it into strips to make a lattice crust or just roll it out as a top crust.

6. Combine the egg and water to make an egg wash and brush the edges of the pie crust to seal. Brush the top of the crust with egg wash and sprinkle with the sugar. Bake in a 375 degree oven for 45 minutes. Remove to a rack, and cool before refrigerating.

– Wine Notes –
A Stainless Steel Fermented Chardonnay or a Reserve Sauvignon Blanc from Long Island would be my choice.

Pan-Seared Sea Scallops over Spring Mirepoix

(a mirepoix is a mixture of aromatic vegetables used to flavor a dish)

4 portions

1½ lbs fresh sea scallops
1 lemon, juice and zest
1 tsp kosher salt
½ tsp ground pepper

Spring Mirepoix
1 bunch asparagus
1 bunch radishes
1 bunch green onions
4 small young carrots
2 cups baby spinach
2 Tbsp fresh thyme
¼ cup chopped parsley
1 Tbsp kosher salt
1 tsp ground pepper

Cooking
1 cup flour
1 Tbsp olive oil
2 Tbsp butter
2 Tbsp olive oil

1. Trim the small muscle from the side of each scallop. Toss the scallops with the lemon juice and zest, salt, and pepper in a bowl. Refrigerate until service.

2. Wash all the vegetables. Break the stems off the asparagus and cut into ¼" pieces. Trim and dice the radishes. Trim the green onions and slice thinly. Peel and dice the carrots. Toss all the vegetables into a large bowl with the thyme, parsley, salt, and pepper.

3. Remove the scallops from the marinade and dry with paper towels. Toss them with the flour in a dry bowl. Heat a large sauté pan and add the olive oil and butter. Cook the scallops quickly at high heat, turning the heat down as you turn the scallops. Do not crowd. Remove scallops and keep warm.

4. Add the olive oil to the same pan along with the chopped vegetables, except the spinach. Cook at medium heat until the vegetables begin to soften, about 5 minutes, then add the spinach and cook another 2 minutes.

5. Portion out the vegetable mirepoix onto 4 plates or a platter. Place the scallops on top and serve. Garnish with lemon wedges.

– Wine Notes –
The aromas of fresh spring vegetables and quickly seared scallops would be complemented by a Viognier from France's Rhone Valley or one from the Mendocino region of California, but a local Chardonnay would also work well.

Spinach Quiche with Goat Cheese

6 to 8 portions

9" Deep Pie Crust
1½ cups flour
½ tsp salt
1 tsp sugar
4 Tbsp cold butter
4 Tbsp cold shortening
5 Tbsp ice water

Filling
2 bags field spinach (1 lb)
2 cups water
1 tsp kosher salt

4 eggs
¾ cup heavy cream
1 cup milk
1 tsp kosher salt
½ tsp ground pepper
Juice from **1** lemon
4 oz goat cheese
2 Tbsp grated parmesan cheese

1. For the pie crust, add the flour, salt, and sugar to the bowl of a food processor and pulse until blended. Add the cold butter and shortening and pulse until it resembles coarse cornmeal. Add the ice water and pulse a few times to form a dough. Turn out onto a floured surface and form into a ball. Flatten the ball into a disc, wrap in plastic film, and refrigerate for 30 minutes.

2. Trim the stems off of the spinach and wash in a sink of cold water, lifting the spinach out of the water to allow the sand to settle. Pick the leaves off the stems and drain.

3. Bring the water to a boil in a soup pot and add the salt. Add the spinach, cover, and bring back to a boil. Drain in a colander and squeeze out all of the moisture possible with your hands. Chop coarsely and set aside.

4. Whisk the eggs in a large bowl and add the cream and milk. Whisk in the salt, pepper, and lemon juice. Crumble the goat cheese and add to the egg mixture along with the chopped spinach.

5. Roll out the pie crust and place into a 9" pie plate with high fluted sides. Pour in the spinach mixture and top with the grated Parmesan. Place in a 375 degree oven and bake for 40 minutes, or until firm.

Moroccan Lamb Tagine

4 to 6 portions

2 lbs lamb stew meat
2 tsp kosher salt
1 tsp ground pepper
2 Tbsp olive oil

1 large onion, peeled and diced
3 cloves garlic, minced
1 Tbsp cHarissa seasoning*
2 tsp fresh ginger, minced
1 can (15 oz.) diced tomatoes
1 cup chicken stock

2 Tbsp sesame seeds
12 whole almonds
½ cup dried apricots
½ cup pitted prunes
1 can (15oz.) chick peas

¼ cup chopped cilantro
1 lemon, juice and zest
1 pkg. cous-cous, cooked by package directions

*cHarissa seasoning is a local North Fork product similar to the Moroccan spice blend *Ras-el-hanout*.

1. Toss the lamb in a bowl with the salt and pepper. Heat a Dutch oven, add the oil, and brown the meat at high heat. Cook in batches to avoid overcrowding. Remove the browned meat and lower the heat.

2. Add the onion to the Dutch oven and cook at low heat for 3 minutes before adding the garlic, cHarissa, and ginger. Continue cooking and add back the lamb with all its juices along with the tomatoes and chicken stock. Bring to a boil, cover, and place in a 300 degree oven until the meat is tender, about 1 hour.

3. In a dry sauté pan, toast the sesame seeds for 3 minutes at medium heat and remove. Toast the almonds in the same manner and set aside. Soak the apricots in hot water for 5 minutes and chop coarsely. Drain the rinse the chick peas.

4. Remove the Dutch oven from the oven and add the sesame seeds, almonds, apricots, prunes, chick peas, cilantro, and lemon juice and zest. Bring back to a boil on the stove and check for seasoning. Serve on a platter over a bed of cous-cous.

Note: *This recipe is a simplified version of a recipe developed by my friend and fellow chef, Jay Miller. The tagine is both a cooking vessel and an ancient recipe for braised lamb. Although tagines are available, the Dutch oven seems to work best in today's modern kitchen.*

– Wine Notes –

This highly seasoned, rich stew, might taste good when accompanied by a Sirah from Paso Robles in California or a Crozes Hermitage from the Rhone Valley of France.

Moroccan Carrot and Orange Salad

4 to 6 portions

1 lb carrots
2 navel oranges
¼ cup chopped cilantro

Dressing
1 orange, zest and juice
1 Tbsp lemon juice
2 tsp minced garlic
¼ cup honey
½ tsp kosher salt
Dash cayenne pepper
¼ cup olive oil
1 pkg. baby arugula

1. Peel and grate the carrots into a bowl using the large holes on a box grater. Peel and section the oranges, removing all the pulp. Cut the sections into bite-sized pieces and add to the carrots. Toss in the cilantro.

2. For the dressing, remove the zest from the orange and squeeze the juice into a small bowl. Add the lemon juice, garlic, honey, salt, and cayenne. Whisk in the olive oil and add to the carrot mixture.

3. Wash and dry the arugula in a salad spinner. Divide it between 4-6 salad plates and portion out the carrot salad on top. Garnish with an orange twist and chopped cilantro.

Edgar Allen's Tossed Salad

4 to 6 portions

1 pkg. mesclun greens
1 cucumber
1 granny smith apple
1 pint grape tomatoes
1 bunch green onions
1 ripe avocado
1 lemon, zest and juice

Dressing
3 Tbsp papitas
¾ cup grapeseed oil
¼ cup rice wine vinegar
2 Tbsp balsamic vinegar
1 Tbsp honey
1 Tbsp minced garlic
½ tsp chile oil
¼ tsp sea salt
¼ tsp ground pepper

1. Wash greens in cold water, dry in a salad spinner, and wrap in paper towels to chill. Peel the cucumber, slice it in half, and scrape out the seeds. Slice it into bite-sized pieces. Peel and core the apple and dice into ½" pieces.

2. Cut the grape tomatoes in half. Trim the green onions and slice them into ⅛" inch pieces. Cut the avocado in half, remove the pit, and score the flesh. Scoop it out with a spoon.

3. Add the cucumber, apple, tomatoes, onions, and avocado to a large bowl and toss with the lemon zest and juice.

4. For the dressing, heat a dry sauté pan and toast the pepitas for 3 minutes. Place them in the bowl of a food processor. Add the grapeseed oil, rice vinegar, balsamic vinegar, honey, garlic, chile oil, salt, and pepper. Process until smooth and transfer to a mason jar.

5. At service time, toss the mesclun with the fruits and vegetables in the bowl and gently toss in about half the dressing. Serve on salad plates. **Note:** *This recipe was contributed by Sarah and Jay Miller. Edgar Allen is the name of their cat.*

Greek-Style Lamb Steaks with Barley Pilaf

6 portions

6 lamb steaks*

Marinade
¼ cup olive oil
2 lemons, zest and juice
2 tsp dried oregano
1 Tbsp minced garlic
2 tsp kosher salt
1 tsp ground pepper

Barley pilaf
1 cup barley

2 Tbsp olive oil
¼ cup chopped walnuts
2 tsp minced garlic
1 pkg. baby bella mushrooms, quartered

1 bag spinach (10 oz)
½ cup chicken stock
1 bunch green onions, minced
2 tsp kosher salt
1 tsp ground pepper
1 lemon, zest and juice

1. Prepare the marinade by combining the olive oil, lemons, oregano, garlic, salt, and pepper in a small bowl.

2. Place the steaks in a shallow pan and spoon the marinade over them. Marinate in the refrigerator for 2 hours or more, but not overnight.

3. For the barley pilaf, bring 1 quart of water to a boil and add the barley. Simmer until barley is tender, about 20 minutes and drain.

4. Heat a large sauté pan and add the olive oil. Stir in the walnuts and garlic. Cook at medium heat for 3 minutes and add the mushrooms. Continue cooking until mushrooms give up their moisture, about 15 minutes.

5. Wash the spinach, remove the stems, and cut or tear the leaves into 2" pieces. Add the spinach to the mushrooms along with the chicken stock. Increase the heat and cook for another 3 minutes. Stir in the cooked barley and the green onions. Season with the salt, pepper, and lemon zest and juice.

6. At service time, remove the steaks from the marinade and dry with paper towels. Cook them on a grill pan in batches (or on an outdoor grill) at high heat until medium rare, about 5 minutes per side. Serve with the barley and a green vegetable.

Note: These lamb steaks, resembling beef sirloin steaks, are delicious. Purchase a whole leg of American lamb and ask your butcher to cut it into slices 1" thick from one end to the other. You will get about 6 steaks from the center for grilling. Use the less tender cuts from either end for braising.

– Wine Notes –
These garlicky, marinated steaks with lemon and oregano flavors over a hearty barley pilaf can use a big wine with lots of fruit. A Napa or Sonoma Valley Cabernet would be fine, but also something more exotic, such as a Zweigelt from Austria.

Sesame-Crusted Salmon with French Lentils

4 portions

1½ lbs boneless skinless salmon fillet

1 egg white
2 Tbsp cornstarch
½ cup sesame seeds

For the Lentils
1 cup French lentils
2 cups water
½ onion, peeled
2 bay leaves
2 sprigs thyme
Zest of **1** lemon

2 Tbsp olive oil
1 bunch green onions, trimmed and sliced
2 cups fresh tomatoes, diced
2 Tbsp chopped dill
2 Tbsp chopped parsley
2 tsp kosher salt
1 tsp ground pepper

3 Tbsp olive oil

1. Cut the salmon into 4 equal portions and remove any bones.

2. Combine the egg white and cornstarch in a small dish and brush over the top of the salmon. Place the sesame seeds in a pie plate and press the salmon fillets into the seeds. Refrigerate until service time.

3. Rinse the lentils and put them into a saucepan. Add the water, onion, bay leaves, thyme, and lemon zest. Bring to a boil and simmer, covered, until lentils are just tender, about 25 minutes. Remove the onion, thyme, and bay leaves. Drain and set aside.

4. At service time, heat a large sauté pan and add the olive oil. Stir in the green onions and cook for 3 minutes before adding the diced tomatoes and the cooked lentils. Continue cooking on low heat and add the dill, parsley, salt, and pepper.

5. Heat another large sauté pan and add the olive oil. Place the salmon fillets, crust side-down, in the hot pan and cook until brown, about 3 minutes. Turn the salmon, reduce the heat, and cook until the salmon is fully cooked, another 5 minutes. Serve over the lentil mixture and garnish with lemon and sprigs of dill.

– Wine Notes –
A Puilly Fume from the Loire Valley, or a dry white Bordeaux.

Moroccan Lamb Tagine

Dr. Jay Miller with Lamb Tagine

EASTER

Easter is an important Christian holiday but also has roots in antiquity as a Spring ritual. We are discovering foods from the past that are healthier than many of our modern processed foods and also happen to be delicious. This Easter dinner uses some of the ingredients of antiquity.

Potato, Leek, and Wild Leek (Ramps) Soup

4 portions

4 leeks

4 cups chicken stock
1 cup water

2 cups wild leeks (ramps)*

2 Tbsp olive oil
2 Tbsp flour
Chicken stock mixture

6 cups red potatoes,
      skin on, diced
1 bay leaf
2 sprigs fresh thyme
1 cup heavy cream
2 tsp kosher salt
1 tsp ground pepper
¼ cup chopped chives

1. Trim the stem end of the leeks and cut off the green leaves (reserve leaves). Cut the white part into quarters and rinse under cold water. Slice into ¼" pieces and set aside.

2. Wash the green leaves and cut into 1" pieces. Add the chopped green leaves to a soup pot along with the chicken stock and water. Simmer for 30 minutes and strain.

3. Trim the stem ends off the wild leeks and rinse. Chop both the white and green parts and set aside (substitute 1 chopped onion and 1 tsp. minced garlic if wild leeks are not available).

4. Heat a soup pot and add the olive oil. Stir in the chopped leeks (white part) and the chopped wild leeks. Cook at low heat until tender, about 5 minutes. Stir in the flour and continue cooking. Add the reserved chicken stock mixture and turn up the heat to medium.

5. Add the diced potatoes, the bay leaf, and thyme. Simmer until the potatoes are tender. Remove the bay leaf and thyme and add the heavy cream. Season with the salt and pepper, and taste for seasoning. Garnish with the chopped chives.

Wild leeks, or Ramps, are a spring specialty available during April on the East coast. They have a unique flavor that is a combination of onion and garlic. Here on the North Fork they are grown by Satur Farms and are available at some specialty stores.

Deviled Eggs with Smoked Salmon and Mache

4 portions

6 eggs
¼ cup smoked salmon,
     chopped
2 Tbsp cream cheese
1 Tbsp sour cream
1 tsp Dijon mustard
1 tsp lemon juice
¼ tsp kosher salt
Dash cayenne pepper
2 Tbsp minced chives

For the salad
6 oz mache (lambs ears)
1 lime, zest and juice
1 lemon, zest and juice
½ tsp kosher salt
¼ tsp ground pepper
¼ cup olive oil

1. Cover the eggs with water in a saucepan. Bring to a boil, cover, and remove from the heat. Let stand for 15 minutes and plunge into a bowl of ice water.

2. Peel the eggs and cut them in half. Remove the yolks and put them in a bowl. Reserve the whites.

3. Mash the yolks with a dinner fork and add the smoked salmon, cream cheese, sour cream, and mustard. Continue to mash and season with the lemon juice, salt, pepper, and chives.

4. Spoon this mixture into the egg whites. Garnish with small pieces of smoked salmon and fresh dill if desired. Refrigerate until service.

5. For the salad, wash the mache in cold water and dry in a salad spinner (substitute baby spinach if mache is not available).

6. Make the dressing by combining the lime juice and zest with the lemon juice and zest. Add the salt and pepper and whisk in the olive oil. Toss with the mache and place on a platter with the devilled eggs or arrange on individual plates.

Braised Lamb Shanks in Merlot with Whole Farro

4 portions

4 lamb shanks
2 tsp kosher salt
1 tsp ground pepper
2 Tbsp canola oil

2 onions, peeled and chopped
4 carrots, peeled and sliced
2 Tbsp minced garlic
2 Tbsp tomato paste
2 Tbsp flour

2 cups merlot wine
1 cup chicken stock

1 can (28 oz) San Marzano whole tomatoes in puree
2 sprigs rosemary
2 sprigs thyme

1 cup whole farro
2 cups chicken stock
1 tsp kosher salt
½ tsp ground pepper

1. Sprinkle the lamb shanks with the salt and pepper. Heat a Dutch oven and add the canola oil. Brown the lamb at high heat on all sides, cooking in batches so as not to crowd. Remove and set aside. ***Note:*** *lamb shanks come in a wide variety of sizes depending on whether they come from the U.S., New Zealand, or Australia. One large shank is adequate for one portion, but smaller ones may require two per person.*

2. Reduce the heat and pour off any excess fat over about 2 Tbsp. Add the onions, carrots, and garlic. Sauté for 5 minutes and add the tomato paste. Continue cooking and stir in the flour.

3. Cook another 3 minutes and add the wine and chicken stock. Bring back to a boil, then reduce the heat.

4. Chop the tomatoes and add them to the sauce along with the puree. Add back the lamb shanks and season with the rosemary and thyme. Bring to a boil, cover, and place in a 300 degree oven for 2 hours.

5. Remove the shanks and test for tenderness. They should almost fall off the bone. Skim the fat from the sauce and check for seasoning, but do not strain. Serve over the lamb.

6. For the whole farro, cover with cold water and soak for 20 minutes. Drain and place in a saucepan with the chicken stock. Bring to a boil and simmer, uncovered, until the liquid is absorbed, about 30 minutes. Season with the salt and pepper and serve.

Note: *Farro is a whole cereal grain reputed to be the oldest domesticated grain in existence, dating back to 7000 BCE. Sometimes called spelt or emmer wheat, these grains are very healthy, as they contain essential amino acids and do not contain saturated fat. They are also delicious, with a chewy texture and earthy flavor.*

– Wine Notes –
A Napa or Sonoma Valley Cabernet Sauvignon, or a Chateauneuf Du Pape.

Sautéed Kale, Asparagus, Radishes, and Peas

4 portions

1 bunch kale

1 bunch asparagus
1 bunch radishes
1 bunch green onions

2 cups shelled fresh peas
    (or 1 pkg. frozen.)
2 Tbsp olive oil
2 tsp kosher salt
1 tsp ground pepper
½ cup mint leaves,
    chopped

1. Trim the stem ends from the kale and wash in a sink of cold water. Drain in a colander and remove the leaves from the stems by sliding a paring knife along the stem from bottom to top. Cut the leaves into large pieces.

2. Trim the asparagus stems, rinse, and cut the asparagus into ½" pieces. Trim the radishes and slice. Trim the onions and slice into ¼" pieces.

3. Heat a large sauté pan and add the oil. Toss the asparagus, radishes, onions, and peas in the hot pan and cook, uncovered, for 5 minutes, being careful not to burn (cook in batches if too crowded).

4. Add the kale, cover, and continue cooking at medium heat for another 5 minutes. Stir in the salt, pepper, and mint leaves.

Arborio Rice Pudding

4 portions

2½ quarts milk
1 tsp salt
1¼ cups Arborio rice

5 eggs
1½ cups sugar
¾ cup heavy cream
1 tsp vanilla extract

Topping
¼ cup sugar
½ cup dark brown sugar
1 Tbsp ground cinnamon
1 tsp ground nutmeg

1. Add the milk and salt to a heavy saucepan and gradually bring up to a simmer. Stir in the rice and cook at medium heat until it thickens and thick bubbles appear, about 1 hour. Stir often with a wooden spoon to prevent burning.

2. Beat the eggs in a bowl and whisk in the sugar, cream, and vanilla. Add this to the thick rice mixture and cook, stirring, for 3 minutes. Do not boil.

3. Pour into a casserole or individual soufflé dishes. Whisk the sugar, brown sugar, cinnamon, and nutmeg together in a bowl and sprinkle liberally over the top of the rice pudding. Caramelize the crust by placing the casserole or soufflé dishes under a hot broiler for about 5 minutes. The pudding can be served warm at this point, or it can be chilled overnight and cut into squares when serving.

Most any kind of white rice can be used, but arborio rice creates a very creamy, custard-like texture. This is one of the simplest and best dessert recipes that I've ever seen. The secret is to cook it slowly until very thick. If desired, add raisins at the end.

MAY

— United States Of Barbecue —
By Jake Adam York

Mud Creek, Dreamland, Twixt-n-Tween,
the cue-joints rise through smoke
and glow like roadhouses on Heaven's way.
Or so the local gospels raise them,
each tongue ready to map the ramshackle
of shacks and houses, secret windows
and business-sector hip in some new
geography of truth. If the meek shall,
then a rib-mobile may shame the fixed pit
in a reading from the book of skill,
the grill-less one cook himself to legend
rib by rib. The great chain's links
are live and hermetic as bone
and where cue burns hotter than politics,
every mouth's the forge of change,
all scholars temporary and self-proclaimed.
One says he half-sublimes each time he eats
a rib and expects to go in a puff of smoke
when he finds the perfect pig:
he wanders like a ghost, his eyes
trying everything, a genuine R & D,
and once a day he proclaims the latest find,
a homegrown Moses canting
a vernacular talmud changeable as wind.
A word could crumple him, some backyard

master slapping mustard on a country rib
to turn the state of things entire.
So every word reverberates and mystery's
sown again. Rib or rump, dry-rub or ketchup
the eternal terms turn and barbecue's rooted
or pulled anew. Theories proliferate
like flies after rain, but that's the usual business
where Georgia and the Carolinas river in,
the wind spirits Mississippi or Caríb,
and piedmont's melted to the uplands
in open hearths and coke ovens, stitched tight
in cotton fields, and a kudzu vine's
the proper compass. Beef or pork,
catfish, quail or armadillo,
we've tried it all, loved it with brushes,
kiss of vinegar, tongue of flame,
so whatever it may not be,
we've covered all it is. Vegetarian
exception opens eggplant, means tofu's
the next horizon, purity an envelope
that's always opening. So summer afternoons
and Saturdays when the fires go up,
smoke rises to a signal and shapes
the single common word,
hand-made silence talking on every tongue.

The month of May begins with a celebration of Mother's Day and ends with honoring our fallen soldiers on Memorial Day.

Mother's Day used to be the busiest restaurant day of the year as traditional husbands took Mom out to dinner to give her a day off from household chores and the drudgery of cooking. Today, men are just as likely to be cooking as women, and preparing a home-cooked meal is considered a pleasure and a source of entertainment.

Memorial Day weekend is the unofficial beginning of the "season" on the North Fork and is also the time when we move our cooking operations to the deck or the back yard. The chargrill, whether gas-fired or charcoal/wood-fired, is the central piece of cooking equipment for the summer. In recent years our BBQ skills have increased dramatically. We are slow cooking on indirect heat, cooking with smokers that infuse the flavors of hickory, mesquite, and cherry wood into our food, and using ingredients that we never thought possible on a grill.

Prime Meal

Crabmeat-Stuffed Belgian Endive

Chargrilled "Spatchcocked" Chicken with lemon and thyme

Grilled Vegetables

Individual Cheesecakes with Apricot Sauce

Recommended wine: *Stainless Steel Chardonnay*

Selected Recipes

1. *Grilled Bourbon Steak with Hash Browns*
2. *Grilled Flat Iron Steak with Twice-Baked Potato*
3. *Grilled Veal Chops with Sage, Rosemary, and Spring Vegetables*
4. *Argentine-Style Mixed Grill with Chimichurri Sauce and Grilled Tomatoes*
5. *Argentine-Style Potato Salad*
6. *Cedar-Planked Wild Salmon with Vegetable Bundles*
7. *Chargrilled Whole Wheat Pizza*
8. *Grilled Rack of Asparagus with Shrimp and Chunky Vinaigrette*
9. *Asparagus Spring Rolls with Dipping Sauce*
10. *Roasted Asparagus with Pancetta and Quinoa Crepes*

PRIME MEAL

– *First Course* –
Crabmeat-Stuffed Belgian Endive

4 portions

8 oz jumbo lump crabmeat
1 mango, peeled, diced
¼ cup chopped cilantro
2 tsp minced ginger
2 Tbsp olive oil
1 Tbsp lime juice
½ cup Kalamata olives,
    pitted, chopped
½ tsp kosher salt
¼ tsp ground pepper
Dash Tabasco sauce
2 heads Belgian endive
1 pkg. baby spinach or arugula

1. Empty crabmeat into a bowl and gently break it apart, removing any cartilage.

2. Combine the mango, cilantro, ginger, olive oil, lime juice, olives, salt, pepper, and Tabasco in a separate bowl. Fold in the crabmeat and refrigerate.

3. Trim the stem end from the endive and separate the leaves. Rinse under cold water, drain, and dry with paper towels. Fill the leaves with the crabmeat mixture. Place the spinach (or arugula) on a platter or individual plates and arrange the stuffed endive on top.

– Entree –
Chargrilled Spatchcocked Chicken with Lemon and Thyme

(Spatchcocking refers to butterflying a whole chicken so that it rests flat on a grill)

4 portions

One 4 lb chicken
2 tsp kosher salt
1 tsp ground pepper

Marinade
4 lemons
1 Tbsp minced garlic
2 Tbsp thyme leaves
1 Tbsp rosemary leaves
¼ cup chopped cilantro
1 red onion, peeled and
    sliced
¼ tsp hot red pepper flakes
¼ cup canola oil

Vegetables
1 green pepper
1 red pepper
1 yellow pepper
1 zucchini
1 red onion
1 eggplant
4 plum tomatoes
1 Tbsp kosher salt
1 tsp ground pepper

1. Place the chicken breast-side down on a cutting board. Using a stiff knife, cut along both sides of the backbone. Open up the chicken and make a small notch in the hard breastbone cartilage, then bend the two sides back to expose the cartilage. Pull this out with your hands so the chicken will lay flat.

2. Cut off the wing tips and remove any excess fat and skin. Season the chicken on both sides with the salt and pepper and place in a shallow casserole.

3. Remove the zest from the lemons and place in a bowl. Squeeze the lemons into the bowl and add the rinds. Add the garlic, thyme, rosemary, cilantro, sliced onion, red pepper flakes, and canola oil. Pour the marinade over the chicken and refrigerate at least 2 hours, turning once.

4. Remove the chicken from the marinade, dry with paper towels, and set aside. Pour the marinade into a small saucepan and bring to a boil. Remove from the heat and reserve for the vegetables.

5. For the vegetables, split the peppers, remove the seeds, and trim the ends. Cut the zucchini in half lengthwise and then into quarters. Peel and slice the onion into thick slices.

6. Trim the ends from the eggplant and slice into thick rounds. Cut the tomatoes in half through the stem. Put all the vegetables on a foil-lined sheet pan and brush with the reserved marinade. Sprinkle with the salt and pepper and set aside.

7. Prepare the charcoal grill. Rub the grill with an oil soaked paper towel and wait for white coals before beginning to cook. Spray the chicken with no-stick and place it on the grill skin-side down. After 3 minutes, turn the chicken 90 degrees to form crosshatch marks.

8. Cook another 5 minutes, turn the chicken over, and move it away from direct heat. Cover and cook until the internal temperature reaches 165 degrees, about 1 hour. During this time the vegetables can be cooked alongside the chicken, or you can wait for the chicken to be done. The vegetables will only take about 15 minutes to cook.

9. At service time, cut the chicken into 4 quarters and place it on a platter with the grilled vegetables. Split 2 lemons in half and grill them cut- side down to use as garnishes along with sprigs of rosemary.

– Wine Notes –

A dry rose from Provence in France or one of the great dry roses of Long Island made from the merlot or the cabernet franc grape. These wines are great for grilled poultry and vegetables with their crisp acidity and forward fruit flavor.

– *Dessert* –
Individual Cheesecakes with Apricot Sauce

4 portions

3 Tbsp melted butter
½ cup graham cracker crumbs

---

1 lb cream cheese
2 eggs
1 cup sugar
1 tsp lemon zest
1 Tbsp lemon juice
½ tsp vanilla extract

Apricot Sauce
½ cup (4 oz.) apricot preserves
1 Tbsp apricot brandy
2 Tbsp sugar
2 Tbsp water

1. Spray four 12 oz. soufflé dishes lightly with no-stick. Spoon the melted butter into the bottom and sprinkle the graham cracker crumbs over the butter. Press down on the crumbs with a small glass.

2. Cut the cheese into quarters and add it to the bowl of an electric mixer with a paddle attachment. Beat at low speed and add the eggs, sugar, lemon zest and juice, and the vanilla. Scrape down the bowl and beat at high speed until very smooth, about 4 minutes.

3. Preheat the oven to 350 degrees and bring 2 quarts of water to a boil in a saucepan. Divide the batter between the soufflé dishes and place them in a small roasting pan. Put them into the oven and pour the boiling water into the roasting pan to come up about half way on the sides of the soufflé dishes.

4. Bake the cheesecakes in the water bath for 45 minutes, then turn the oven off and let the cheesecakes rest with the door closed for another 30 minutes. Remove and cool for a few minutes before turning them out onto plates while still warm.

5. For the sauce, combine the apricot preserves, brandy, sugar, and water in a small saucepan. Simmer, stirring, for 10 minutes. Pour over the cheesecakes at service time.

Bourbon Steak with Hash-Browned Potatoes

4 portions

2 lbs boneless, thick cut, sirloin steak

Marinade
2 Tbsp brown sugar
2 Tbsp chili sauce
1 Tbsp Dijon mustard
1 Tbsp Worcestershire sauce
1 Tbsp minced garlic
2 Tbsp minced shallots
1 Tbsp red wine vinegar
1 tsp kosher salt
1 tsp ground pepper
¼ cup Kentucky bourbon

Bourbon Sauce
1 Tbsp butter
¼ cup chopped shallots
¼ cup Kentucky bourbon
¼ cup beef stock
1 Tbsp balsamic vinegar
2 Tbsp cold butter

Hash Browns
4 medium sized russet potatoes
1 bunch green onions, finely chopped
1 Tbsp chopped fresh rosemary
2 tsp kosher salt
1 tsp ground pepper
4 Tbsp melted butter

1. The steak should be about 1½" thick. Cut it into 4 equal portions or, if desired, leave it whole. Place the steak in a shallow casserole.

2. Combine the marinade ingredients in a small bowl and pour them over the steak. Refrigerate from 4-8 hours, turning once.

3. Remove the steaks from the marinade, dry them with paper towels, and let them come to room temperature before grilling. Prepare a charcoal grill and wipe down the grill with an oil-soaked paper towel. Close to service time, spray the steaks with no-stick and grill over hot coals, brushing with the marinade as they cook to desired doneness.

4. For the sauce, melt the butter in a small saucepan and add the shallots. When they are soft, add the bourbon and beef stock. Bring to a boil and let it reduce to half its volume. Swirl in the vinegar and cold butter just before serving.

Hash-browned Potatoes

1. Place the potatoes, skin on, in a saucepan and cover with water. Bring to a boil and simmer until the potatoes are just tender, about 25 minutes. Remove and cool the potatoes.

2. Peel the potatoes and grate them into a bowl using the large holes of a box grater. Gently stir in the onions, rosemary, salt, and pepper.

3. To cook individual portions, spray an omelet pan with no-stick and place it on high heat. Add 1 Tbsp. of the melted butter and a handful of the shredded potatoes. Press them into the pan with a rubber spatula and turn them when they brown. To cook all at once, use a large cast iron skillet and the same instructions.

4. Place each portion in a warm oven and repeat cooking the rest (these potatoes can also be cooked on the chargrill by wrapping them in heavy foil).

Grilled Flat Iron Steak with Twice-baked Potato

4 portions

2 lbs flat iron steak, trimmed to make two 1 lb steaks

Marinade
¼ cup olive oil
1 lemon, zest and juice
1 Tbsp dried oregano
2 Tbsp minced garlic
1 Tbsp smoked paprika
2 tsp kosher salt
1 tsp ground pepper
Few drops Tabasco sauce

Twice-Baked Potato
4 large russet potatoes
4 strips bacon
½ cup extra sharp cheddar cheese
1 bunch green onions, trimmed
1 Tbsp butter
1 cup sour cream
2 tsp kosher salt
1 tsp ground pepper
¼ tsp ground nutmeg

– Wine Notes –
A red wine with a good balance of fruit, tannins, and acidity will match this dish. I like a reserve Merlot from the North Fork.

1. Remove the line of gristle that runs through the center of the whole top blade if the butcher hasn't already. You will end up with two very tender steaks with no fat or gristle. At service time they can be sliced into 4 portions.

2. Combine the olive oil, lemon zest and juice, oregano, garlic, paprika, salt, pepper, and Tabasco in a small bowl. Place the steaks in a shallow casserole and pour the marinade over them. Refrigerate at least 2 hours but not more than 8 hours. Turn steaks once during this time.

3. Scrub the potatoes under cold water and poke holes in them with a dinner fork. Spray them with no-stick and place on a foil-lined sheet pan. Bake in a 400 degree oven for 1 hour and 15 minutes. Remove and cool.

4. Place the bacon on another small sheet pan lined with parchment paper. Cook in the same oven for about 15 minutes, or until crisp. Remove, cool on a paper towel, and chop coarsely.

5. Grate the cheddar cheese, chop the green onions, and set both aside. Cut the tops off the potatoes and scoop the flesh into a bowl, leaving a ¼" wall around the sides of the potatoes.

6. Mash the scooped potato flesh with a potato masher and add the butter, sour cream, salt, pepper, and nutmeg. Fold in the chopped bacon, cheddar cheese, and the green onions.

7. Fill the potato shells generously with the potato mixture. Do not press the stuffing into the potato so as to compact it. At service time, place the potatoes in a 400 degree oven for 15 minutes and serve.

8. Remove the steaks from the marinade and let them come to room temperature, drying them with paper towels. When the charcoal grill is hot, grill the steaks over high heat to desired doneness. Let them rest for 15 minutes before carving into thin slices against the grain.

Grilled Veal Chops with Sage, Rosemary, and Spring Vegetables

4 portions

4 veal chops, 1½" thick
½ cup extra virgin olive oil
8 sage leaves
1 Tbsp fresh rosemary
4 cloves sliced garlic
2 tsp kosher salt
1 tsp ground pepper

Spring Vegetables
1 lb fingerling (or new) potatoes
1 bunch young carrots, stems on
1 bunch asparagus
1 zucchini
1 bunch green onions
1 Tbsp kosher salt
1 tsp ground pepper

1. Heat a small saucepan and add the olive oil. Add the sage, rosemary, and garlic and cook at low heat for 5 minutes before turning off the heat. Combine the salt and pepper in a little bowl.

2. Sprinkle the veal chops with the salt and pepper and let them come to room temperature.

3. Tear an 18" square of heavy foil, lay it out, and spray with no-stick. Rinse the potatoes and place them on the foil. Brush with the flavored oil and sprinkle with the salt and pepper mixture. Seal the foil loosely around them.

4. Wash and peel the carrots, leaving some of the stem on. Wrap them in the same manner as the potatoes and set aside. Rinse and trim the asparagus and place it on a foil-lined sheet pan.

5. Cut the ends off the zucchini and split in half lengthwise. Cut in quarters and place on the sheet pan. Rinse and trim the onions and put them on the sheet pan. Brush all of the vegetables with the flavored oil and sprinkle with the salt and pepper mix.

6. Prepare a charcoal grill and allow the coals to turn white. Put the foil-wrapped potatoes and carrots on the side of the grill, cover, and cook for 15 minutes.

7. Brush the veal chops with the flavored oil and remove the grill lid. Place them over the hottest part of the grill and cook to desired doneness. Place the remaining vegetables alongside the veal and cook for about 5 minutes. Serve on a platter and garnish with sprigs of rosemary and sage leaves.

– Wine Notes –
Veal with sage suggests the earthy aromas of Burgundy. A Gevrey Chambertin if for a special occasion or a Bourgogne Rouge from a good negociant if it is more of an everyday dinner.

Grilled Flat Iron Steak

Argentine-Style Mixed Grill

Argentine-Style Mixed Grill
with Chimichurri Sauce and Grilled Tomatoes

6 to 8 portions

Grilled Tomatoes

4 large beefsteak tomatoes
(or 8 smaller ones)
1 Tbsp olive oil
1 tsp kosher salt
½ tsp ground pepper

Meats

1 whole chicken, cut up
2 lbs beef short ribs
2 lbs beef skirt steak
2 lbs fresh chorizo sausage

Chimichurri Sauce

1 cup cilantro
1 cup flat leaf parsley
5 cloves minced garlic
½ tsp hot red pepper flakes
2 Tbsp fresh oregano
2 Tbsp minced shallots
1 lemon, zest and juice
3 Tbsp white wine vinegar
1 tsp kosher salt
1 tsp ground pepper
¾ cup olive oil
1 lb hickory chips

– Wine Notes –

A Malbec from Argentina would match the grilled assortment of food perfectly along with matching the cultural theme. A California Syrah with big fruit and alcohol content would also be good.

1. Remove the core from the tomatoes and slice in half crosswise. Brush the tops with the olive oil and season with the salt and pepper. Cook on the outer edge of the grill while the meat is cooking at low temperature.

2. Bone the chicken breasts, leaving the skin on. Slice the breasts in half lengthwise to make 4 cutlets. Separate the legs from the thighs by cutting through the thigh joint. Fold back the wing tips or trim them off. Place all the meat and poultry on foil-lined sheet pans and set aside.

3. Place the cilantro, parsley, garlic, red pepper flakes, oregano, shallots, lemon zest and juice, vinegar, salt, and pepper into the bowl of a food processor. Pulse until coarsely chopped and drizzle in the olive oil. Brush the meat and poultry with this sauce and refrigerate for 2 hours or more. Reserve the rest of the sauce to serve with the meal.

4. Prepare your charcoal grill, waiting for white coals to develop. Soak the hickory chips in water for 30 minutes or more. Push the coals to one side and place a shallow pan of water next to the coals. Drain the hickory chips and put them on top of the coals.

5. Rub the grill with an oil-soaked paper towel. Place the chicken thighs, legs, and wings on the grill over the pan of hot water along with the short ribs and sausage. Cover the grill and cook at slow, indirect heat for 3 hours, allowing the hickory smoke to flavor the meat. Add more hickory chips if necessary.

6. When the poultry and meat are tender and well done, remove and keep in a warm place. Remove the water bath and add fresh coals to the fire. At service time, grill the skirt steaks and the chicken breasts over the hot coals. Place all the meat and poultry on a platter and serve with the chimichurri sauce. Garnish with grilled lemon halves and cilantro.

Argentine-Style Potato Salad

6 to 8 portions

Potato Salad

2 lbs Yukon gold (or other thin-skinned potato)
1 Tbsp kosher salt
4 eggs
4 medium carrots
1 lb green beans
2 tsp kosher salt
1 bunch green onions
1 cup stuffed olives

Dressing

½ cup mayonnaise
2 Tbsp chopped dill
1 lemon, zest and juice
1 tsp ground mustard
2 tsp kosher salt
1 tsp ground pepper
2 Tbsp olive oil
½ cup chopped cilantro

2. Scrub the potatoes, place in a saucepan, and cover with water. Add the salt, bring to a boil, and simmer until tender, about 20 minutes. Remove, cool, and cut into 1" chunks, leaving the skin on.

3. Place the eggs in a saucepan, cover with water, and bring to a boil. Remove from the heat, cover, and let rest for 15 minutes. Plunge into ice water, peel, and chop coarsely.

4. Peel and dice the carrots and cut the green beans into 1" pieces. Blanch the vegetables in boiling, salted water until just cooked, about 5 minutes. Drain and chill in an ice bath.

5. Trim and peel the onions, cutting them into thin slices. Cut the stuffed olives in half (almond-stuffed or garlic-stuffed are best).

6. For the salad dressing, combine the mayonnaise with the dill, lemon zest and juice, mustard, salt, and pepper. Whisk in the olive oil. Combine the potatoes, eggs, vegetables, green onions, and olives in a large bowl. Toss lightly with the dressing and the chopped cilantro.

Argentine-Style Potato Salad

Cedar-Planked Wild Salmon with Vegetable Bundles

4 portions

4 cedar planks
1½ lbs fresh wild salmon fillets

Spice Rub
1 tsp lemon pepper seasoning
2 tsp smoked paprika
½ tsp powdered garlic
2 tsp brown sugar
½ tsp dried thyme
1 tsp kosher salt

Flavored Oil
½ cup extra virgin olive oil
3 cloves sliced garlic
1 sprig rosemary
2 sprigs thyme
1 Tbsp kosher salt
2 tsp ground pepper

Vegetable Bundles
½ lb green beans
1 bunch young carrots,
    stems on
2 parsnips
1 bunch asparagus

– Wine Notes –
Wild salmon are caught in the spring on the west coast, so a wine from that region would be appropriate. An Oregon pinot gris or a Napa Valley Chardonnay would fit the bill.

---

1. Soak the cedar planks in water for 2 hours (they can be purchased from a housewares store, but you can also use untreated cedar roofing shingles from a lumber store). Cut the salmon into four 6 oz. portions. It is not necessary to remove the skin.

2. Prepare the spice rub by combining the lemon pepper, paprika, garlic, sugar, thyme, and salt in a small bowl. Rub each piece of salmon, covering the top and sides. Refrigerate for 30 minutes or more.

3. For the flavored oil, heat the olive oil in a small saucepan and add the garlic, rosemary, and thyme. Heat to a simmer and cook for 10 minutes. Remove from the heat and set aside. Mix the salt and pepper together in a small bowl and set aside.

4. For the vegetables, trim the ends off the green beans. Trim and peel the carrots and parsnips, and cut them into 3" strips. Trim the ends off the asparagus.

5. Tie each vegetable into a small bundle with string. Bring 2 quarts of water to a boil and quickly blanch each bundle, cooking for about 2 minutes each.

6. Prepare a charcoal grill and wait for the coals to turn white. Remove the cedar planks from the water and place them on the hot grill. Cover and cook for about 3 minutes per side. Remove them from the fire and spray with no-stick.

7. Place the salmon on 1 or 2 of the planks and brush with the flavored oil. Put the vegetable bundles on the rest of the planks, brush with the oil, and season with the salt and pepper.

8. Put the planks back on the grill, cover, and cook for about 15 minutes, or until the fish begins to flake apart (it is not necessary to turn the fish or vegetables). Serve the fish and vegetables on the cedar planks if desired. Garnish with lemon and herbs.

Chargrilled Whole Wheat Pizza

Two 8-slice pizzas

Pizza Dough
1½ cups warm water (110 degrees)
1 pkg. active dry yeast
1 tsp sugar
1 Tbsp olive oil
1 tsp salt
2 cups whole wheat flour
2 cups all- purpose flour
1 tsp olive oil

Pizza Sauce
1 Tbsp olive oil
1 cup chopped onion
2 tsp minced garlic
1 can (15 oz.) crushed tomatoes
¼ cup chopped basil
1 bay leaf
1 tsp dried oregano
1 tsp sugar
1 tsp kosher salt
½ tsp ground pepper

Toppings
1 pkg. baby bella mushrooms
1 lb mozzarella cheese
1 red bell pepper
½ cup pitted Kalamata olives
2 oz Parmigiano-Reggiano cheese
1 Tbsp olive oil

1. For the dough, place the water in the bowl of a mixer with a dough hook. Add the yeast and sugar and let rest for 10 minutes. Add the olive oil, salt, and 1 cup each of the flours. Mix at medium speed and gradually add the rest of the flour. If the dough does not form a ball and cling to the dough hook, add a little more flour, 1 tablespoon at a time.

2. Remove the dough and place it in a lightly oiled bowl. Cover with a towel and let rise until double in bulk, about 1 hour. Punch the dough down and divide it in half to form 2 balls of dough. Place these on a floured surface, cover with a towel, and let rise another 30 minutes.

3. For the sauce, heat a saucepan on medium heat, add the oil, then the chopped onions. As the onions soften, add the garlic. Continue cooking and stir in the tomatoes, basil, bay leaf, oregano, sugar, salt, and pepper. Simmer on low heat for 30 minutes.

4. To prepare the toppings, slice the mushrooms and cut the mozzarella into thin 2" square slices. Cut the pepper into strips, measure out the olives, and grate the cheese.

5. Prepare the grill, allowing the charcoal to turn white and wiping the grill with an oil-soaked paper towel. Put the cover on the grill to preheat for a few minutes.

6. Flatten the 2 balls of dough on a floured surface. Roll each into a large circle with a rolling pin, and brush one side lightly with oil. Place one pizza dough, oil side-down, on the hot grill. Cover and cook about 3 minutes, then flip and brown on the other side, being careful not to burn. Remove, and repeat with the other dough.

7. Divide the sauce between the two pizzas, leaving a 1" border around the edge. Place the toppings on the sauce along with the mozzarella cheese. Sprinkle the grated cheese on top. At service time, place each pizza back on the hot grill, cover, and cook until the cheese melts, about 5 minutes.

Grilled Rack of Asparagus
with Shrimp and Chunky Vinaigrette

4 portions

24 bamboo skewers
1½ lbs jumbo shrimp,
   in the shell
2 bunches thick asparagus

Marinade
¼ cup olive oil
1 Tbsp chopped oregano
1 Tbsp minced garlic
2 tsp kosher salt
1 tsp ground pepper
¼ tsp red pepper flakes

Chunky Vinaigrette
1 red pepper, split, seeded,
and diced
1 yellow pepper, split,
   seeded, and diced
1 fennel bulb, sliced thin
1 red onion, peeled and
   sliced thin
2 Tbsp chopped capers
2 limes, zest and juice
1 jalapeno pepper, seeded
and minced
1 tsp kosher salt
½ tsp ground pepper

¼ cup olive oil
1 pkg. baby arugula

1. Soak the skewers in water for 30 minutes or more. Peel and devein the shrimp, removing the tails. Place 6 or 7 shrimp on each skewer, folding the shrimp and running the skewer through the tail and body.

2. Rinse and trim the stems off the asparagus. Line up 6 asparagus spears on a cutting board and run skewers through the top and bottom to form a raft.

3. Combine the olive oil, oregano, garlic, salt, pepper, and red pepper flakes in a bowl. Lay the skewered shrimp and asparagus on a foil-lined sheet pan and brush them both with the marinade.

4. For the vinaigrette, combine the red and yellow peppers, fennel, onion, capers, lime zest and juice, jalapeno, salt, and pepper in a bowl. Stir in the olive oil and chill.

5. Prepare a charcoal grill, being sure to wipe the grill rack with an oil-soaked paper towel. Spray the shrimp and the asparagus with no-stick and grill over high heat, turning once.

6. Wash and dry the arugula in a salad spinner. Place it on individual dinner plates with the chunky vinaigrette on top. Lay the asparagus raft on top and pull out the skewers. Finish with the shrimp on top of the asparagus.

– Wine Notes –
Asparagus is a difficult wine match as it has an astringent vegetal character that doesn't complement a wine's better qualities. I would recommend a Sauvignon Blanc from Long Island or one from New Zealand.

Asparagus Spring Rolls with Dipping Sauce

1 lb thin asparagus
1 bunch green onions
1 red bell pepper
1 mango
1 cup fresh snow pea
    shoots
½ cup peanuts
½ cup fresh snow pea
    shoots, chopped
¼ cup cilantro
1 Tbsp minced ginger
1 pkg. (12 oz) 9"-diameter
    spring roll skins

Dipping Sauce
¼ cup soy sauce
¼ cup rice wine vinegar
1 Tbsp honey
1 tsp minced garlic
1 Tbsp minced ginger
1 tsp sesame oil
Dash Tabasco sauce

1. Wash and trim all of the vegetables. Line a sheet pan with foil and arrange the cut vegetables on it for assembly: Cut the asparagus into 4" strips; trim the green onions and cut them into 4" strips; split the red pepper, remove the seeds and trim off the ends. Flatten and cut into 4" strips; peel the mango, remove the flesh, and cut it into long thin slices; cut the snow pea shoots into 4" pieces.

2. Add the peanuts, snow pea shoots, cilantro, and ginger to the bowl of a food processor and pulse until coarsely chopped. Place in a small bowl and set aside.

3. Cover a cutting board with plastic film, with the vegetables nearby. Fill a large bowl with hot tap water. Soak 1 piece of spring roll skin in the water for 30 seconds and place on the cutting board. Fold the bottom of the skin up to make a straight edge.

4. Arrange the asparagus, onions, red pepper, mango, and snow pea shoots on the rice paper, all pointing in the same direction, with the tops of the asparagus hanging over the straight edge. Place 1 tablespoon of the peanut mixture on top. Fold the bottom of the spring roll skin over the vegetables and roll the wrapper tightly, with the asparagus tips hanging out.

5. Place a small cup in the middle of a serving plate for the dipping sauce. Cut the spring rolls in half on the bias and stand them on the plate leaning against the cup in the middle for support.

6. For the dipping sauce, combine the soy sauce, vinegar, honey, garlic, ginger, sesame oil, and Tabasco in a small bowl. Let it rest for 30 minutes to develop flavor. Place the dipping sauce in the cup at the center of the spring rolls and pass as an hors d'oeuvre or place on the table.

*My granddaughter Madison, eager to have some
Chargrilled Whole Wheat Pizza*

Asparagus Spring Rolls with Dipping Sauce

Roasted Asparagus and Pancetta with Fontina and Quinoa Crepes

4 portions

Crepes
½ cup quinoa
1 cup water
½ cup pecans
2 eggs
1¼ cups milk
1 cup flour
½ tsp kosher salt
2 green onions, minced
4 Tbsp butter, melted

Asparagus
2 bunches asparagus
2 Tbsp olive oil
1 tsp kosher salt
½ tsp ground pepper
2 oz thinly sliced pancetta
7 oz Fontina cheese, grated

1. Bring the water to a boil in a small saucepan and stir in the quinoa. Simmer 15 minutes and set aside. Heat a dry sauté pan and add the pecans. Let them toast at medium heat for 3 minutes and remove. Add the pecans to a food processor and process until finely ground.

2. Beat the eggs in a bowl and whisk in the milk. Combine the flour and salt and gradually whisk into the egg mixture. Stir in the cooked quinoa, the ground pecans, and the green onions.

3. Heat an omelet pan and spray with no-stick. Brush the bottom with melted butter and turn up the heat to high. Add ¼ cup of the crepe batter and cook until bubbles form and the edges are brown. Turn with a rubber spatula, cook another 2 minutes and remove.

4. Repeat with the rest of the batter, brushing the pan with melted butter between each crepe. Stack the crepes on a plate and keep warm.

5. Line a sheet pan with heavy foil and spray with no-stick. Trim the ends off the asparagus, rinse, and line up the spears on the sheet pan all facing the same way in one layer. Brush them with the olive oil and sprinkle with the salt and pepper.

6. Lay the thin slices of pancetta on top of the asparagus. Place the pan in a 425 degree oven for 15 minutes. The asparagus will be cooked and the pancetta just turning crisp. Remove from the oven.

7. Line another sheet pan with foil and spray lightly with no-stick. Lay out the crepes and place 3 or 4 spears of asparagus on top of each one along with the crisp pancetta. Sprinkle the grated Fontina cheese on top and put the pan back in the hot oven. Cook until the cheese melts and serve.

Note: *If you use an 8-inch omelet pan instead of a 6-inch pan, the crepes will be larger and you can roll them up with the asparagus and cheese inside if desired. These crepes go well with poached eggs and steamed kale.*

JUNE

— Procrustinacean —
By Graeme King

"Order!" shouted lobster as a loudmouthed limpet swore,
"Hurry up!" said the ghost crab, "I've a date up on the shore."
Shellfish gathered for a meeting, full of disbelief,
Yet another rumor had been floating round the reef.

Conch had heard from winkle (and told pipi shell, of course)
News had spread upon the tide: a brand new seafood sauce!
Oysters shivered in their shells, and baby scallops cried,
Crayfish waved a sign that said "The reef is suicide!"

"Who's this guy called Heinz?" asked abalone in a huff,
"Yeah," said prawn, "aren't fifty-odd varieties enough?"
"I say war," cried oyster, "all crustaceans must unite!
Ring the bells across the swells to come and join the fight!"

"Why should they have bouillabaise?" asked cockle to his mate,
"Surely they are satisfied with meat upon their plate?
We should be the only ones to taste this scrumptious dish,
Humans? Ha! We owe them nothing, let them all eat fish!"

June is the month for backyard graduation parties, weddings, expectations for a busy summer, the fishing season, and for strawberries. The annual strawberry festival in Mattituck, sponsored by the Lions Club, is the biggest single event on the North Fork. It is a time when the farm stands are showing more produce, switching from plants to vegetables and fruits.

June is also when we begin to see more seafood arriving from Canada, the East coast, and our local waters. Flounder, fluke, bluefish, blowfish, weakfish, and cod become available. Lobster, sea scallops, and mussels often come from the maritime provinces of Canada, while clams and oysters are found here on the North Fork. Soft shell crabs, coming from Chesapeake Bay, are at their peak. Cooking a pot of bouillabaisse or grilling local duck is a good way to test your culinary skills and usher in the new season.

Finally, There seem to be lots of birthday parties in June. A tray of carrot cupcakes is a good way to celebrate after a dinner of North Fork food.

Prime Meal
Baked Stuffed Clams Oreganata

Grilled Duck Breast with Rhubarb Compote

Strawberry Feast Cake

Recommended wine: *Pinot Noir*

Selected Recipes
1. North Fork Bouillabaisse
2. Almond-Crusted Fluke with Braised Leeks
3. Grey Sole Poached in Artichoke Sauce
4. Baked Stuffed Artichokes
5. Panko-Crusted Blowfish with Strawberry Salsa
6. Grilled Tuna Steak with Red Wine Sauce
7. Vidalia Onion and Goat Cheese Pie
8. Strawberry Spinach Salad
9. Puree of Strawberry Soup
10. Carrot Cupcakes with Cream Cheese Frosting
11. Pan-Fried Soft Shell Crabs with Fresh Pea Risotto

PRIME MEAL

– First Course –
Baked Stuffed Clams Oreganata

4 portions

2 dozen cherrystone clams

2 Tbsp butter
1 Tbsp minced garlic
½ **cup** minced shallots
½ **cup** minced green pepper
2 plum tomatoes, diced

Reserved chopped clams
2 tbsp chopped oregano
¼ **cup** chopped parsley
½ **tsp** ground pepper
2 cups panko crumbs
Reserved clam juice
2 oz thinly sliced pancetta

1. Scrub the clams under cold water. Open them with a clam knife, reserving the juice and the shells (if clams prove difficult to open, run them under hot tap water for 3 minutes). Chop the clam meat coarsely and refrigerate. Let the sediment in the juice settle, and wash the shells.

2. Heat a large sauté pan and add the butter. Stir in the garlic, shallots and green pepper, and cook at low heat for 5 minutes. Add the tomatoes and chopped clams and increase the heat to medium.

3. Cook another 5 minutes and season with the oregano, parsley, and ground pepper. Remove from the heat and stir in the panko crumbs. Moisten the mixture with clam juice; the mixture should be thick but not dry.

4. Stuff the clam shells with the clam mixture. Cut the pancetta in squares and place them on top of the clams. Bake in a 400 degree oven for 15 minutes and serve.

– *Entree* –
Grilled Duck Breast with Rhubarb Compote

4 portions

2 lbs boneless duck breasts, skin-on
1 tsp kosher salt
½ tsp ground pepper
1 tsp five spice powder

Rhubarb Compote
1 Tbsp olive oil
½ cup minced shallots
1 Tbsp minced garlic
2 Tbsp minced ginger
1 cup water
¾ cup sugar
4 cups diced rhubarb
1 Tbsp rice wine vinegar
½ tsp kosher salt
¼ tsp ground pepper

1. Separate the duck breasts into 4 pieces. Trim off extra fat, leaving the skin on top. Score the skin with the point of a sharp knife into a crosshatch pattern. Combine the salt, pepper, and spice powder and rub over the duck breasts. Refrigerate until service time.

2. Heat a shallow saucepan and add the olive oil. Stir in the shallots and garlic and cook on medium heat for 3 minutes. Add the ginger, water, and sugar, and continue cooking until the sugar dissolves.

3. Add the rhubarb and cook another 3 minutes (do not overcook it). Remove the rhubarb with a slotted spoon and set aside. Bring the liquid to a boil and cook until it reduces to about 1 cup. Lower the heat and add back the rhubarb along with the vinegar, salt, and pepper. Remove from the heat.

4. Prepare a charcoal fire and rub the grill with an oil-soaked paper towel. Grill the duck breasts skin-side down until brown and crisp, then turn and cook another 5 minutes for medium rare. The internal temperature should be 130 degrees.

5. Let the duck breasts rest for 15 minutes and slice on the bias, leaving the skin on. Place a little of the rhubarb compote on the plate with the duck and pass the rest.

Note: *This dish goes well with Jasmine rice and stir fried vegetables.*

– *Wine Notes* –
The lean, medium rare duck breast requires the vibrant acidity of a pinot noir and the rhubarb will provide a background of fruit. An Oregon pinot noir from the Willamette Valley, a Cote de Beaune from France, or a reserve pinot noir from Long Island will be a good match.

– *Dessert* –
Strawberry Feast Cake

8 to 10 portions

4 large eggs
1⅓ cups sugar
1½ cups flour
1½ tsp baking powder
½ cup water
2 quarts ripe strawberries
2 cups heavy cream
½ cup confectioners sugar
1 tsp vanilla extract
1 cup strawberry preserves

1. Beat the eggs and sugar in the bowl of an electric mixer, using the whip attachment, at high speed for a full 15 minutes. Sift the flour and baking powder together in a bowl.

2. Preheat the oven to 350 degrees and spray a 10" springform pan with no-stick. With the mixer on low speed, add the water to the egg mixture, then gradually add the flour mixture. Do not overmix.

3. Pour the batter into the springform pan and bake for 30 minutes, or until a skewer comes out clean when inserted into the middle of the cake. Remove from the oven, let the cake cool, and remove the springform pan.

4. When the cake is completely cool, cut it into three layers using a long serrated bread knife. Place the bottom layer on a cake stand.

5. Trim the tops off the strawberries, rinse, and slice into a bowl, saving 8 whole berries as a garnish. Whip the cream with an electric mixer until soft peaks form. Add the confectioners sugar and vanilla and beat until stiff.

6. Spread a thin coating of strawberry preserves on the bottom layer of the cake, then place sliced berries in a circle on top of the preserves. Spread a layer of whipped cream on the berries and lay the second layer of cake on top. Repeat with the preserves, the berries, and the whipped cream.

7. Place the third layer of cake on top, coat it with whipped cream, and garnish it with the reserved whole berries. Refrigerate before serving.

Grilled Duck Breast with Rhubarb Compote

Strawberry Feast Cake

North Fork Bouillabaisse

6 to 8 portions

Seafood
2 live lobsters (1¼ lbs. each)
1 lb jumbo shrimp, in the shell
8 oz cod fillet, cut into 4
  pieces
8 oz monkfish fillet,
  cut into 4 pieces
1 dozen littleneck clams
1 lb mussels
8 oz sea scallops
1 pint frozen fish stock*

Cooking ingredients
2 Tbsp olive oil
¼ cup brandy
1 cup white wine
2 Tbsp olive oil
1 leek, white part, diced
1 Tbsp minced garlic
1 fennel bulb, diced
1 can (28oz.) San Marzano
  tomatoes
1 orange, zest and juice
¼ tsp hot red pepper flakes
Pinch saffron threads
½ cup basil, sliced

... Indeed, a rich and savory stew 'tis;
And true philosophers, methinks,
Who love all sorts of natural beauties,
Should love good victuals and good drinks.
And Cordelier or Benedictine
Might gladly, sure, his lot embrace,
Nor find a fast-day too afflicting,
Which served him up a bouillabaisse ...
  — William Makepeace Thackeray

1. Hold the lobster, shell side down, on a cutting board and plunge the point of a chefs knife between the tail and the body, then split the lobster in half. Remove the head sac and discard. Cut the claws and the feet off the body.

2. Bring 2 quarts of water to a boil and add the lobster claws. Bring back to boil and simmer for 10 minutes. Remove and cool.

3. Heat a large sauté pan and add the olive oil. Cook the split lobsters shell-side down at high heat until the shells turn bright red. Heat the brandy briefly on the stove, light it with a match, and pour it over the lobsters. Remove the lobsters and set aside (they will not be fully cooked).

4. Add the shrimp, in their shells, to the same pan, adding a little more oil if necessary. Cook the shrimp at high heat for 5 minutes, tossing them in the pan to prevent burning. Remove the shrimp and add the sea scallops, searing them at high heat until just browned. Remove and set aside.

5. Deglaze the pan by adding the wine and scraping up the drippings with a wooden spoon while the pan is still on the heat. Strain the juices into a small saucepan and add the frozen fish stock. Bring this to a boil and set aside.

6. Remove the meat from the lobster claws and set aside. Peel and devein the shrimp. Cut the lobster tails into thirds and discard the lobster bodies.

7. Heat a large, shallow saucepan and add the olive oil. Stir in the leeks, garlic, and fennel. Cook at low heat for 5 minutes and add the reserved fish stock.

8. Chop the tomatoes with a chef's knife, and add them and their puree to the saucepan. Add the orange zest and juice, the red pepper flakes, and the saffron. Simmer at medium heat for 20 minutes.

9. Add the mussels to the simmering sauce and raise the heat. Cover the sauce until the mussels open, then remove them with a slotted spoon and set aside. Add the clams and continue cooking until they open, removing them also.

10. Lower the heat and add the cod and monkfish. Remove the fish after it is just cooked, about 3 minutes. Add the partially cooked lobster tails, shrimp, and scallops. Continue cooking for another 5 minutes.

11. Place all of the cooked seafood on a platter and keep warm. Add the sliced basil to the sauce and check for seasoning. Serve the broth in individual bowls, adding the seafood to it or keeping them separate. Garnish with toasted croutons and rouille sauce.

Note: Other firm-fleshed fish can be substituted depending on what is available at the time. Striped bass, blackfish, and black sea bass are examples. The frozen fish stock is available from the local fish markets and is superior to canned versions. Using whole fish and making your own stock is also an option.

Croutons and Sauce Rouille

– Wine Notes –
The French origins of bouillabaisse might call for a French rosé, but since this is a North Fork version, we might drink a dry rosé made from Cabernet Franc or Merlot. Also a stainless steel fermented Chardonnay from Long Island.

1 French baguette
2 Tbsp olive oil
1 jarred roasted red pepper
2 cloves garlic
1 slice of baguette
1 egg yolk
1 Tbsp Dijon mustard
1 tsp lemon juice
½ tsp kosher salt
¼ tsp ground pepper
½ cup olive oil

1. Cut the baguette into rounds, reserving 1 piece for the sauce. Place these on a foil-lined sheet pan and toast in a 400 degree oven for 10 minutes. Remove them from the oven and brush with olive oil.

2. Add the roasted red pepper, garlic, egg yolk, mustard, lemon juice, salt, and pepper to the bowl of a food processor. Cut the slice of baguette into cubes and add it to the processor.

3. Pulse the whole mixture until it is coarsely chopped, then drizzle in the olive oil. Brush some of the sauce on the croutons and serve the rest on the side.

Almond-Crusted Fluke with Braised Leeks

4 portions

1½ lbs fluke filet
1 tsp kosher salt
½ tsp ground pepper

Almond Crust
1 cup sliced almonds
Zest from **1** lemon
¼ cup chopped parsley
1 cup flour
1 egg, beaten
1 Tbsp water

Braised Leeks
4 leeks
3 Tbsp butter
½ cup shallots, chopped
2 cloves garlic, sliced
1 tsp kosher salt
1 tsp sugar
1 Tbsp fresh thyme leaves
1 bay leaf
1 cup white wine
1 cup fresh sweet peas
    (or substitute frozen)

– Wine Notes –
A Sancerre from the Loire Valley would match the refined nature of this dish. A trocken (dry) Riesling from Germany would also be delicious. My local choice would be a Sauvignon Blanc.

1. Cut the fluke into 8 small filets. Sprinkle with the salt and pepper and refrigerate.

2. Heat a dry sauté pan and add the almonds. Cook until lightly toasted, about 3 minutes. Add the almonds, lemon zest, and parsley to the bowl of a food processor and pulse to a coarse texture. Place this mixture in a shallow pan.

3. Add the flour to another shallow pan and combine the beaten egg and water in a small bowl. Line a sheet pan with foil and spray with no-stick.

4. Dredge each fish filet in flour, then brush one side with egg wash and press it into the almond mixture, coating one side of the fish filet. Lay the filet, crust side up on the sheet pan and repeat with the other filets. Refrigerate.

5. Cut off the green leaves of the leeks just above the white part. Trim off the root and split in half. Rinse under cold water and drain.

6. Heat a large sauté pan and add the butter. Place the leeks In the pan, cut side down. Sauté 3 minutes at medium heat before adding the shallots and garlic. Continue cooking and add the salt, sugar, thyme, and bay leaf.

7. Add the wine, cover, and simmer at low heat for 20 minutes. Remove the cover and bring to a boil, letting the liquid reduce a little. Stir in the peas, cook briefly, and remove from the heat.

8. Put the sheet pan with the breaded fluke into a 425 degree oven and cook for 15 minutes. The top should be brown and the fish beginning to flake.

9. Using a slotted spoon, place the leek mixture on 4 plates and put the fish on top. Garnish with lemon wedges and a sprig of fresh thyme. Serve with boiled potatoes.

Grey Sole Poached in Artichoke sauce

4 portions

1½ lbs gray sole filets
1 tsp kosher salt
½ tsp ground pepper

Artichoke Sauce
2 Tbsp butter
2 shallots, minced
1 stalk celery, minced
1 carrot, peeled and
  diced
1 pkg. frozen artichoke
  hearts
1½ cups chicken stock
¼ cup heavy cream
1 tsp kosher salt
½ tsp ground pepper

1. Cut the sole filets lengthwise through the lateral line. You should end up with 8 small filets. Season with the salt and pepper and fold into small squares. Spray a shallow casserole with no-stick and place the filets in it.

2. Heat a saucepan and add the butter. Stir in the shallots, celery, and carrots and cook at low heat for 5 minutes. Coarsely chop half of the package of frozen artichoke hearts and add them to the pan with the vegetables (reserve the rest of the artichokes for poaching).

3. Add the chicken stock and continue cooking at medium heat for 10 minutes. Puree the mixture in a food processor and return to the pan. Stir in the cream and season with the salt and pepper.

4. Strain the artichoke sauce over the fish filets in the casserole, and add the rest of the artichoke hearts. Cut a piece of foil to fit the top of the casserole, spray it with no-stick, and place it down tight over the fish. Cook in a 400 degree oven until the fish turns opaque, about 25 minutes.

Note: *serve with the following recipe for stuffed artichokes.*

Almond-Crusted Fluke with Braised Leeks

Baked Stuffed Artichoke

Baked Stuffed Artichokes

4 or 8 portions

4 large artichokes
1 lemon
2 quarts cold water

Stuffing
½ cup pine nuts
2 Tbsp olive oil
1 bunch green onions, chopped
3 cloves garlic, minced
Chopped artichoke stems
1 small jar pimientos (4 oz.), chopped
¼ cup capers
1 small can flat anchovies, minced
¼ cup parsley
½ tsp ground pepper
½ cup panko crumbs

– Wine Notes –
Artichokes and asparagus are difficult to match with wine. A Viognier or Riesling may be the best choice.

1. Pour the cold water into a large bowl, cut the lemon in half, and squeeze it into the water. Toss in the rind also.

2. Cut the stems off the artichokes at the base. Peel and trim the stems and put them into the bowl of lemon water. Cut the tops off the artichokes 1" down from the top and break off all outside leaves.

3. Split the artichokes in half through the stem with a large chef's knife and put all the halves in the lemon water. Remove each artichoke half and, using a sharp paring knife, cut out the fuzzy choke and pull out the prickly leaves on top of it. Be careful not to cut into the base. Place each half back in the water as you finish to prevent browning.

4. Lay the artichoke halves in a shallow saucepan, cut-side up. Place the peeled stems in the pan also. Pour in the lemon water to cover the artichokes.

5. Bring the liquid to a boil and simmer, uncovered, until the artichokes are very tender, about 25 minutes. Carefully lift them out, drain, and place onto a foil-lined sheet pan. Chop the artichoke stems and set aside.

6. Heat a dry sauté pan and add the pine nuts. Toast them for 3 minutes at medium heat, remove, and chop coarsely. Add the olive oil to the pan and stir in the green onions and garlic. Cook on low heat for 5 minutes and add the reserved chopped artichoke stems.

7. Continue cooking and add the pimientos, capers, anchovies, parsley, and pepper. Add back the toasted pine nuts along with the panko crumbs and remove from the heat.

8. Stuff the cooked artichoke halves generously with the stuffing and place them back on the lined sheet pan. At service time, heat them in a 400 degree oven for 15 minutes.

Note: *These are excellent when served with the preceding recipe for sole poached in artichoke sauce, but they can also be served as-is for a first course.*

107

Panko-Crusted Blowfish with Strawberry Salsa

4 to 6 portions

2 lbs blowfish

Breading
1 cup flour
1 tsp kosher salt
½ tsp ground pepper
1 egg, beaten
½ cup milk
2 cups panko crumbs

Strawberry Salsa
2 cups strawberries
1 jalapeno pepper
½ yellow pepper
½ green pepper
½ cup red onion, peeled
   and diced

1 orange, zest and juice
1 lime, zest and juice
2 Tbsp olive oil
½ tsp kosher salt
¼ cup chopped cilantro
Few drops Tabasco sauce

Cooking
2 Tbsp olive oil
2 Tbsp butter
1 pkg. baby arugula

1. Remove the bones from the blowfish with a small sharp knife, leaving 2 small fillets for each fish (it is not necessary to bone the blowfish, but doing so makes them easier to cook and to eat).

2. Combine the flour, salt, and pepper in a shallow dish. Whisk the egg and milk together in a bowl and place the panko crumbs in another shallow dish. Dredge the blowfish in the flour, then in the egg wash, and finally in the panko crumbs. Place on a foil-lined sheet pan and refrigerate.

3. For the salsa, coarsely chop the strawberries and put them into a bowl. Split the jalapeno, remove the seeds, and mince finely (use only half for a milder salsa). Finely dice the yellow and green peppers and add to the strawberries along with the diced red onion.

4. Stir in the orange zest and juice, the lime zest and juice, the olive oil, salt, cilantro, and Tabasco sauce. Check for seasoning and refrigerate.

5. At service time, heat a large sauté pan and add the olive oil and butter. Sauté the breaded blowfish quickly on medium heat, turning them with tongs to prevent burning. Cook in batches if necessary. Serve the blowfish on a bed of arugula with the salsa on the

– Wine Notes –
I recommend one of the great dry roses from the North Fork.
A village Chablis from France would also be good.

Grilled Tuna Steak with Red Wine Sauce and Portabella Mushrooms

4 thick tuna steaks (about 2 lbs total)
1 tsp kosher salt
½ tsp ground pepper
4 portabella mushroom caps
1 Tbsp Dijon mustard

Red Wine Sauce
2 Tbsp olive oil
½ cup chopped shallots
½ cup chopped celery
1 Tbsp minced garlic
1 pkg. baby bella mushrooms
2 sprigs thyme
1 tsp crushed black peppercorns
1 cup red wine (pinot noir is best)
¾ cup beef stock
2 Tbsp balsamic vinegar
½ cup chopped shallots
1 Tbsp cornstarch
2 Tbsp cold water

1. Season the tuna steaks with the salt and pepper and refrigerate. Remove the stems and scrape the gills out of the mushroom caps with a spoon. Spread the mustard on the insides of the mushrooms and set aside.

2. For the sauce, heat a shallow saucepan and add the oil. Stir in the shallots, celery, and garlic. Cook at low heat for 3 minutes. Trim the mushrooms and cut them into quarters. Add them to the pan and cook, uncovered, at medium heat until the mushrooms give up their moisture, about 10 minutes.

3. Add the thyme, peppercorns, red wine, and beef stock. Cook at medium heat for 20 minutes and strain into a clean saucepan, pressing out all the juices with a wooden spoon.

4. Put the pan on high heat and add the balsamic vinegar and the shallots. Continue to boil until the liquid is reduced by half. Dissolve the cornstarch in the water and add to the sauce. When slightly thickened, reduce the heat to low and check for seasoning.

5. Prepare a charcoal grill and wait until the coals turn white. Rub the grill with an oil-soaked paper towel. Spray the tuna steaks with no-stick and place on the hottest part of the grill. Turn 90 degrees to create grill marks and turn the tuna over, cooking quickly to keep the center rare.

6. Grill the mushroom caps along with the tuna, cooking them with the underside facing up. Serve with the red wine sauce on the tuna and the mushrooms.

Note: *Wild rice is a good accompaniment for this dish.*

– Wine Notes –
A robust Pinot Noir from Carneros, a red Burgundy, or a reserve Pinot Noir from the North Fork would match the sauce and the earthy mushroom flavors.

Vidalia Onion and Goat Cheese Pie

6 to 8 portions

Pie Crust
1½ cups flour
½ tsp salt
1 tsp sugar
4 Tbsp cold butter
4 Tbsp (¼ cup) cold
  shortening
5 tbsp ice water

Filling
2 large Vidalia onions
2 Tbsp olive oil

1 leek, white part, sliced
2 sprigs thyme
6 parsley stems
1 bay leaf
3 cloves peeled garlic
2 tsp kosher salt
1 tsp ground pepper
Dash hot red pepper
  flakes

Custard
2 eggs
½ cup heavy cream
½ cup milk

Toppings
2 oz goat cheese
6 strips anchovy
6 strips pimiento (roasted
  red pepper)
12 pitted Kalamata olives

1. Add the flour, salt, and sugar to the bowl of a food processor and pulse until combined. Add the cold butter and shortening and pulse until the mixture resembles coarse cornmeal.

2. Add the ice water and pulse to form a dough. Turn out on a floured board and knead a few times, then flatten into a disc. Wrap in plastic film and refrigerate 30 minutes.

3. Peel the onions, cut them in half, and slice thinly with the grain. Heat a large sauté pan and add the oil. Add the sliced onions and cook at medium heat for 3 minutes.

4. Tie together the leek, thyme, parsley, and bay leaf to make a bouquet garni. Add to the onions along with the garlic, salt, pepper, and red pepper flakes. Reduce the heat to low, cover, and cook for 30 minutes. Remove the bouquet garni and the garlic.

4. For the custard, whisk together the eggs, cream, and milk in a bowl and set aside.

6. Roll out the pie crust and place it in a 9" deep pie pan. Poke holes in the crust with a dinner fork and put it in a 425 degree oven for 5 minutes. Add the cooked onions to the pie and pour the custard mixture over the onions. Continue baking at 425 degrees for another 15 minutes.

7. Remove the pie from the oven and arrange the goat cheese, anchovies, pimiento, and olives on the top. Lower the oven temperature to 375 degrees and bake for another 30 minutes, or until the filling is set and a skewer comes out clean.

Grilled Tuna Steak with Portabella

Vidalia Onion and Goat Cheese Pie

Strawberry Spinach Salad

4 to 6 portions

Dressing
2 Tbsp raspberry vinegar
1 lemon, zest and juice
2 Tbsp minced shallots
1 tsp honey
½ tsp kosher salt
½ tsp ground pepper
2 chopped strawberries
¼ cup extra virgin olive oil

Salad
4 oz baby spinach
1 pint fresh strawberries
½ cup sliced almonds
4 oz goat cheese

1. Combine the vinegar, lemon zest and juice, shallots, honey, salt, pepper, and strawberries in a bowl and whisk in the olive oil (or combine all ingredients in a Mason jar and shake vigorously).

2. Plunge the spinach in cold water to wash and remove the stems. Dry in a salad spinner, wrap in paper towels, and refrigerate.

3. Rinse the strawberries, remove the hulls, and slice into a bowl. Heat a dry sauté pan and add the almonds, toasting them for 3 minutes.

4. Toss the spinach and strawberries with the dressing and portion onto individual salad plates. Garnish with the toasted almonds and the goat cheese.

Puree of Strawberry Soup

4 to 6 portions

1 quart strawberries
1 cup freshly squeezed
    orange juice (3 oranges)
¼ cup mint leaves
¼ tsp ground cinnamon
1 Tbsp honey
⅛ tsp ground allspice
1 lemon, zest and juice
1 lime, zest and juice
2 cups buttermilk

1. Rinse the berries and cut off the stems, reserving 8 whole berries for garnish. Place the strawberries, orange juice, mint, cinnamon, honey, and allspice in the bowl of a food processor and puree. Transfer to a large bowl.

2. Add the lemon zest and juice and the lime zest and juice. Stir in the buttermilk and refrigerate. Serve in chilled bowls and garnish with the whole strawberries, mint leaves, lemon, and lime slices.

Carrot Cupcakes with Cream Cheese Frosting

24 cupcakes

1 lb carrots
¾ cup brown sugar
1 cup fresh pineapple,
    diced
¾ cup dried apricots
¼ cup brandy
24 paper cupcake liners
2 cups flour
1 tsp baking soda
2 tsp ground cinnamon
½ tsp salt
3 eggs
1 cup sugar
¾ cup canola oil
1 tsp vanilla extract
¾ cup chopped walnuts

Frosting

8 oz cream cheese
5 Tbsp butter
1 Tbsp sour cream
1 tsp vanilla extract
Pinch of salt
1 cup confectioners sugar
Carrot curls

1. Trim and peel the carrots. Grate them into a bowl using the large holes of a box grater. Stir in the brown sugar and set aside.

2. Trim a fresh pineapple and cut a wedge out of it (save the rest for another use). Peel and dice the pineapple into small pieces to make 1 cup. Chop the dried apricots and soak them in a small dish with the brandy.

3. Line 2 muffin tins with the paper liners and preheat the oven to 350 degrees.

4. Whisk the flour, baking soda, cinnamon, and salt together in a bowl. In a separate bowl, whisk the eggs until frothy, then whisk in the sugar, oil, and vanilla. Stir in the flour mixture to form a batter.

5. Fold in the pineapple and apricots along with their juices. Fold in the grated carrots and the walnuts, making sure the mixture is well combined.

6. Using a ⅓ cup measure and a spoon, fill the cupcake liners with the batter about ¾ full. You should have enough for 24 cupcakes. Bake at 350 degrees for 40 minutes. They should be firm and a skewer inserted should come out clean. Cool on a rack before frosting.

7. For the frosting, place the cream cheese and the butter in the bowl of an electric mixer. Using the paddle attachment, mix at medium speed until light and fluffy. Reduce the speed to low and add the sour cream, vanilla, and salt. Gradually add the confectioners sugar and beat until smooth.

8. Frost the cupcakes and garnish with carrot curls.

Carrot Cupcakes

My granddaughter Shaina and sister Danielle
celebrating Shaina's birthday with carrot cupcakes

Pan-Fried Soft Shell Crabs with Fresh Pea Risotto

4 portions

To bread the crabs
4 live jumbo soft shell crabs
   (cleaned at fish market)
1 cup flour
1 tsp kosher salt
½ tsp ground pepper
1 tsp Old Bay seasoning
2 eggs, beaten
2 Tbsp water
2 cups cracker meal
1 Tbsp smoked paprika

For the risotto
3 cups chicken stock
2 Tbsp olive oil
½ cup chopped shallots
1 cup Arborio rice

1 cup white wine

½ cup pine nuts
2 cups snow pea shoots
1 cup fresh peas
2 Tbsp cold butter

¼ cup canola oil
Lemon wedges
Chopped parsley

1. Place the flour in a shallow pan and mix in the salt, pepper, and Old Bay. Whisk the eggs and water together in a separate bowl. Add the cracker meal to a shallow casserole and stir in the paprika.

2. Dredge the crabs in the flour, then in the egg mixture, and then press them into the cracker meal. Place on a tray and refrigerate.

3. For the risotto, heat the chicken stock in a saucepan and set aside. Heat another saucepan and add the olive oil. Stir in the shallots and the Arborio rice.

4. Continue cooking at medium-high heat and add the wine. When it evaporates, begin adding the chicken stock ½ cup at a time, stirring with a wooden spoon. Continue cooking until the rice is tender, about 20 minutes.

5. Toast the pine nuts in a dry sauté pan and add them to the risotto. Chop the snow pea shoots and add them to the risotto along with the fresh peas. Stir in the cold butter and check the risotto for seasoning.

6. Heat a large sauté pan and add the canola oil. When hot, but not smoking, add the crabs to the pan belly side-down. Cook until golden, about 3 minutes, and turn with a metal spatula. Do not crowd the pan.

7. To serve, place a large spoonful of the risotto in the center of each plate and put a crab on top. Garnish with a wedge of lemon and chopped parsley.

July

— The Envious Lobster —
By H.F. Gould

A lobster from the water came,
And saw another, just the same
In form and size, but gaily clad
In scarlet clothing, while she had
No other raiment to her back,
Than her old suit of greenish black.

"So ho!" she cried, " 'tis very fine!
Your dress was yesterday like mine,
And in the mud, below the sea,
You lived, a crawling thing, like me.
But now, because you've come ashore
You've grown so proud, that what you wore,
Your strong old suit of bottle-green
You think improper to be seen!
To tell the truth, I don't see why
You should be better dressed than I;
and I should like a suit of red
As bright as yours, from feet to head.
I think I'm quite as good as you;
And I'll be dressed in scarlet, too!"

"Will you be boiled," the owner said,
"To be arrayed in glowing red?
Come here, my discontented Miss,
And hear the scalding kettle hiss!
Will you go in, and there be boiled
To have your dress so old and soiled,
Exchanged for one of scarlet hue?"

"Yes!" cried the lobster, "that I'll do,
And thrice as much, if needs must be
To be as gaily clad as she!"
Then, in she made a fatal dive
And never more was seen alive.
Now, those who learn the lobster's fate,
Will see how envy could create
A vain desire within her breast,
And pride of dress could do the rest,
That brought her to an early death:
'Twas love of show that cost her breath.

July begins with a celebration of Independence Day on July 4th. Before the fireworks begin, we eat everything from hot dogs to fried chicken to T-bone steaks. But it is also a time when the abundance of local produce makes the North Fork come alive.

At Ross' North Fork Restaurant, I waited until July to offer our signature Lobster Stew. We had to wait until local snap peas, leeks, peppers, corn, and lobster became available. We would then buy our ingredients from the farm stand at the peak of freshness, cook them at the last possible minute, and serve them for our customers to enjoy. On Monday, when we were closed, I would celebrate the July 4th holiday on our deck with my family, enjoying lobster stew and a bottle of barrel-fermented Long Island chardonnay.

Prime Meal

Roasted Beet, Orange, Walnut, and Arugula Salad

———

Ross' Summer Lobster Stew

———

Fourth of July Mousse

Recommended wine: *Barrel-Fermented Chardonnay*

Selected Recipes

1. *Cedar-Roasted Lobster Stew with Sea Scallops*
2. *Lobster Risotto*
3. *Pan-Seared Striped Bass with Grilled Corn Polenta*
4. *Poached Halibut with Mussels, Leeks and Wax Beans*
5. *Grilled Duck Breast with Orecchiette*
6. *Roasted Cod with Thyme and Lemon Corn Sauce*
7. *Cherrystone Clam Pie*
8. *Zucchini Spaghetti with Pesto*
9. *Seared Sea Scallops with Zucchini Pancakes*
10. *Pulled Pork and Barbecued Beans*
11. *Brewed Bratwurst with Caraway Sauerkraut*

PRIME MEAL

– *First Course* –
Roasted Beet, Orange, Walnut and Arugula Salad

4 portions

1 bunch red (or mixed color) beets, about 1 lb.
1 Tbsp canola oil

Dressing
1 navel orange
¼ cup champagne vinegar
2 tsp Dijon mustard
1 Tbsp minced shallots
¼ tsp kosher salt
¼ tsp ground pepper
½ cup extra virgin olive oil

Roasted Walnuts
1 tsp five spice powder
¼ cup sugar
2 Tbsp honey
2 Tbsp water
1 cup walnut halves
1 pkg. baby arugula
2 navel oranges

1. Trim the stems and roots off the beets. Wash thoroughly and brush with oil. Wrap loosely in foil, place on a sheet pan, and roast at 400 degrees for 45 minutes, or until a skewer runs through easily. Remove from the oven and cool. Peel and cut into bite-sized wedges.

2. Remove the zest from the orange with a fine grater and squeeze the juice. Whisk together the orange juice, zest, vinegar, mustard, shallots, salt, and pepper. Gradually whisk in the olive oil and set aside.

3. Bring the spice powder, sugar, honey, and water to a boil in a small saucepan. Add the walnuts and cook until most of the liquid evaporates. Spray a foil-lined sheet pan with no-stick and place the walnut mixture on it. Roast for 5 minutes at 400 degrees.

4. Wash the arugula in cold water and dry in a salad spinner. Toss with ¼ cup of the dressing in a salad bowl and portion onto 4 salad plates. Toss the beets in 2 tablespoons of the dressing and arrange on the plates.

5. Cut the oranges into segments and add to the salad plates. Garnish with the roasted walnuts and pass the remaining dressing.

– Entree –
Summer Lobster Stew

4 to 6 portions

4 live lobsters (1¼ lb each)

1 Tbsp canola oil
¼ cup brandy

1 cup chopped onion
½ cup chopped celery
½ cup chopped carrot
1 plum tomato, diced
Reserved lobster broth
1 tsp Old Bay seasoning
2 bay leaves
1 tsp kosher salt
6 whole peppercorns

4 Tbsp butter
2 leeks, white part, diced
2 carrots, peeled and
        thinly sliced
1 Tbsp minced garlic
2 plum tomatoes, diced
8 small new potatoes,
        skin-on, cut in half

1 cup heavy cream
4 ears very fresh corn on
        the cob
½ lb sugar snap peas
¼ cup chopped parsley

1. Bring 6 quarts of water to a boil in a large stock pot. Plunge the lobsters into the pot, cover, and bring back to a boil. Simmer for 5 minutes and remove the lobsters with tongs, reserving the broth (the lobsters will not be fully cooked). Break off the lobster claws and the tails and put them back in the simmering water for 10 minutes and remove. Reserve 2 quarts of the cooking water.

2. Split the lobster bodies in half and remove the head sac. Scrape out any tomalley and coral and reserve.

3. Heat a large sauté pan, add the oil, and place the lobster bodies shell-side down in the pan. Cook at high heat until the shells turn bright red. Warm the brandy in a small pan, light it with a match, and pour over the lobster bodies.

4. Add the onion, celery, and carrot to the pan and continue cooking on medium heat. Add the tomato and enough of the lobster broth to cover the bodies. Season with the Old Bay, bay leaves, salt, and peppercorns. Simmer for 30 minutes and strain.

5. In a large, shallow saucepan, melt the butter and add the leeks and carrots. Cook at low heat for 3 minutes and add the garlic and tomatoes. Increase the heat to medium and add the potatoes and 4 cups of the lobster stock. Simmer until the potatoes are tender, about 15 minutes.

6. Remove the meat from the lobster claws and tails and cut into bite-sized pieces. Shuck the corn and cut the kernels off the cob with a sharp paring knife. Rinse and pull the strings off the sugar snap peas.

7. Add the cream, lobster meat, corn, and peas to the simmering potato mixture. Stir in the chopped parsley and check for seasoning. Serve in large pasta bowls.
   Note: *if local sugar snap peas aren't available, substitute fresh local string beans. Cut them into bite-size pieces and blanch in boiling water before adding to the stew.*

Continued...

John and Lois Ross are joined by friends Jane and Cliff Utz and
Larry and Barbara Salmieri for Lobster Stew.

– Wine Notes –

The rich nature of lobster and the creamy sauce deserve a well-balanced Chardonnay with a little oak aging. When a big celebration was part of this meal, we would open a bottle of French Meursault.

Optional garnishes:

<u>Croutons</u> – cut a baguette into rounds and place them on a foil-lined sheet pan. Brush with olive oil and spread the reserved tomalley and coral on them. Roast in a 400 degree oven for 10 minutes.

<u>Clams or mussels</u> – steam 16 littleneck clams or ½ lb. of mussels in 2 cups of the lobster cooking water until they open. Place them on the sides of the pasta bowls.

Note: *This recipe is called Ross' Lobster Stew because it was a signature menu item at my restaurant, Ross' North Fork Restaurant, in Southold. The cooking method has evolved over the years into a number of versions, but the original inspiration has not changed. Cook this only during the season when the ingredients are at their best.*

– *Dessert* –
Fourth of July Mousse

4 to 6 portions

1 Tbsp plain gelatin
⅛ tsp salt
¼ cup sugar
2 eggs, separated
1¼ cups milk

½ tsp vanilla extract

Reserved egg whites
¼ cup sugar
1 cup heavy cream

Raspberry Sauce
½ pint fresh raspberries
¼ cup currant jelly
2 tsp sugar

1 tsp cornstarch
1 Tbsp cold water
½ pint fresh blueberries

1. Whisk together the gelatin, salt, and sugar and pour into a small saucepan. Beat the egg yolks and the milk and add to the saucepan. Cook over low heat until the gelatin and sugar are dissolved, about 5 minutes.

2. Remove from the heat and add the vanilla. Chill until the mixture begins to thicken.

3. Beat the reserved egg whites with an electric mixer until foamy, then add the sugar and beat until stiff peaks form. Fold this into the chilled gelatin mixture.

4. Beat the heavy cream with an electric mixer until stiff and fold into the gelatin mixture with a rubber spatula. Spoon the mousse into serving goblets or glass dishes and chill until well set, about 1 hour.

5. For the raspberry sauce, combine the raspberries, currant jelly, and sugar in a saucepan, bring to a boil, stirring with a wooden spoon, and remove from the heat. Transfer to the bowl of a food processor and puree. Strain back into the saucepan.

6. Dissolve the cornstarch in the water and stir into the raspberry mixture. Bring back to a boil and remove from the heat. Refrigerate until chilled.

7. At service time, spoon the raspberry sauce over the mousse and garnish with the blueberries.

Cedar-Roasted Lobster Stew with Sea Scallops

4 portions

4 cedar boards (or untreated cedar roofing shingles)

2 live lobsters (1¼ lbs. each)

1 lb fresh sea scallops
6 ears corn on the cob, shucked
¼ cup canola oil

1 cup white wine
1 cup water
1 lb fresh mussels

3 Tbsp butter
½ cup chopped shallots
1 Tbsp minced garlic
½ cup chopped celery
¼ cup flour
1 lb potatoes, peeled and diced
1 cup heavy cream
½ cup chopped parsley

1. Soak the cedar boards in water for at least 1 hour. Prepare the charcoal grill, waiting for white coals, and rubbing the grill with an oil-soaked paper towel.

2. Split the live lobsters by holding them down on a cutting board, shell-side down. Plunge the tip of a chefs knife between the body and the tail, then split the lobster in two. Remove the head sac and cut off the claws.

3. Remove the cedar boards from the water and place them on the hot grill. Cook, turning once, for about 4 minutes total, being careful not to burn. Brush the boards with canola oil and place the lobsters on the wood, shell-side down.

4. Put the sea scallops on metal skewers and place them next to the lobsters on the boards. Brush the corn with oil and place it around the edges of the grill. Cover the grill and let everything cook for 15 minutes. If the wood catches fire, sprinkle a little water on it. Remove everything to a sheet pan and bring to the kitchen.

5. Pour the wine and water into a large, shallow saucepan and bring to a boil. Add the reserved lobster claws, bring back to a boil, and simmer for 10 minutes. Remove and cool. Add the mussels, cover, and bring back to a boil. As they open, remove them with a slotted spoon. Reserve the broth.

6. Remove the meat from the lobster tails and claws and cut it into bite-sized pieces. Scrape out the tomalley and coral and reserve. Cut the corn off the cobs with a paring knife and set aside. Put the lobster bodies and the corn cobs into the broth, simmer for 30 minutes, and strain.

7. Melt the butter in a large, shallow saucepan and add the shallots, garlic, and celery. Cook briefly and stir in the flour. Whisk the broth into the pan and continue cooking at medium heat until it thickens. Add the diced potatoes, simmer until tender, then stir in the heavy cream.

8. Add the lobster meat, scallops, and corn kernels. Chop the
    reserved tomalley and coral and add to the sauce. Simmer until
    all seafood is cooked. Check for seasoning and serve in pasta
    bowls. Garnish with the mussels and parsley.

Cedar-Roasted Lobster Stew

Cedar-Roasted Lobster Stew

Lobster Risotto

4 to 6 portions

2 live lobsters, 1¼ lbs. each

Lobster Stock
2 Tbsp olive oil
1 onion, peeled and chopped
1 stalk of celery, chopped
1 carrot, chopped
2 cloves garlic, sliced
1 tsp Old Bay seasoning
1 bay leaf
6 whole black peppercorns

Risotto
2 Tbsp olive oil
½ cup chopped shallots
1½ cups Arborio rice
1 cup white wine
6 cups lobster stock (from above)
2 cups fresh sweet peas (or 1 pkg. frozen)
1 Tbsp chopped fresh tarragon
2 tsp kosher salt
1 tsp ground pepper

1. Bring 4 quarts of water to a boil in a large stock pot. Plunge the lobsters into the pot, cover, and bring back to a boil. Simmer for 5 minutes and remove lobsters with a pair of tongs, reserving the broth.

2. Break off the claws and the tails and put them back in the simmering broth for 10 more minutes. Split the bodies, remove the head sac, and set aside.

3. Heat a wide, shallow saucepan and add the oil. Place the split lobster bodies in the pan shell-side down. Cook at high heat for 3 minutes and reduce the heat.

4. Add the onion, celery, carrot, and garlic. Continue to cook for 5 minutes and ladle in 8 cups of the lobster broth. Season with the Old Bay, bay leaf, and peppercorns. Simmer for 30 minutes and strain.

5. Remove all the meat from the lobster claws and tails and cut it into small, bite-sized pieces and set aside.

6. Heat a wide, shallow saucepan and add the olive oil. Stir in the shallots and rice and cook at medium heat, stirring, for 3 minutes. Add the wine and cook until it is almost completely evaporated.

7. Ladle in the lobster stock, one ladle at a time, allowing each addition to reduce before adding more. Continue cooking, stirring with a wooden spoon, until rice is tender, about 25 minutes.

8. Bring the remaining lobster broth to a boil and quickly blanch the peas. Strain the peas and add them to the rice along with the tarragon, salt, and pepper. Fold in the cooked lobster meat and serve in pasta bowls.

– Wine Notes –

Lobster and Chardonnay seem to be very good companions in many different styles. Sometimes the wine is more important than the food and vice versa. Lobster risotto is a good way to show off a rare white Burgundy or expensive Napa Chardonnay, but you can also enjoy lobster with a barrel-fermented local Chardonnay.

Pan-Seared Striped Bass with Grilled Corn Polenta

4 portions

1½ lbs striped bass,
   boneless, skin on
1 tsp kosher salt
½ tsp ground pepper

Polenta
2 Tbsp olive oil
1 cup chopped onion
1 tsp minced garlic
Kernels from **2 ears** of
   fresh corn
1 tsp kosher salt
½ tsp ground pepper

2 cups water
1 tsp kosher salt
1 cup stone-ground
   cornmeal
1 Tbsp butter
½ cup grated parmesan
   cheese

4 ears fresh corn on
   the cob, shucked
¼ cup olive oil

1. Cut the bass into 4 equal pieces about 1" thick. Sprinkle with the salt and pepper and refrigerate.

2. Heat a sauté pan and add the olive oil. Stir in the onion, garlic, corn, salt, and pepper. Cook over medium heat for 5 minutes and remove from the heat.

3. Bring the water and salt to a boil in a saucepan and stir in the cornmeal. Lower the heat, stirring, for 5 minutes, or until large bubbles form and the cornmeal is cooked. Remove from the heat and stir in the corn mixture, the butter, and the grated cheese.

4. Spray a shallow casserole with no-stick and scrape the polenta into it with a rubber spatula. Refrigerate until firm.

5. Prepare a charcoal grill and rub the grill with an oil-soaked paper towel. Cut the polenta into squares and remove from the casserole. Brush the squares with oil and grill over high heat, turning to make grill marks. Brush the corn on the cob with oil and grill alongside the polenta.

6. For the bass, spray a large sauté pan with no-stick and place on high heat on the stove. Add 1 Tbsp. olive oil and wait until it shimmers. Spray the bass skin with the no-stick and lay it skin-side down in the pan. Press the fish down with a metal spatula to insure the skin is crisp.

7. Cook about 4 minutes and turn with a thin metal fish spatula. Cook another 4 minutes on medium heat and check for doneness. Remove and serve with the corn and polenta.
   Note: *The bass can also be grilled over charcoal with the skin on, but make sure the grill has been rubbed liberally with oil before cooking.*

– Wine Notes –

Striped bass is a full-flavored fish with a fairly high oil content. A white wine with good structure and acidity will match well. I like a dry Spatlese Trocken Riesling from Germany because it is a big wine with lots of fruit, acidity, and a mineral character. An Italian Gavi from the Piedmont would also be good.

Poached Halibut with Leeks, Shallots, Mussels and Wax Beans

4 portions

1½ lbs halibut fillet, bones and skin removed
1 tsp kosher salt
½ tsp ground pepper

2 Tbsp butter
2 leeks, white part, diced
2 shallots, minced
2 cloves garlic, minced
2 Tbsp fresh marjoram, chopped

1 cup sauvignon blanc wine

2 cups yellow wax beans, cut into 2" pieces
½ lb mussels, rinsed

½ cup heavy cream
1 lemon, zest and juice
¼ cup chopped parsley

1. Cut the halibut into 4 equal pieces, season with the salt and pepper, and set aside.

2. Place a large sauté pan on low heat and add the butter. Add the leeks, shallots, garlic, and marjoram. Cover and cook on low heat for 5 minutes (this is called "sweating").

3. Remove the lid, place the halibut on top of the vegetables, and pour the wine over all. Cut a piece of foil (or parchment) to fit the sauté pan and spray with no-stick. Push the foil down so that it is right on top of the fish.

4. Put the regular cover back on the pan and cook at medium heat until the fish begins to flake, about 4 minutes. Carefully remove the fish and set aside.

5. Bring 1 quart of water to a boil and blanch the beans until they are crisp-tender, and drain. Add the mussels to the sauté pan the fish were in, cover, and bring to a boil.

6. Cook at high heat until the mussels open, about 5 minutes. Remove the mussels and lower the heat. Add the cream and the lemon zest and juice. Stir in the parsley and check for seasoning.

7. Put the cooked fish back in the pan along with the wax beans. Remove most of the mussels from their shells and add to the pan. Save some of the mussels in their shells for garnish, if desired. Bring the pan to a boil and serve in pasta bowls.

Note: *Other firm fleshed fish will work with this recipe. Cod, haddock, blackfish, and striped bass are examples. Halibut works so well because of its delicate flavor which doesn't overshadow the aromatic vegetables.*

– Wine Notes –

The firm flesh and delicate flavor of halibut along with the cooking method of poaching, will go best with a Sauvignon Blanc-based wine. A white Bordeaux from Pessac-Leognan or Graves, or a Sancerre from the Loire Valley would fit perfectly. A local North Fork Sauvignon Blanc would also do well.

— Attack of the Squash People —
By Marge Piercy

And thus the people every year
in the valley of humid July
did sacrifice themselves
to the long green phallic god
and eat and eat and eat.

They're coming, they're on us,
the long striped gourds, the silky
babies, the hairy adolescents,
the lumpy vast adults
like the trunks of green elephants.
Recite fifty zucchini recipes!

Zucchini tempura; creamed soup;
sauté with olive oil and cumin,
tomatoes, onion; frittata;
casserole of lamb; baked,
topped with cheese; marinated;
stuffed; stewed; driven
through the heart like a stake.

Get rid of old friends: they too
have gardens and full trunks.
Look for newcomers: befriend
them in the post office, unload
on them and run. Stop tourists
in the street. Take truckloads
to Boston. Give to your Red Cross.
Beg on the highway: please
take my zucchini, I have a crippled
mother at home with heartburn.

Sneak out before dawn to drop
them in other people's gardens,
in baby buggies at churchdoors.
Shot, smuggling zucchini into
mailboxes, a federal offense.

With a suave reptilian glitter
you bask among your raspy
fronds sudden and huge as
alligators. You give and give
too much, like summer days
limp with heat, thunderstorms
bursting their bags on our heads,
as we salt and freeze and pickle
for the too little to come.

Grilled Duck Breast with Orecchiette

4 to 6 portions

2 boneless duck breasts, skin on (about 3 lbs.)

Marinade
¼ cup sherry vinegar
1 Tbsp minced garlic
½ cup. olive oil
1 tsp kosher salt
1 tsp ground pepper
¼ tsp Tabasco sauce

Vegetables
2 portabella mushroom caps
1 green pepper
1 red pepper
1 yellow pepper
1 red onion

2 zucchini
¼ cup olive oil
1 Tbsp fresh oregano
2 tsp kosher salt
1 tsp ground pepper

1 pkg. orecchiette (12 oz.)
1 bunch broccoli rabe

1 cup sundried tomatoes
1 cup basil leaves
4 oz Parmigiano-Reggiano cheese

1. Cut the duck breasts into 4 halves and trim excess fat, leaving the skin on. Score the skin with a sharp knife point in a cross-hatch pattern.

2. Combine the vinegar, garlic, oil, salt, pepper, and Tabasco. Place the duck in a shallow casserole and pour the marinade over them. Refrigerate 1 hour or more.

3. Scrape the gills out of the mushroom caps with a spoon. Cut the peppers in half, remove the seeds, and trim the ends. Peel the onion and cut into thick slices.

4. Split the zucchini in half lengthwise and cut into quarters. Place the olive oil, oregano, salt, and pepper in a large bowl and toss all the vegetables together.

5. Prepare a charcoal grill and wait for the coals to turn white. Rub the grill with an oil-soaked paper towel. Remove the duck from the marinade and pat it dry with a paper towel. Place it on the hot grill skin-side down and cook for about 5 minutes before turning it over. Cook another 3 minutes and remove (it should be medium rare).

6. Place all of the vegetables on the grill, cover, and cook until lightly charred. Remove the vegetables and the duck to the kitchen. Bring 4 quarts of water to a boil and add the orecchiette. Wash and trim the broccoli rabe and chop it coarsely. When the orecchiette is almost cooked, add the broccoli rabe, bring it back to a boil, and drain.

7. Soak the sundried tomatoes in hot tap water for 5 minutes and drain. Chop them and set aside. Cut up the grilled vegetables into 2" pieces and place in a large bowl. Add the sundried tomatoes.

8. Slice the duck breasts and cut the slices into bite-sized pieces. Add them to the bowl with the vegetables. Add the cooked orecchiette and the broccoli rabe to the bowl and gently toss with the other ingredients.

9. Heat the leftover marinade in a small saucepan and pour over the pasta mixture in the bowl. Roll up the basil leaves and cut into thin ribbons (chiffonade) and add them to the bowl. Shave the parmesan cheese with a vegetable peeler and garnish the bowl with it.

– Wine Notes –

This pasta dish with duck and lots of vegetables is for summer, as is a dry rose from Long Island. You might also enjoy a medium bodied Pinot Noir or a Beaujolais with this dish.

Roasted Cod with Thyme and Lemon Corn Sauce

4 portions

1½ lbs fresh cod fillet
¼ cup canola oil
4 sprigs thyme
1 lemon, zest and juice
½ tsp kosher salt
½ tsp ground pepper
¾ cup panko crumbs
1 tsp lemon pepper
    seasoning

Corn Sauce
4 ears corn on the cob
2 Tbsp butter
1 Tbsp fresh thyme
Zest from **1** lemon
1 tsp minced garlic
1 tsp kosher salt
½ tsp ground pepper
Juice from **1** lemon

1. Cut the cod into 4 equal sized fillets and remove any small bones. Place in a shallow casserole and refrigerate.

2. Heat the oil in a small saucepan and add the thyme. Shut off the heat and let stand for 15 minutes. Add the lemon zest and juice, salt, and pepper. Cool to room temperature, then pour over cod fillets. Refrigerate for 30 minutes or more.

3. Combine the panko and lemon pepper seasoning. Remove the cod from the thyme oil and place on a foil-lined sheet pan. Sprinkle the panko crumbs on the cod and press into the flesh with your hands. Drizzle a little of the thyme oil on the fish.

4. Shuck the corn and strip the kernels with a sharp paring knife. Heat a sauté pan and add the butter. When it just begins to brown, add the corn kernels. Stir in the thyme, lemon zest, and garlic.

5. Continue to cook for 5 minutes and remove from the heat. Using a slotted spoon, transfer half the corn to the bowl of a food processor and pulse until smooth. Add the pureed corn back to the pan and season with the salt, pepper, and lemon juice.

6. At service time, roast the cod in a 400 degree oven until the fish turns opaque and begins to flake, about 15 minutes. Spoon the corn sauce onto the plates and put the cod on top. If desired, split 2 lemons in half, brush them with oil, and grill them cut side-down until lightly charred. Serve on the side as a garnish.

– **Wine Notes** –
The mild flavor of cod with lemon and corn would be great with a village Chablis from France or a crisp, clean stainless steel Chardonnay from Long Island.

Cherrystone Clam Pie

6 to 8 portions

Pie Crust
2½ cups flour
1 tsp salt
1 cup chilled shortening
½ cup ice water

Filling
2 dozen cherrystone clams
2 lbs russet potatoes
2 cups chopped kale leaves
4 strips bacon, diced
1 onion, chopped
1 Tbsp fresh rosemary, chopped
1 tsp ground pepper
2 Tbsp flour
1 Tbsp butter
1 egg
1 Tbsp water

1. Place the flour and salt in a stainless bowl. Cut the chilled shortening into small pieces and add to the flour mixture. Cut in the shortening with a pastry blender so that it resembles coarse cornmeal (if desired, add to a food processor and pulse until combined).

2. Sprinkle the ice water into the bowl and stir with a fork to form a dough. Turn out the dough onto a floured surface and knead with your hands to form 2 balls of dough. Flatten these into discs, wrap in plastic film, and refrigerate for 30 minutes.

3. Shuck the clams over a bowl, reserving the juice (if they are difficult to open, soak them In very hot tap water for 5 minutes). Chop the clams coarsely and refrigerate. Let the sediment settle in the clam juice, then pour it into a saucepan.

4. Peel the potatoes, cut them into chunks, and add them to the clam juice in the saucepan. If necessary, add a little water to the pan to cover the potatoes. Simmer the potatoes until fully cooked.

5. Add the chopped kale to the pan and continue cooking for another 3 minutes. Drain in a colander, place back in the pan, and mash by hand with a potato masher.

6. Heat a sauté pan and add the diced bacon. Cook until the bacon renders its fat and add the chopped onion, rosemary, and pepper. When the onions are soft, combine the onions and the mashed potato mixture in a large bowl. Stir in the flour and the chopped clams.

7. Roll out the pie dough and place it in a 10" pie pan. Add the clam filling and dot with the butter. Combine the egg with the water and brush it around the edge of the pie crust.

8. Place the top crust on the pie and brush it with the egg wash. Poke a few holes in the crust to let out steam. Bake in a 400 degree oven for 45 minutes and serve.

Note: *a local craft beer goes very well with this dish.*

Shredded Zucchini with Pesto

4 portions

4 medium-sized zucchini

Pesto
¼ cup pine nuts
2 cups chopped basil
1 cup chopped parsley
1 Tbsp minced garlic
½ tsp kosher salt
¼ tsp ground pepper
¾ cup extra virgin olive oil
½ cup grated Parmigiano-
  Reggiano cheese

Cooking
2 Tbsp olive oil
4 cloves garlic, sliced
1 onion, thinly sliced
Shredded zucchini
½ cup grated Parmigiano-
  Reggiano cheese
½ cup pesto

1. Rinse the zucchini and trim the ends. Shred the zucchini into a large bowl, using the large holes in a box grater. Wrap the shredded zucchini in a kitchen towel and twist to extract as much moisture as you can. Empty the zucchini into a colander and let it drain.

2. Place a dry sauté pan on the heat and add the pine nuts. Toast them at medium heat for about 3 minutes and remove.

3. Add the pine nuts, basil, parsley, garlic, salt, and pepper to the bowl of a food processor and pulse until coarsely chopped. Drizzle in the olive oil and process until smooth. Transfer to a bowl and stir in the cheese.

4. Heat a large sauté pan and add the olive oil. Add the sliced garlic and cook until it browns, then remove it with a slotted spoon. Immediately add the onion and zucchini and cook over high heat for 3 minutes, tossing to prevent burning.

5. Remove from the heat, and stir in the cheese and ½ cup of the pesto. Serve in bowls with more pesto on the side.

Seared Sea Scallops with Zucchini Pancakes

4 portions

Zucchini Pancakes

4 medium-sized zucchini
1 bunch green onions, minced
¼ cup chopped basil
1 cup flour
1 tsp baking powder
2 tsp kosher salt
1 tsp ground pepper
2 eggs, beaten
½ cup grated Parmigiano-Reggiano cheese
½ cup olive oil

Lemon Basil Aioli Sauce

½ cup mayonnaise
1 tsp minced garlic
1 lemon, zest and juice
2 Tbsp chopped basil
1 tsp kosher salt
Dash Tabasco sauce

Seared Sea Scallops

1½ lbs fresh sea scallops
1 cup flour
1 tsp kosher salt
½ tsp ground pepper
½ cup olive oil
2 Tbsp fresh lime juice
1 Tbsp Rose's lime juice (bottled)
¼ cup chopped parsley

1. Trim the ends off the zucchini, rinse, and dry. Shred into a large bowl using the large holes in a box grater. Place the shredded zucchini in a kitchen towel and twist into a tight ball, squeezing out as much moisture as you can. Combine the zucchini with the green onions and the basil.

2. In a separate bowl, whisk the flour, baking powder, salt, and pepper together and add to the zucchini mixture. Add the beaten eggs and the grated cheese to the zucchini mixture and stir it with a rubber spatula.

3. Heat a large sauté pan and add 2 tbsp. of the oil. Measure ½ cup of the zucchini mixture into your hand and mold it before placing it in the hot pan. Cook at medium heat until the pancakes are brown, then turn with a spatula and finish cooking. Repeat until all the batter is used, keeping the pancakes warm in a slow oven.

4. For the aioli sauce, combine the mayonnaise, garlic, lemon zest and juice, basil, salt, and Tabasco in a small bowl.

5. For the scallops, combine the flour, salt, and pepper in a bowl. Trim the tough muscle from the side of the scallops, rinse, and pat dry. Toss in the flour mixture just before cooking.

6. Heat a large sauté pan over high heat. Add about 2 Tbsp. of the olive oil. When it shimmers, place the scallops in the pan, leaving space between them. Cook the scallops quickly in batches and remove.

7. When the scallops are all browned, put them back in the hot pan and add the lime juice, the Rose's lime juice, and the parsley. Toss quickly and remove.

8. Place the pancakes on the dinner plates with the scallops on top and around them. Serve the aioli sauce on the side.

– Wine Notes –

The sweet flavor of sea scallops with the garlicky aioli sauce might go very well with one of the dry white blended wines of Long Island. They often have a Chardonnay base, accompanied by a little Gewurztraminer for added flavor.

Pulled Pork and Barbecued Beans

8 to 10 portions

For the beans

1 lb Great Northern dried
    beans
½ lb bacon, diced
1 onion, peeled and chopped
1 jalapeno pepper,
    seeded and minced
½ cup tomato paste
½ cup dark brown sugar
½ cup molasses

2 cups chicken stock
1 Tbsp kosher salt
2 tsp ground pepper
¼ tsp cayenne pepper

For the pork

3 lb fresh pork butt, bone-in
2 Tbsp smoked paprika
1 tsp celery seed
½ tsp cayenne pepper
1 tsp garlic powder
¼ tsp ground cloves
¼ cup dark brown sugar
1 Tbsp kosher salt
1 tsp ground pepper

1 orange, rind and juice
¼ cup Pernod liqueur
½ cup red wine vinegar

1 cup commercial BBQ sauce

1. Rinse the beans, cover with cold water, and refrigerate overnight.

2. Heat a Dutch oven and add the bacon. When it begins to brown, add the onions and jalapeno pepper. As the onions soften, add the tomato paste, brown sugar, and molasses.

3. Drain the beans and add to the Dutch oven along with the chicken stock, salt, pepper, and cayenne. Bring to a boil on the stove, cover, and place in a 300 degree oven for 3 hours. If it becomes a little dry, add 1 cup of water. Cook another 30 minutes, uncovered, to get a crusty top.

4. Combine the paprika, celery seed, cayenne, garlic, cloves, brown sugar, salt, and pepper in a small bowl. Rub this mixture on all sides of the pork butt.

5. Place the seasoned pork in a casserole. Combine the orange juice, Pernod, and vinegar and pour over the meat. Add the orange rind to the casserole and cover with heavy foil. Cook in a 300 degree oven for 3 hours. The meat should easily fall off the bone. If not, continue cooking for another 30 minutes.

6. When the pork butt is cool enough to handle, break it apart with 2 forks. Separate the fibers with your fingers and discard any fat and gristle.

7. Place the pork fibers in a bowl and stir in about 1 cup of commercial BBQ sauce. Serve on slider buns with the beans on the side.

Note: *This recipe, for both the beans and the pork, works very well when cooked on the outdoor charcoal grill. Cook in a covered grill over indirect heat for about the same time as above. For a smoked flavor, add water-soaked hickory chips at intervals along the way, adding fresh charcoal if necessary.*

*– **Recommended beverage** –*
A local craft beer

Brewed Bratwurst with Caraway Sauerkraut

6 to 12 portions

Bratwurst

2 bottles dark beer
1 onion, peeled and chopped
½ cup whole grain Dijon mustard
1 Tbsp caraway seeds
1 tsp ground coriander
12 fresh bratwurst

Sauerkraut

2 Tbsp butter
1 cup chopped onion
1 Tbsp caraway seeds
1 Tbsp whole grain Dijon mustard
2 cups fresh sauerkraut, rinsed and drained
1 tsp ground pepper
Kaiser rolls
Chopped dill pickles
Whole grain mustard
Sliced Swiss cheese

1. Add the beer, onions, mustard, caraway seeds, and coriander to a soup pot. Bring to a boil and simmer for 5 minutes. Add the fresh bratwurst and continue simmering, covered, for another 20 minutes. Remove from the heat and leave the bratwurst in the hot marinade for 30 minutes.

2. Heat a shallow saucepan and add the butter. Stir in the onions and caraway seeds, and cook until the onions soften. Add the mustard, sauerkraut, and pepper, and continue cooking on low heat for 20 minutes.

3. Remove the bratwurst from the marinade and split in half lengthwise. Place on a charcoal grill and cook until brown and crisp on the outside. Serve as-is with the sauerkraut, or toast the Kaiser rolls on the grill and serve with sauerkraut plus the mustard, chopped dill pickles, and Swiss cheese.

– Recommended beverage –
A local craft beer or a full-bodied German beer

Barbecued pork and beans

August

— Laughing Corn —
By Carl Sandburg

There was a high majestic fooling
Day before yesterday in the yellow corn.

And day after to-morrow in the yellow corn
There will be high majestic fooling.
The ears ripen in late summer
And come on with a conquering laughter,
Come on with a high and conquering laughter.

The long-tailed blackbirds are hoarse.
One of the smaller blackbirds chitters on a stalk
And a spot of red is on its shoulder
And I never heard its name in my life.

Some of the ears are bursting.
A white juice works inside.
Cornsilk creeps in the end and dangles in the wind.
Always—I never knew it any other way—
The wind and the corn talk things over together.
And the rain and the corn and the sun and the corn
Talk things over together.

Over the road is the farmhouse.
The siding is white and a green blind is slung loose.
It will not be fixed till the corn is husked.
The farmer and his wife talk things over together.

During August, the heat rises and the summer vacation season is in full swing. Going to the beach, spending a day on the boat (or someone else's boat), and visiting the wineries are all more enjoyable when you pack some delicious cold food to take along and serve picnic-style.

Abundant produce continues with the full ripening of sweet (or supersweet) corn, the arrival of peaches, melons, and lots of berries. Beefsteak, heirloom, grape, and cherry tomatoes are at their best, along with eggplants, peppers, beans, and more. August is the heart of the season when cooking local ingredients is mandatory and you begin to appreciate the beauty of the North Fork.

Prime Meal
A picnic lunch served cold –

Lobster Rolls; Chargrilled Chicken Breasts with Corn Relish;

Caponata; German Potato Salad; Guacamole; Watermelon Salad

Recommended wine: *A dry Rosé or a dry Riesling*

Selected Recipes
1. Roasted striped bass with Aioli Potato Crust
2. Cold Stuffed Beefsteak Tomato with Marinated Crabmeat
3. Tomato Sauces – Roasted, Fresh, and Classic
4. Eggplant Rollatine
5. Eggplant Parmesan with Goat Cheese
6. Baked Stuffed Eggplant
7. Chargrilled Salad Niçoise
8. Blackened Sea Bass with Peach Salsa
9. Grilled Porterhouse Pork Chops with Peach BBQ Sauce
10. Wine-Poached Peaches with Raspberry Sauce (Peach Melba)

PRIME MEAL

– *A picnic lunch served cold* –

Lobster Rolls

6 to 8 portions

3 live lobsters (1¼ lb each)
¼ cup minced shallots
½ cup minced celery
1 lemon, zest and Juice
Few drops Tabasco sauce
2 Tbsp chopped tarragon
½ cup mayonnaise
1 tsp kosher salt
½ tsp ground pepper
8 top-cut hot dog rolls

1. Bring 6 quarts of water to a boil in a large stock pot. Plunge the lobsters into the water, cover, and return to the boil. Reduce the heat and simmer for 20 minutes. Remove the lobsters, rinse under cold water, and break off the claws and tails with your hands (reserve bodies for stock if desired).

2. Split the tails with a chefs knife and remove the meat. Remove the intestinal vein and cut the meat into ½" pieces. Crack the claws and remove the claw meat, including the knuckles. Cut into pieces and add all of the lobster meat to a large bowl.

3. Combine the shallots, celery, lemon zest and juice, Tabasco, mayonnaise, salt, and pepper in a small bowl. Stir together and add to the lobster meat, tossing gently to combine. Transfer to a plastic container, cover, and refrigerate.

4. Just before serving, portion lobster salad into hot dog rolls (if you are close to a grill, toast the rolls first).

My granddaughter Vivien, preferring a cheese sandwich to lobster rolls

Chargrilled Chicken Breasts with Corn Relish

6 to 8 portions

2 lbs boneless, skinless
   chicken cutlets
¼ cup olive oil
3 Tbsp kosher salt
1 Tbsp ground pepper
6 ears of fresh corn
1 zucchini
1 yellow squash
1 green pepper
1 red pepper
1 red onion

Dressing
1 jalapeno pepper
2 cloves garlic
2 limes, zest and juice
¼ cup olive oil
¼ cup chopped cilantro

1. Line a sheet pan with foil and prepare the chicken and vegetables for grilling. Combine the salt and pepper in a small bowl (professional chefs call this "chefs salt"). Put the olive oil in another bowl. Brush the chicken cutlets with oil, sprinkle with the salt mixture and place on the sheet pan.

2. Shuck the corn; trim the ends off the zucchini and squash and split in half; split the peppers, remove the seeds, and flatten; peel and cut the onion into thick slices.

3. Brush all the vegetables with the oil and sprinkle with the seasoning. Place them on the sheet pan with the chicken.

4. Prepare a charcoal grill and wait until the coals turn white. Rub the grill with an oil-soaked paper towel. Place the chicken over the hot coals and surround it with the vegetables, cooking in batches if necessary. Turn the chicken and vegetables once, letting them char a little before removing to a sheet pan and returning to the kitchen.

5. Cut the chicken into bite-sized pieces and place in a large bowl. Slice the corn off the cob with a paring knife and add to the chicken. Dice the zucchini, squash, peppers, and onion and add to the bowl.

6. For the dressing, cut the jalapeno pepper in half, scrape out the seeds, and mince finely. Mince the garlic and combine with the jalapeno. Add the zest and juice from the limes and whisk in the olive oil.

7. Add the dressing to the chicken mixture and toss gently. Toss in the cilantro and check for seasoning. Place in covered plastic containers and refrigerate.

Caponata

6 to 8 portions

2 large eggplants
½ **cup** kosher salt

½ **cup** pine nuts

2 **Tbsp** olive oil
1 **cup** chopped onion
2 **Tbsp** minced garlic
1 large tomato, diced

½ **cup** Kalamata olives,
    pitted
4 minced anchovies
2 **Tbsp** capers
¼ **cup** currants
¼ **cup** pimientos
1 **tsp** kosher salt
1 **tsp** ground pepper
Dash hot red pepper
    flakes
¼ **cup** chopped basil

1. Cut the ends off the eggplants and dice into ½" cubes (do not peel). Place them in a colander and sprinkle the salt over them. Let sit for 30 minutes, rinse under cold water, and dry with paper towels.

2. Heat a dry sauté pan and add the pine nuts. Toast them for about 3 minutes and set aside.

3. Heat a large sauté pan and add the oil. When the oil shimmers, add the eggplant and cook until it begins to brown. Turn down the heat and add the onion, garlic, and tomato. Continue to cook, stirring, for 5 minutes.

4. Add the toasted pine nuts, olives, anchovies, capers, currants, pimientos, salt, pepper, and hot red pepper flakes. Continue cooking for another 5 minutes, stir in the chopped basil and remove from the heat. Transfer to covered containers and refrigerate.

German Potato Salad

6 to 8 portions

2 **lbs** new potatoes

¼ **lb** bacon, diced
1 red onion, peeled and
    chopped

1 **Tbsp** sugar
¼ **cup** red wine vinegar
2 **tsp** kosher salt
1 **tsp** ground pepper
½ **cup** minced green
    onion

1. Bring 2 quarts of water to a boil and add the potatoes in their skins. Let them simmer until tender, about 15 minutes. Drain, cool, and cut into ¼" thick slices. Place in a large bowl.

2. Heat a sauté pan and add the bacon. When crisp, remove with a slotted spoon and set on a paper-towel-lined plate. Add the onion to the pan and continue cooking at medium heat.

3. Stir in the sugar, vinegar, salt, pepper, and green onion. Add to the bowl with the potatoes and toss gently. Check for seasoning, transfer to plastic containers, and refrigerate.

Guacamole

6 to 8 portions

4 ripe avocados
2 limes

1 jalapeno pepper
1 tsp minced garlic
¼ cup chopped cilantro
¼ cup minced red onion
Few drops Tabasco sauce
1 tsp Worcestershire sauce
1 tsp kosher salt
½ tsp ground pepper

1 bag multigrain taco chips

1. Cut the avocados in half lengthwise and remove the pit with the point of a large knife. Score the flesh with a paring knife and scoop it out with a spoon into a bowl. Remove the zest from 1 lime and add it to the bowl along with the juice from both limes. Toss gently with the avocado.

2. Split the jalapeno pepper, scrape out the seeds, and mince finely. Add it to the avocado along with the garlic, cilantro, red onion, Tabasco, Worcestershire, salt, and pepper.

3. Mash the ingredients with a dinner fork, leaving the guacamole a little chunky. Place in a covered container and refrigerate. Serve with the taco chips.

Yellow and Red Watermelon Salad

6 to 8 portions

4 cups red seedless watermelon
4 cups yellow seedless watermelon
4 oz feta cheese
½ cup pitted Kalamata olives
1 cup mint leaves, chopped

Dressing
1 lemon, zest and juice
1 lime, zest and juice
2 Tbsp honey
¼ cup olive oil
1 tsp kosher salt
½ tsp ground pepper
Few drops Tabasco sauce

1. Cut the watermelons in half, then in thick slices. Remove the rind with a paring knife, cut the slices into 1" chunks, and place them in a large bowl.

2. Add the feta cheese, olives, and mint leaves and toss gently.

3. Combine the lemon zest and juice, the lime zest and juice, and the honey. Add the salt, pepper, and Tabasco and whisk in the olive oil. Toss with the watermelon mixture just before serving.

Roasted Striped Bass with Aioli Potato Crust

4 portions

1½ lbs striped bass fillet, bones and skin removed
1½ lb Yukon gold potatoes
1 Tbsp chopped rosemary
1 tsp kosher salt
½ tsp ground pepper

Aioli Sauce
1 Tbsp minced garlic
2 Tbsp panko crumbs
1 Tbsp white wine vinegar
2 egg yolks
¾ cup olive oil
1 Tbsp lemon juice
½ tsp kosher salt
Dash cayenne pepper
1 Tbsp smoked paprika

1. Cut the bass into 4 thick portions. Line a sheet pan with foil and spray with no-stick. Put the fish on the sheet pan and refrigerate.

2. Bring 2 quarts of water to a boil and add the potatoes (in their skins). Simmer until just cooked, about 20 minutes. Refrigerate until cool.

3. Peel the potatoes and grate them into a large bowl using the large holes of a box grater. Add the rosemary, salt, and pepper and toss gently.

4. For the sauce, add the garlic, panko, and vinegar to the bowl of a food processor and pulse until smooth. Scrape down the sides with a rubber spatula and add the egg yolks.

5. Continue processing and drizzle in a little olive oil. Gradually pour in the rest of the oil in a steady stream to form a thick emulsion. Pulse in the lemon juice, salt, and cayenne. Transfer to a small bowl.

6. Preheat an oven to 400 degrees and place the sheet pan with the fish on the table. Coat each fillet of fish with the aioli sauce, saving any left over to serve on the side. Sprinkle the shredded potatoes over and around the sides of the fish to a thickness of about 1 inch. Do not press the potatoes down.

7. Sprinkle the potatoes with the smoked paprika and roast in the 400 degree oven for about 25 minutes. The potatoes will turn brown and the fish will begin to flake apart. Make a small cut with a paring knife to check for doneness. Serve on a bed of steamed Swiss chard or other leafy green vegetable.

– Wine Notes –

With a heavy topping of potatoes and the garlicky aioli sauce, this version of striped bass requires a barrel-fermented Chardonnay from Napa, Sonoma, or the Maconnais in Burgundy. Our many high quality reserve Chardonnays from Long Island would also be perfect.

Cold Stuffed Beefsteak Tomato with Crabmeat

6 portions

6 ripe beefsteak tomatoes
1 lb jumbo lump crabmeat
2 Tbsp chopped green onions
1 Tbsp chopped tarragon
1 tsp chopped thyme leaves
2 Tbsp chopped parsley

Dressing

2 lemons
¼ cup extra virgin olive oil
1 tsp kosher salt
½ tsp ground pepper
½ tsp dry mustard
Pinch cayenne pepper
1 pkg. baby arugula

1. Rinse the tomatoes. Remove the core and cut off the tops about ¼ of the way down. Slice a small piece off the bottom so the tomato rests flat. Scoop out the pulp, leaving a ¼" wall. Dice the pulp and the top, drain, and reserve. Turn the tomatoes upside down on a paper towel to drain.

2. Turn the crabmeat out of its container into a bowl. Separate the meat and pick out any cartilage. Add the green onion, tarragon, thyme, and parsley, and toss gently.

3. For the dressing, remove the zest from 1 lemon and set aside. Squeeze the juice from both lemons into a bowl. Whisk in the olive oil and season with the salt, pepper, mustard, and cayenne.

4. Stir in the lemon zest. Add the dressing to the crab mixture along with the reserved chopped tomato. Toss gently and refrigerate.

5. At service time, wash arugula and dry in a salad spinner. Place the arugula on a platter or on individual salad plates. Stuff the tomatoes with the crab mixture and place them on the arugula.

Three Tomato Sauces

Roasted Cherry Tomato Sauce

4 cups cherry tomatoes
2 tsp kosher salt
1 tsp ground pepper
1 tbsp minced garlic
2 tbsp olive oil

4 oz thinly sliced pancetta

12 leaves fresh basil
Pasta of choice
½ cup Parmigiano-Reggiano
    cheese

1. Cut the cherry tomatoes in half and put them in a large bowl. Combine the salt, pepper, garlic, and olive oil in a small bowl and pour it over the tomatoes. Toss lightly.

2. Spray a foil-lined sheet pan with no-stick and pour the tomatoes onto the sheet pan. Arrange them cut side down. Separate the slices of pancetta and lay them on the sheet pan with the tomatoes. Put the pan in a 250 degree oven and roast for 2 hours.

3. At service time, cook the pasta, drain, and add back to the pasta pot. Chop the cooked pancetta and add it to the pasta along with the tomatoes and all their juices. Slice the basil into thin strips (chiffonade) and add it to the pasta. Serve in pasta bowls and garnish with the cheese.

Fresh Plum Tomato Sauce

2 lbs ripe plum tomatoes
¼ cup olive oil
2 Tbsp minced garlic
2 tsp kosher salt
1 tsp ground pepper
½ cup chopped basil

1. Cut out the core and make an X in the bottom of each tomato. Bring 2 quarts of water to a boil and plunge the tomatoes in the boiling water for 2 minutes and remove.

2. Cool briefly, slip off the skins, and cut in half crosswise. Squeeze out the seeds with your hands and chop the tomatoes coarsely.

3. Heat a saucepan and add the olive oil. Add the garlic and cook for 1 minute before adding the chopped tomatoes, salt, and pepper. Bring to a boil and simmer, uncovered, for 30 minutes. Stir in the basil and serve with a pasta of choice.

Marcella Hazan's Classic Tomato Sauce

2 lbs ripe plum tomatoes
5 Tbsp cold butter
Half an onion, peeled
2 tsp kosher salt

1. Cut off the stem end and make an X in the bottom of each tomato. Plunge the tomatoes in 2 quarts of boiling water for 2 minutes and remove. Cool briefly, slip off the skins, and cut in half crosswise. Squeeze out the seeds, chop coarsely, and place in a saucepan.

2. Add the butter and the onion and simmer, uncovered, for 1 hour. Season with the salt and serve over your choice of pasta. If desired, puree the sauce in a food processor.
Note: *these sauces all go well with the following eggplant recipes.*

148

Eggplant Rollatine

4 to 6 portions

2 large eggplants
¼ cup kosher salt
1 cup flour
1 tsp kosher salt
1 tsp ground pepper
4 eggs
1 cup grated parmesan
    cheese
¼ cup olive oil

Filling
15 oz container ricotta
    cheese
½ cup mozzarella, shredded
1 cup grated parmesan
    cheese
1 egg, beaten
½ cup chopped basil
1 tsp kosher salt
½ tsp ground pepper

Assembly
2 cups fresh tomato sauce
(choose from previous page)
½ cup shredded mozzarella
    cheese
½ cup grated parmesan
    cheese

1. Trim the ends off the eggplants, peel, and cut them lengthwise into ¼" thick slices. Place the slices of eggplant on a rack over a sheet pan and sprinkle the salt on both sides. Let them rest for 30 minutes or more, then rinse under cold water and dry with paper towels (this is called purging).

2. Prepare a fresh tomato sauce from one of the recipes on the previous page.

3. Combine the flour, salt, and pepper in a shallow pan. Whisk the eggs and grated cheese together in a bowl. Heat a large sauté pan and add half of the oil.

4. Dip the eggplant slices in the flour, then in the egg mixture, then into the hot pan. Cook about 3 minutes per side until eggplant is golden. Do not burn. Cook in batches, adding more oil when necessary, and remove to a paper-towel-lined sheet pan.

5. For the filling, combine the ricotta, mozzarella, and parmesan cheese in a large bowl. Stir in the egg, basil, salt, and pepper.

6. To assemble, spread about a third of the tomato sauce in a shallow casserole. Spoon the cheese mixture onto each slice of eggplant and roll it up. Place each eggplant roll in the casserole, seam-side down, resting against each other.

7. Spoon the remaining sauce over all. Sprinkle the mozzarella and parmesan over the top and bake at 350 degrees for 30 minutes.

– Wine Notes –

Eggplant is not an easy wine match, but the two cheeses and the tomato sauce add richness and acidity. A Chianti from Tuscany or a Barbera from the Piedmont would be my first choices. A Cabernet Franc from Long Island would also be good.

Eggplant Parmesan with Goat Cheese

4 to 6 portions

2 large eggplants
¼ cup kosher salt

2 cups flour
2 eggs
2 Tbsp water
2 cups plain breadcrumbs
1 Tbsp dried oregano
1 tsp powdered garlic
1 tsp kosher salt
1 tsp ground pepper

8 oz soft goat cheese
¼ cup grated parmesan
   cheese
1 egg, beaten
¼ cup chopped basil
1 tsp kosher salt
½ tsp ground pepper

2 beefsteak tomatoes
8 oz fresh mozzarella
   cheese

1. Trim the ends off the eggplants and peel if desired. Cut them cross-wise into ½" thick rounds and place on a rack over a foil-lined sheet pan. Sprinkle both sides of the eggplants with the salt and let rest for 30 minutes or more. Rinse under cold water, drain, and dry with paper towels.

2. Add the flour to a shallow pan. Break the eggs into a bowl and whisk in the water. Place the breadcrumbs in a shallow pan and season with the oregano, garlic, salt, and pepper.

3. Line a sheet pan with foil and spray with no-stick. Dip the eggplant slices in the flour, then in the egg wash, and finally press them into the breadcrumbs. Lay the eggplant on the sheet pan and place in a 400 degree oven for 30 minutes, turning them once.

4. Combine the goat cheese and the parmesan cheese in a bowl. Stir in the egg, basil, salt, and pepper and set aside.

5. Remove the core from each tomato and cut into thick slices. Cut the mozzarella into thick slices.

6. Assemble individual portions in ceramic ramekins or on a foil-lined sheet pan. Place a slice of eggplant on the bottom and spread the goat cheese mixture over it.

7. Place another eggplant slice on top, with a slice of tomato and a slice of mozzarella. Repeat until all ingredients are used. Place in a 400 degree oven for 15 minutes and serve. Garnish with basil leaves.

Note: Accompany with one of the fresh tomato sauces if desired.

— The Eggplant Epithalamion —
By Erica Jong

Once upon a time on the coast of Turkey
there lived a woman who could cook eggplant 99 ways.
She could slice eggplant thin as paper.
She could write poems on it and batter-fry it.
She couls bake eggplant and broil it.
She could even roll the seeds in banana-
flavored cigarette papers
and get her husband high on eggplant.
But he was not pleased.
He went to her father and demanded his bride-price back.
He said he'd been cheated.

He wanted back two goats, twelve chickens
and a camel as reparation.
His wife wept and wept.
Her father raved.

The next day she gave birth to an eggplant.
It was premature and green
and she had to sit on it for days
before it hatched.
"This is my hundredth eggplant recipe," she screamed.
"I hope you're satisfied."

Baked Stuffed Eggplant

4 portions

2 large eggplants

---

1 Tbsp lemon juice
1 Tbsp kosher salt

¾ cup barley
1 tsp kosher salt

---

2 Tbsp olive oil
1 onion, peeled and chopped
1 Tbsp minced garlic
1 pkg. baby bella mushrooms, quartered
1 zucchini, diced
1 red pepper, diced

---

2 plum tomatoes, diced
1 Tbsp fresh thyme leaves
1 Tbsp chopped fresh oregano
¼ cup chopped parsley
Dash hot red pepper flakes
2 tsp kosher salt
1 tsp ground pepper

---

4 oz goat cheese
1 small jar roasted red peppers
½ cup pitted Kalamata olives

1. Cut off the stem end of the eggplants and split them in half. Trim a thin slice off the bottom so that they rest firmly in place. Cut around the inside with a paring knife, leaving a ¼"-thick wall all around.

2. Scoop out the flesh with a spoon and brush the inside with lemon juice. Dice the filling, place it in a colander, and sprinkle with the salt. Let it rest for 30 minutes, then rinse under cold water, drain, and dry on paper towels.

3. Bring 2 quarts of water to a boil and add the salt. Stir in the barley, reduce the heat to medium, and cook until tender, about 20 minutes, drain, and set aside.

4. Heat a large sauté pan and add the oil. Add the onions, cook for 3 minutes and stir in the garlic and mushrooms. Cook until the mushrooms begin to brown and add the zucchini, red pepper, and the reserved eggplant filling.

5. Stir in the tomatoes, thyme, oregano, parsley, red pepper flakes, salt, and pepper. Continue cooking another 5 minutes before adding the cooked barley.

6. Stuff the eggplant shells with the filling. Arrange slices of goat cheese, red pepper strips, and olives on top in an attractive pattern. Place on a foil-lined sheet pan and roast at 375 degrees for 30 minutes.

Chargrilled Salad Niçoise

4 to 6 portions

1½ lbs fresh tuna steak
1 tsp kosher salt
½ tsp ground pepper

Vegetables
1 lb green beans, trimmed
6 medium-sized red
    potatoes, cut in half
6 eggs
2 cups grape tomatoes
1 red onion

Dressing
1 cup olive oil
2 lemons, zest and juice
2 Tbsp minced shallots
1 Tbsp Dijon mustard
1 Tbsp fresh thyme
1 Tbsp fresh oregano
1 tsp minced garlic
1 tsp kosher salt
1 tsp ground pepper

Garnish
1 cup pitted Kalamata
    olives
1 can flat anchovies
12 leaves fresh basil
¼ cup olive oil

– Wine Notes –
This summer dish enjoyed on the deck needs a crisp, dry rosé from Long Island or a slightly chilled Beaujolais from France.

1. Season the tuna steak with salt and pepper and refrigerate.

2. Bring 2 quarts of water to a boil. Blanch the green beans for 3 minutes and remove with a slotted spoon. Plunge them in ice water to cool. Add the potatoes to the same water and blanch for 5 minutes. Remove and cool.

3. Cover the eggs with cold water in a saucepan and bring to a boil. Remove from the heat, cover, and let rest for 15 minutes. Cool under cold water and peel.

4. Rinse the grape tomatoes and cut in half. Peel the onion and cut into thick slices.

5. For the dressing, combine the lemon zest and juice, shallots, mustard, thyme, oregano, garlic, salt, and pepper in a bowl. Whisk in the olive oil and set aside.

6. Add 2 Tbsp. of the dressing to the tomatoes and set aside. Prepare a charcoal grill, wait until the coals turn white, and rub the grill with an oil-soaked paper towel. Brush the tuna steak with oil and cook over high heat, turning once. Cook quickly to keep it rare on the inside.

7. Brush the potatoes and green beans with oil and place them on the grill (put the beans on a piece of heavy foil if necessary). Grill the onion until lightly charred.

8. As the vegetables come off the grill, toss them in a large bowl with some of the dressing, then arrange them on a platter. Cut the tuna into large chunks and add to the platter.

9. Cut the boiled eggs in half and add to the platter along with the tomatoes. Drizzle dressing over all and garnish with anchovies, olives, and fresh basil leaves.

Blackened Sea Bass with Peach Salsa

4 portions

1½ lbs black sea bass, boneless, skinless

Spice rub
2 tsp smoked paprika
½ tsp garlic powder
½ tsp onion powder
1 tsp dried thyme, crushed
¼ tsp cayenne pepper
1 tsp kosher salt
½ tsp ground black pepper

Peach salsa
4 fresh peaches
2 Tbsp canola oil
1 onion, peeled and chopped
1 jalapeno pepper, seeded, minced
2 tsp fresh ginger, minced
¼ cup sugar
1 lemon, zest and juice
½ tsp kosher salt
¼ cup chopped cilantro

1. Combine the paprika, garlic powder, onion powder, thyme, cayenne, salt, and pepper in a small bowl. Rub the spice mixture on both sides of the fish and refrigerate 30 minutes prior to cooking.

2. To make the salsa, bring 2 quarts of water to a boil and plunge the peaches into the water for 1 minute. Remove with a slotted spoon, cool, and peel. Cut the peaches in half, remove the pits, and dice into ½" pieces.

3. Heat a large sauté pan and add the oil. Stir in the onions, jalapeno, ginger, and sugar. Cook until the onions are soft and the sugar is dissolved, about 5 minutes. Add the peaches, lemon, and cilantro. Continue cooking for 3 minutes, remove from the heat, and taste for seasoning.

4. Heat a chargrill and wait for white coals. Rub the grill with an oil-soaked paper towel. Spray the fish fillets with no-stick and place on the hottest part of the grill. Cook until the flesh turns opaque, about 3 minutes per side. Serve with the peach salsa on the side.

Note: *Pan-searing this fish is also very good. Leave the skin on and cook quickly in 2 tablespoons of very hot olive oil, skin side-down. Press down on the fish for a crispy skin.*

Baked Stuffed Eggplant

Chargrilled Salad Niçoise

— "From Blossoms" —
By Li-Young Lee

From blossoms comes
this brown paper bag of peaches
we bought from the boy
at the bend in the road where we turned toward
signs painted Peaches.

From laden boughs, from hands,
from sweet fellowship in the bins,
comes nectar at the roadside, succulent
peaches we devour, dusty skin and all,
comes this familiar dust of summer, dust we eat.

O, to take what we love inside,
to carry within us an orchard, to eat
not only the skin, but the shade,
not only the sugar, but the days, to hold
the fruit in our hands, adore it, then bite into
the round jubilance of peach.

There are days we live
as if death were nowhere
in the background; from joy
to joy, to joy, from wing to wing,
from blossom to blossom to
impossible blossom, to sweet impossible blossom.

Grilled Porterhouse Pork Chops with Peach Barbecue Sauce

6 portions

6 porterhouse pork chops, 1½" thick
1 tsp kosher salt
½ tsp ground pepper

Peach Barbecue Sauce
6 fresh peaches

2 Tbsp canola oil
1 cup chopped onion
1 Tbsp minced garlic
1 Tbsp minced ginger
1 cup catsup
¼ cup peach preserves

2 Tbsp cider vinegar
1 tsp kosher salt
½ tsp ground pepper
Dash Tabasco sauce

3 peaches for garnish

1. Season the pork chops with the salt and pepper and refrigerate.

2. Bring 2 quarts of water to a boil and plunge the peaches into the water for 1 minute. Remove, cool, peel, and chop coarsely.

3. Heat a saucepan and add the oil. Stir in the onions, garlic, and ginger. Cook for 3 minutes at low heat and add the catsup, peach preserves, and chopped peaches.

4. Simmer, uncovered, for 30 minutes and add the vinegar, salt, pepper, and Tabasco. Continue cooking for another 10 minutes and remove from the heat.

5. Prepare a charcoal grill with hot white coals. Rub the grill with an oil-soaked paper towel. Spray the pork chops with no-stick and place them on the hottest part of the grill. Turn them 90 degrees to make grill marks, then move them to the cooler part of the grill.

6. Paint the chops with the peach BBQ sauce, cover the grill, and cook slowly for about 30 minutes. A meat thermometer should read 145 before taking them off the grill.

7. Split 3 peaches in half, unpeeled, and remove the pits. Brush them with oil and grill, cut-side down, for 5 minutes. Serve them with the pork chops and barbecue sauce on the side.

Note: *Grilled thick slices of sweet potato go well with this dish.*

– Wine Notes –
A local Cabernet Franc would match the spicy sauce and complement the mild-flavored pork. From France, a Rhone wine would be good or a Syrah from California.

Wine-Poached Peaches with Raspberry Sauce (Peach Melba)

6 fresh peaches
2 cups rose wine
¼ **cup** sugar
3 strips lemon rind

Raspberry sauce
2 cups fresh raspberries
¼ **cup** confectioners sugar
1 tsp lemon juice

Garnishes
Vanilla Ice Cream
½ **cup** toasted sliced almonds

1. Cut the peaches in half, leaving the skin on. Remove the pits (leave them in if they don't come out easily).

2. Add the wine to a saucepan along with the sugar and lemon rind. Cook until the sugar dissolves, then add the peaches. Simmer until the peaches are tender, about 15 minutes.

3. Remove the peaches with a slotted spoon and slip off the skins. Refrigerate the peaches in the syrup.

4. Combine the raspberries, sugar, and lemon juice in the bowl of a food processor. Process until smooth, then strain into a bowl, pushing the fruit through the strainer with a wooden spoon.

5. Place vanilla ice cream in the bottom of a dessert dish with the peaches surrounding it. Spoon the sauce over the top and sprinkle toasted almonds over all.

September

— To Autumn —
By William Blake

O Autumn, laden with fruit, and stain'd
With the blood of the grape, pass not, but sit
Beneath my shady roof; there thou may'st rest,
And tune thy jolly voice to my fresh pipe,
And all the daughters of the year shall dance!
Sing now the lusty song of fruits and flowers.

The narrow bud opens her beauties to
The sun, and love runs in her thrilling veins;
Blossoms hang round the brows of Morning, and
Flourish down the bright cheek of modest Eve,
Till clust'ring Summer breaks forth into singing,
And feather'd clouds strew flowers round her head.

The spirits of the air live in the smells
Of fruit; and joy, with pinions light, roves round
The gardens, or sits singing in the trees.
Thus sang the jolly Autumn as he sat,
Then rose, girded himself, and o'er the bleak
Hills fled from our sight; but left his golden load.

September is an exciting time on the North Fork, when it seems that we have a truly local cuisine. The Maritime Festival in Greenport reminds us of our heritage of whaling, shipbuilding, commercial fishing fleets, oyster factories, bunker fishermen, and sport fishing. For many years the chowder contest was a popular event at the festival, with local restaurants competing for the "Best in Show" trophy.

Though diminished in quantity, we still have great local fish and shellfish to enjoy. The farm stands are bursting with new arrivals after Labor Day: butternut squash, acorn squash, cauliflower, broccoli, carrots, hardy greens, and potatoes. The cool fall air and the beginning of the grape harvest make me want to cook local duck and pair it with a local wine. The vineyards are very busy as they begin to bring in the new vintage, and their tasting rooms are crowded with people discovering new wines and enjoying the beauty of the North Fork.

Prime Meal

Deviled Oysters with Spinach and Pancetta

---

*Steamed and Roasted Long Island Duck with Roasted Plum Sauce,
Wild Rice and Glazed Carrots*

Peach-Blueberry-Blackberry Cobbler

Recommended wine: *Long Island Merlot*

Selected Recipes

1. *Manhattan Clam Chowder*
2. *New England Clam Chowder*
3. *Portuguese-Style Scallop and Fish Chowder*
4. *Grilled Corn and Chicken Chowder*
5. *Oysters Rockefeller and Clams Casino*
6. *Grilled Pork Tenderloin with Sweet Potatoes and Pears*
7. *Fried Calamari with Romesco Sauce*
8. *Roasted Butternut Squash with Farfalle and Sage Pesto*
9. *Cauliflower Gratin with Fingerling potatoes and Applewood-Smoked Bacon*

Judging for the "Best in Show" award for best chowder at the 2012 Maritime Festival in Greenport. Clockwise from left to right are: Tom Scalia, Chris Smith (hidden), Mary Morgan (hidden), Lois Ross, John Ross, Starr Boggs, Paula Croteaux, and Albie de Kerillis.

The chowder contest was a major source of funds to support the festival, as people would enter the tent, pay a small fee, and sample a dozen or more chowders prepared by local restaurants. The 2012 winner was a clam and corn chowder prepared by chef Darren Boyle of the Shelter Island restaurant, Salt.

PRIME MEAL

– *First Course* –
Deviled Oysters with Spinach and Pancetta

4 portions

2 dozen oysters

3 oz thinly sliced pancetta

1 pkg. (6 oz) fresh spinach
6 radishes

1 Tbsp Pernod liqueur

1 Tbsp Dijon mustard
½ cup melted butter
2 cups panko crumbs
2 tsp kosher salt
1 tsp ground pepper

Reserved oyster meats
¼ cup olive oil
Lemon wedges

1. Scrub the oysters under cold water. Shuck them with an oyster knife and place the meats and any juice in a bowl. Rinse the bottom shells and reserve (if opening the oysters proves difficult, snip off the thin end with pliers, then slip the knife in the opening and slide it around the shell, twisting as you go).

2. Spray a large sauté pan with no-stick and place it on medium heat. Add the pancetta and cook until crisp, then remove and put it on a paper towel-lined plate.

3. Wash the spinach in cold water and drain. Remove the stems and cut the leaves into thin strips. Trim the radishes and grate them using the large holes of a box grater.

4. Add the spinach and radishes to the above sauté pan, cover, and cook at high heat for 2 minutes. Remove and place in a colander to drain.

5. Place the clean bottom shells of the oysters on a foil-lined sheet pan. Using tongs, fill the shells with the spinach mixture, then sprinkle the Pernod over the spinach.

6. Combine the melted butter and the mustard in a bowl. Add the panko, salt, and pepper to a shallow pan. Dip the oyster meats in the butter mixture, then in the panko crumbs. Work in small batches and place the breaded oysters on a tray.

7. Heat a clean sauté pan and add the oil. Cook the breaded oysters at medium heat until golden, about 2 minutes per side. Cook in batches to avoid crowding.

8. Put the cooked oysters on top of the spinach-filled shells. Chop the reserved pancetta and sprinkle on top. Just before service, place the pan of oysters in a 400 degree oven for 5 minutes. Garnish with lemon wedges.

– Wine Notes –
A dry Chenin Blanc from the Loire Valley or from the North Fork is very good with oysters. A Premier Cru Chablis would also be delicious and complement the rich, sautéed cooking method.

– Entreé –
Steamed and Roasted Long Island Duck

4 to 6 portions

6 lb Long Island Duck
1 Tbsp five spice powder
2 tsp sugar
2 tsp kosher salt
1 Tbsp soy sauce

Half an unpeeled onion
Half an unpeeled orange
1 Tbsp sliced ginger
4 cloves sliced garlic

1 quart water
½ cup honey
¼ cup soy sauce
¼ cup rice wine vinegar

1. Remove the giblets and the fat from the body cavity of the duck. Trim off the flap skin by the neck, cut off the tail, and remove the wing tips. Rinse under cold water, drain, and poke holes in the skin with a sharp fork.

2. Make a spice rub by combining the five spice powder, sugar, salt, and soy sauce. Place the duck, breast side up, in a V-shaped poultry rack set inside a roasting pan. Rub the spices over the duck and inside the cavity.

3. Put the onion, orange, ginger, and garlic in the body cavity. Tie the legs and wings close to the body with string.

4. Place the duck in a 400 degree oven. Bring the water to a boil on the stove and pour it into the roasting pan with the duck. Cover the pan tightly with heavy foil and let the duck steam in the oven for 1 hour.

5. Combine the honey, soy sauce, and vinegar in a small saucepan, bring to a boil, and let it reduce by half.

6. Remove the duck from the oven and transfer it to a sheet pan. Pour off the water from the roasting pan and place the duck back in the V-shaped rack. Brush the duck all over with the honey glaze and roast, uncovered, at 400 degrees for another hour. Baste with the glaze every 15 minutes.

7. Remove the duck and let it rest for 20 minutes before carving. You can also cut it into pieces before serving on plates or a platter. Serve with roasted plum sauce (recipe follows).

– Wine Notes –
For the past 40 years, Long Island Duck paired with Long Island Merlot fits the criteria of a perfect match in flavor and regional integrity. A reserve merlot with oak aging would be best.

Roasted Plum Sauce

12 fresh purple plums
1 Tbsp maple syrup
1 cup merlot wine

2 cups merlot wine
2 Tbsp maple syrup
1 Tbsp honey
¼ cup minced shallots

½ cup beef stock
1 Tbsp cornstarch
2 Tbsp cold water
1 tsp kosher salt
½ tsp ground pepper

1. Cut the plums in half and remove the pits. Place them cut-side down in a shallow casserole. Mix the maple syrup and the wine together and pour over the plums. Roast in a 350 degree oven for 30 minutes.

2. Combine the 2 cups of merlot, maple syrup, honey, and shallots in a saucepan. Bring to a boil and continue cooking until reduced by half.

3. Remove the plums from the oven. Spoon them, with all the juices, into the bowl of a food processor and puree. Add this to the reduced wine mixture and cook on medium heat.

4. Stir in the beef stock and continue cooking. Dissolve the cornstarch in the cold water and add it to the sauce. Bring the sauce to a boil and season with the salt and pepper.

Wild Rice and Glazed Carrots

1 cup long grain wild rice
3 cups water
1 tsp kosher salt

2 bunches young carrots,
    stem on
2 Tbsp butter
1 tsp honey
1 tsp kosher salt
½ tsp ground pepper
1 cup water
2 Tbsp chopped fresh dill

1. For the rice, rinse under cold water and place in a saucepan with the water and salt. Bring to a boil and simmer at low heat, covered, for 45 minutes, or until just tender. Drain any excess liquid and serve.

2. For the carrots, heat a large sauté pan and add the butter. Trim and peel the carrots, leaving them whole with the stem on if they are small. Place them in the butter and cook for 5 minutes before adding the honey, salt, and pepper. Add the water and bring to a boil. Simmer, uncovered, until carrots are tender, about 20 minutes. Stir in the dill and serve.

– Dessert –
Peach-Blueberry-Blackberry Cobbler

8 portions

8 cups fresh peaches,
    peeled and sliced
1 cup fresh blueberries
1 cup fresh blackberries
¼ cup cornstarch
1½ cups sugar
1 tsp salt
1 lemon, zest and juice
1 tsp vanilla extract

Biscuit topping
1½ cups flour
3 Tbsp sugar
¾ tsp baking powder
¼ tsp salt
6 Tbsp cold butter
¾ cup milk

1. Combine the peaches, blueberries, and blackberries in a large bowl. Whisk together the cornstarch, sugar, and salt and add to the berry mixture. Add the lemon zest and juice and the vanilla. Gently toss all ingredients together and let rest while making the topping.

2. Add the flour, sugar, baking powder, and salt to the bowl of a food processor and pulse until combined. Cut the cold butter into small pieces, add to the food processor, and pulse until it resembles coarse cornmeal. Remove to a bowl and stir in the milk with a fork to form a dough.

3. Pour the fruit with all the juices into a 9" by 13" casserole. Spoon the biscuit topping onto the fruit, making 8 portions. Bake in a 400 degree oven for 40 minutes, or until biscuits are brown and fruit is bubbling.

— It's All the Same to the Clam —
By Shel Silverstein

You may leave the clam on the ocean's floor,
It's all the same to the clam.
For a hundred thousand years or more,
It's all the same to the clam.
You may bury him deep in mud and muck
Or carry him 'round to bring you luck,
Or use him for a hockey puck,
It's all the same to the clam.

You may call him Jim or Frank or Nell,
It's all the same to the clam.
Or make an ashtray from his shell,
It's all the same to the clam.
You may take him riding on the train
Or leave him sitting in the rain.
You'll never hear the clam complain,
It's all the same to the clam.

Yes, the world may stop or the world may spin,
It's all the same to the clam.
And the sky may come a-fallin' in,
It's all the same to the clam.
And man may sing his endless songs
Of wronging rights and righting wrongs.
The clam just sets – and gets along,
It's all the same to the clam.

Manhattan Clam Chowder

6 to 8 portions

1 dozen cherrystone clams

4 strips of bacon
1 large onion
2 stalks of celery
2 carrots
½ tsp Old Bay seasoning
2 sprigs fresh thyme
1 bay leaf
1 tsp ground pepper

3 cups water
2 cups diced potatoes
1 can (15 oz) diced
      tomatoes

2 Tbsp cornstarch
¼ cup cold water
¼ cup chopped parsley

1. Rinse the clams in cold water. Shuck them over a bowl using a clam knife or an old paring knife. Reserve the juices (if they are too difficult to open, soak them in very hot tap water for 5 minutes before opening).

2. Lift the clam meats out of the juice, chop coarsely, and refrigerate. Let the sediment settle out of the juice, then pour it off into a pint measure, discarding the sediment.

3. Dice the bacon and add it to a Dutch oven. Cook on medium heat until it is almost crisp, then add the onions, celery, and carrots. Continue cooking and add the Old Bay, thyme, bay leaf, and pepper.

4. Pour in the reserved clam juice and the water (the combined liquid should make about 5 cups). Bring the chowder to a boil and add the potatoes and the tomatoes. Reduce the heat and simmer until the potatoes are tender, about 20 minutes.

5. Dissolve the cornstarch in the cold water and add to the chowder. Stir in the reserved chopped clams and bring back to a boil. Simmer another 10 minutes and add the parsley. Check for seasoning and serve with chowder crackers.

New England Clam Chowder

8 to 10 portions

2 dozen cherrystone clams
4 cups water
1 tbsp celery seed
½ tsp Old Bay seasoning

4 oz salt pork, diced
1 large onion, peeled and
    chopped
½ cup chopped celery
4 cups diced potatoes
Reserved clam broth
1 Tbsp fresh thyme leaves
1 tsp ground pepper

4 cups milk
1 bay leaf
¼ tsp ground nutmeg
5 Tbsp butter
½ cup flour

Reserved chopped clams

1. Rinse the clams in cold water and scrub with a brush. Place them in the soup pot with the water, celery seed, and Old Bay. Cover and bring to a boil.

2. As the clams begin to open, remove the lid and pull them out with a pair of tongs. You should end up with about 5 cups of clam broth. Let the sand settle and pour off the broth into a clean bowl. Cut the cooked clams out of their shells, chop coarsely, and refrigerate.

3. Put a Dutch oven on medium heat and add the salt pork. Once it begins to brown, stir in the onions and celery. As the vegetables begin to soften, add the potatoes and reserved clam broth. Season with the thyme and pepper and continue cooking until potatoes are tender, about 15 minutes.

4. Place the milk, bay leaf, and nutmeg in a small saucepan over medium heat. Do not boil. In a separate small pan, melt the butter and stir in the flour to make a roux. Cook for 3 minutes, then whisk it into the simmering milk. Bring it gradually to a boil, stirring with a wooden spoon.

5. Add the thickened white sauce and the reserved chopped clams to the potato mixture in the Dutch oven. Simmer briefly and check for seasoning.

Portuguese-Style Scallop and Fish Chowder

6 to 8 portions

8 oz fresh sea scallops
8 oz fresh cod fillet
4 oz Portuguese chourico
  sausage

---

2 Tbsp olive oil
1 large onion, peeled and
  chopped
1 Tbsp minced garlic
1 bay leaf
4 small new potatoes, skin-on,
  sliced
2 cups fish stock (frozen from
  local fish market)
2 cups chicken stock

---

1 bunch kale, stems removed,
  chopped
1 can (15 oz) chopped tomatoes
1 can (15 oz) chick peas,
  drained and rinsed
¼ cup chopped cilantro
1 lemon, zest and juice
1 tsp ground pepper

1. Slice the scallops in half crosswise, and cut the cod into 2" chunks. Refrigerate both.

2. Peel the casing off the sausage and slice it into ⅛"-thick rounds.

3. Heat a soup pot and add the oil. Stir in the onions and cook for 3 minutes before adding the garlic and bay leaf. Continue cooking at low heat and add the potatoes, fish stock, and chicken stock. Simmer until potatoes are tender, about 15 minutes.

4. Add the kale, tomatoes, and chick peas and continue cooking another 10 minutes. Stir in the reserved scallops, cod, and sausage. Finish by adding the chopped cilantro, lemon zest and juice, and pepper. Check for seasoning and serve.

*North Fork restaurateur Tom Schaudel receiving
the 2010 Chowder Contest trophy from John Ross*

Grilled Corn and Chicken Chowder

8 portions

1 lb boneless, skinless, chicken cutlets

4 ears fresh corn on the cob

2 Tbsp olive oil

1 red bell pepper

1 Tbsp kosher salt

1 tsp ground pepper

For the chowder

1 Tbsp olive oil

1 large onion, peeled and chopped

1 jalapeno pepper, split, seeded, minced

2 Tbsp minced garlic

1 tsp ground cumin

2 tsp curry powder

4 cups chicken stock

Reserved corn cobs

1 can (15 oz.) diced tomatoes

2 medium sweet potatoes, peeled and diced

1 can (15 oz.) coconut milk

1 lime, zest and juice

¼ cup chopped cilantro

1. Prepare a charcoal grill and wait until the coals turn white. Rub the grill with an oil-soaked paper towel. Shuck the corn and split the red pepper in two, removing the seeds. Place the chicken cutlets, corn, and pepper on a foil-lined sheet pan and brush with the olive oil. Sprinkle all with salt and pepper.

2. Grill the chicken, corn, and red pepper until lightly charred and remove to the kitchen. Cut the chicken into bite-sized pieces, scrape the kernels off the corn (reserve corn cobs), and cut the pepper into 1" pieces.

3. Heat the oil in a Dutch oven and add the onions, jalapeno pepper, and garlic. Cook for 3 minutes, then add the ground cumin and curry powder.

4. Raise the heat and add the chicken stock and the reserved corn cobs. Simmer for 20 minutes and remove the corn cobs.

5. Add the diced tomatoes and the diced sweet potatoes. Simmer until potatoes are tender and stir in the coconut milk.

6. Add the cooked chicken, corn kernels, and red pepper. Add the lime zest and juice and the cilantro. Check for seasoning and serve.

Oysters Rockefeller and Clams Casino

4 to 8 portions

16 oysters
16 cherrystone clams

Oyster Topping
1 head of kale
1 bunch of Swiss chard
1 bunch of field spinach

2 Tbsp butter
1 bunch green onions,
    trimmed and chopped
¼ cup minced shallots
1 Tbsp minced garlic
4 minced anchovies
2 tsp kosher salt
1 tsp ground pepper
¼ tsp Tabasco sauce
2 Tbsp Pernod liqueur
½ cup panko crumbs

Clam Topping
1 tsp olive oil
2 oz thinly sliced pancetta
½ cup minced red pepper
½ cup minced green pepper
¼ cup minced shallots
1 Tbsp minced garlic
1 Tbsp chopped fresh
    oregano

¼ cup white wine
¼ cup grated parmesan
    cheese

1. Scrub the oysters and clams under cold water. Shuck them, leaving them on the half shell, and place on a foil-lined sheet pan. Refrigerate.

2. For the oyster topping, trim the root ends off the kale, Swiss chard, and spinach. Plunge the leaves into a cold water bath, lift them out, and drain. Trim the leaves off the stems and discard the stems.

3. Bring 4 quarts of water to a boil in a pasta pot and add all of the greens. Bring the water back to the boil and drain in a colander. Rinse under cold water to cool, then press out as much moisture as possible. Wrap the greens in a kitchen towel and twist to squeeze out any remaining water. Chop coarsely and set aside.

4. Heat a large sauté pan and add the butter. Stir in the onions, shallots, garlic, and anchovies. Add the chopped greens and continue cooking on low heat. Season with the salt, pepper, and Tabasco, then stir in the Pernod and panko crumbs. Transfer to a bowl and keep warm.

5. For the clam topping, heat a sauté pan and add the oil. Cook the pancetta until crisp and remove to a paper-towel-lined plate. Add the red and green pepper, shallots, garlic, and oregano to the drippings in the pan. Cook at low heat for 3 minutes.

6. Add the wine and parmesan cheese. Chop the pancetta and add to the pan. Transfer to a bowl.

7. At service time, place a tablespoon of the greens mixture on each oyster and a tablespoon of the pepper mixture on each clam. Heat in a 400 degree oven for 5 minutes before serving. Line the serving plates with the excess greens mixture.

Grilled Pork Tenderloin with Pears, Sweet Potato and Blackberry Sauce

4 portions

1 pork tenderloin (about 1½ lbs)

Seasoning rub
1 tsp smoked paprika
1 tsp chili powder
½ tsp garlic powder
½ tsp onion powder
1 tsp kosher salt
Dash cayenne pepper

Twice-Baked Sweet Potato
4 medium sized sweet potatoes
½ cup cream cheese
1 tsp five spice powder
½ tsp ground ginger
½ tsp ground cinnamon
1 tsp kosher salt
½ tsp ground pepper

Pears
4 Bosc pears
1 tsp lemon juice
1 tsp canola oil

Blackberry sauce
½ cup sugar
½ cup balsamic vinegar
½ cup chicken stock
¼ cup blackberry preserves
1 cinnamon stick
3 cloves
½ lemon, rind and juice
½ tsp kosher salt
¼ tsp ground pepper
1 Tbsp cornstarch
2 Tbsp cold water
1 cup fresh blackberries

1. Trim any fat and silverskin from the pork. Combine the paprika, chili powder, garlic powder, onion powder, salt, pepper, and cayenne in a small bowl. Rub the mixture over the pork and refrigerate for at least 30 minutes.

2. Scrub the sweet potatoes, spray with no-stick and roast in a 400 degree oven until soft, about 1 hour. Cut the tops off and scoop out the flesh, reserving the shells.

3. Mash the sweet potato and stir in the cream cheese. Season with the five spice powder, ginger, cinnamon, salt, and pepper. Stuff the shells and reheat just before service.

4. Trim the stem ends off the pears and split the pears in half. Using a spoon, remove the cores and brush with lemon juice. Set aside.

5. Prepare a charcoal fire and wait for the coals to turn white. Brush the pork with oil, place on the hot part of the grill, and cook for about 5 minutes per side. When nicely marked, move to a cooler part of the grill. Cook until internal temperature is 145 degrees, and remove. Grill the pear halves, cut-side down, for 3 minutes and remove.

6. For the sauce, heat a small saucepan and add the sugar. Cook, stirring with a wooden spoon, until the sugar turns into liquid and begins to turn golden in color. Carefully add the vinegar, let the mixture come to a boil, and reduce to a thin syrup.

7. Add the chicken stock, blackberry preserves, cinnamon, cloves, lemon juice and rind, salt, and pepper. Continue cooking at medium heat for 30 minutes. Dissolve the cornstarch in the water and add to the sauce. Bring it back to a boil, remove, and strain into a bowl. Add the fresh blackberries and serve.

8. Slice the pork and arrange on a platter with the grilled pears and the twice-baked sweet potatoes. Spoon some of the sauce on the meat and pass the rest.

Oysters Rockefeller and Clams Casino

Grilled Pork Tenderloin with Pears, Sweet Potato and Blackberry Sauce

Fried Calamari with Romesco Sauce

2 lbs fresh calamari (squid)

2 cups flour
2 cups buttermilk
4 cups cracker meal
1 Tbsp chili powder
1 Tbsp smoked paprika
1 Tbsp kosher salt
1 tsp ground pepper
2 cups canola oil

Romesco Sauce
1 small jar (4 oz.) roasted
        red peppers
½ cup olive oil
6 cloves peeled garlic
½ cup cubed French
        bread
½ cup chopped walnuts
1 tsp smoked paprika
2 Tbsp sherry vinegar
1 tsp kosher salt

1. Clean the calamari by pulling out the head and tentacles from the body. Cut the head off and discard. Remove and discard the pen, the skin, and the fins. Rinse the tubes and the tentacles, and cut the tubes into ¼"-wide rings. Separate the tentacles.
   Note: *frozen calamari is available at most fish markets and does not require cleaning, but when available, fresh is best.*

2. Set up a breading station with the flour in a shallow pan, the buttermilk in a bowl, and the cracker meal in another shallow pan.

3. Season the cracker meal with the chili powder, paprika, salt, and pepper. Dust the calamari pieces in the flour, dip them in the buttermilk, then press them into the cracker crumbs. Bread the pieces a few at a time and lay them on a tray.

4. At service time, heat the oil in a Dutch oven to 350 degrees. Cook the breaded calamari in small batches for about 3 minutes, then place on a paper towel lined sheet pan and keep warm.

5. For the sauce, drain the red peppers and place them in the bowl of a food processor. Heat the olive oil in a small pan and add the garlic. Cook for 3 minutes, then add to the processor along with the bread cubes.

6. Process until chunky and add the walnuts and paprika. Drizzle in the vinegar and the salt. Process until smooth and serve.

– Wine Notes –
This Italian dish might be well matched with a Pinot Grigio or a Tocai Friulano from Italy or a local Chardonnay.

Fried Calamari with Romesco Sauce

Butternut Squash with Farfalle

Butternut Squash with Sage Pesto and Farfalle

4 portions

1 medium-sized butternut
   squash
2 Tbsp olive oil
2 tsp kosher salt
1 tsp ground pepper
1 tsp minced garlic
¼ cup chopped fresh sage

Sage Pesto
½ cup fresh sage, coarsely
   chopped
½ cup chopped flat leaf
   parsley
4 green onions, trimmed
   and sliced
1 tsp minced garlic
½ cup walnuts
½ cup olive oil
¼ cup grated parmesan
   cheese
1 box (12 oz) farfalle
2 Tbsp olive oil
12 sage leaves
½ cup walnuts
¼ cup grated parmesan
   cheese

1. Trim the ends off the squash and peel the skin with a vegetable peeler or a paring knife. Split the squash in half, then in quarters. Remove the seeds and cut the squash into 2" pieces.

2. Toss the squash in a large bowl with the olive oil, salt, pepper, garlic, and sage. Line a sheet pan with foil, spread the squash out on it, and roast in a 400 degree oven for 30 minutes. Remove and set aside.

3. For the pesto, add to the bowl of a food processor the sage, parsley, green onions, garlic, and walnuts. Pulse until coarsely ground and drizzle in the olive oil. Remove to a bowl and stir in the grated cheese.

4. Bring 3 quarts of water to a boil and add the farfalle. When cooked al dente, strain, saving ½ cup of the cooking water.

5. Place a large sauté pan on the heat and add the olive oil. When hot, add the sage leaves and cook for 2 minutes. Remove the sage with tongs to a paper-towel-lined plate.

6. Add to the pan the roasted squash, cooked farfalle, and walnuts. Stir in ½ cup of the pesto, plus some of the pasta water if the mixture is too dry. Serve in pasta bowls with the grated cheese and additional pesto on the side.

Cauliflower Gratin with Fingerling Potatoes and Applewood-Smoked Bacon

4 to 6 portions

1 head cauliflower
1 lb fingerling potatoes
¼ cup canola oil
2 tsp kosher salt
1 tsp ground pepper
1 head of garlic
8 oz Applewood-smoked bacon

Horseradish Bechamel Sauce
2 cups milk
1 tsp kosher salt
½ tsp ground pepper
Dash ground nutmeg
3 Tbsp butter
¼ cup flour
½ cup grated fresh horseradish
1 bunch green onions, finely chopped

Topping
1 cup grated extra sharp cheddar cheese
1 cup grated fontina cheese

1. Working from the bottom, cut the cauliflower into small florets. Cut the fingerling potatoes into 1" pieces, leaving the skin on. Place the oil, salt, and pepper into a large bowl and toss the cauliflower and potatoes together. Place them on a foil-lined sheet pan.

2. Trim the top off the head of garlic and brush it with oil. Wrap loosely with foil and place on the sheet pan with the cauliflower and potatoes. Place the strips of bacon on a separate sheet pan, and put both pans in a 400 degree oven for 30 minutes. The bacon should be crisp and the vegetables fully cooked.

3. For the sauce, heat the milk in a saucepan and add the salt, pepper, and nutmeg. Do not boil the milk. Melt the butter in a small pan and stir in the flour to make a roux. Cook for 3 minutes and whisk into the milk. Let it come to a boil to thicken, then reduce the heat to low. Add the horseradish and set aside.

4. Squeeze the cloves of garlic out of their skins, chop finely, and add to the sauce. Transfer the sauce to a large bowl and add the cooked cauliflower and potatoes. Stir in the chopped green onions.

5. Chop the cooked bacon and add to the bowl. Gently combine everything in the bowl and transfer to a casserole. Sprinkle the grated cheddar and fontina on the top and place in a 400 degree oven for 20 minutes before serving.

OCTOBER

— When the Frost is on the Punkin —
By James Whitcomb Riley

When the frost is on the punkin and the fodder's in the shock,
And you hear the kyouck and gobble of the struttin' turkey-cock,
And the clackin' of the guineys, and the cluckin' of the hens,
And the rooster's hallylooer as he tiptoes on the fence;
O, it's then the time a feller is a-feelin' at his best,
With the risin' sun to greet him from a night of peaceful rest,
As he leaves the house, bareheaded, and goes out to feed the stock,
When the frost is on the punkin and the fodder's in the shock.

They's something kindo' harty-like about the atmusfere
When the heat of summer's over and the coolin' fall is here –
Of course we miss the flowers, and the blossoms on the trees,
And the mumble of the hummin'-birds and buzzin' of the bees;
But the air's so appetizin'; and the landscape through the haze
Of a crisp and sunny morning of the airly autumn days
Is a pictur' that no painter has the colorin' to mock –
When the frost is on the punkin and the fodder's in the shock.

The husky, rusty russel of the tossels of the corn,
And the raspin' of the tangled leaves as golden as the morn;
The stubble in the furries-kindo' lonesome-like, but still
A-preachin' sermuns to us of the barns they growed to fill;
The strawstack in the medder, and the reaper in the shed;
The hosses in theyr stalls below, the clover overhead! –
O, it sets my hart a clickin' like the tickin' of a clock,
When the frost is on the punkin and the fodder's in the shock.

Then your apples all is gathered, and the ones a feller keeps
Is poured around the cellar-floor in red and yaller heaps;
And your cider-makin's over, and your wimmern-folks is through
With theyr mince and apple-butter, and theyr souse and sausage too!
I don't know how to tell it, but ef such a thing could be
As the angels wantin' boardin', and they'd call around on me –
I'd want to 'commodate 'em all, the whole-indurin' flock
When the frost is on the punkin and the fodder's in the shock.

October on the North Fork is all about pumpkins, the harvest, and the wine. Many years ago the farmstands sold a few pumpkins, mostly for halloween jack-o-lanterns and decorations around the house. But when the Krupski family, the Harbes family, and others began expanding their pumpkin crop and turning pumpkin shopping into a family experience, things changed enormously. It started with U-Pick pumpkins, then the corn maze and the roasted corn, and finally, country bands and hayrides for family entertainment.

Along with the pumpkins, the hordes of people coming to the North Fork in October stop for pies and the many fruits and vegetables at their peak: apples; cauliflower; broccoli; Brussels sprouts; kale; and a whole list of squash and pumpkin varieties. The local vineyards begin their harvest of red wine grapes, and visitors flock to the wineries for weekend entertainment, picnics, and wine tasting.

Prime Meal
Pumpkin Chardonnay Soup

---

*Cider-Brined, Herb-Roasted, Bone-in Pork Roast with Hard Cider Sauce,
Yukon Gold Potatoes, Cippolini Onions and Carrots*

Baked Mutsu Apples with Walnuts and Oatmeal

Recommended wine: *A Long Island Cabernet Franc or Craft Beer*

Selected Recipes
1. *Stuffed Jack-B-Little Pumpkins*
2. *Roasted Cauliflower with Pumpkin and Chick Peas*
3. *Spaghetti Squash with Slow-Roasted Tomatoes and Pesto*
4. *Butternut Squash Ravioli with Mushroom Sage Sauce*
5. *German Potato Dumplings with Veal Medallions*
6. *Individual Yankee Pot Roast with Fall Vegetables*
7. *Pork Schnitzel with Potato Apple Pancakes and Chunky Applesauce*
8. *Mixed Hardy Greens and Sausage Pie*
9. *Duck Ragout braised in Pinot Noir*

Pumpkin Chardonnay Soup

PRIME MEAL

– *First Course* –
Pumpkin Chardonnay Soup

8 portions

2 Tbsp olive oil
1 large onion, peeled and
    chopped
1 leek, white part, diced
2 cloves garlic, crushed
1 Tbsp fresh thyme leaves
1 cup chardonnay
6 cups fresh pumpkin, peeled,
    seeded, cut into chunks
1 carrot, peeled, diced
1 turnip, peeled, diced
1 parsnip, peeled, diced
2 medium-sized potatoes,
    peeled, diced
6 cups chicken stock
1 cup heavy cream
1 Tbsp kosher salt
1 tsp ground pepper
½ tsp ground nutmeg

1. Heat a soup pot and add the oil. Add the onion, leek, garlic, and thyme. Cover and cook at low heat for 5 minutes. Remove the cover, turn up the heat, and add the chardonnay. Cook until wine is almost evaporated.

2. Add the pumpkin, carrot, turnip, parsnip, potatoes, and chicken stock. Bring to a boil, reduce the heat and simmer for 30 minutes.

3. Strain the liquid from the soup and set aside. Place the cooked vegetables in the bowl of a food processor and puree. Return the pureed vegetables to the pot along with the reserved liquid (use an immersion blender instead of the food processor if you have one).

4. Add the heavy cream, salt, pepper, and nutmeg, and simmer for another 15 minutes and serve. Garnish with buttered croutons and finely chopped green onions if desired.

Note: *The sugar pumpkin (or cheese pumpkin) is best for this recipe because of its firm texture, but any fresh pumpkin will suffice. Butternut squash is also a good substitute.*

Cider-Brined Bone-In Pork Loin

6 portions

1 center cut pork loin, bone-in, with 5 rib bones

Cider Brine
1 cup brown sugar
1 cup kosher salt
3 bay leaves
2 Tbsp coriander seeds
10 black peppercorns
2 cups water
2 cups apple cider
2 cups ice cubes

6 fresh sage leaves
1 Tbsp thyme leaves
1 Tbsp fennel seeds

1 Tbsp canola oil
1 cup chopped onion
1 stalk of celery, chopped
1 carrot, peeled and chopped

¼ cup flour
2 cups chicken stock
1 cup hard cider

1. Have your butcher cut the chine bone off the pork loin and crack the backbone for ease of carving. Have the ribs "Frenched" by trimming off all the fat and meat from the rib bones.

2. Combine in a large soup pot the brown sugar, salt, bay leaves, coriander, peppercorns, and water. Bring to a boil and simmer for 10 minutes, then stir in the apple cider and the ice cubes to cool. Put the pork roast in the brine and refrigerate overnight.

3. Remove the pork from the brine and dry with paper towels. Make a cut lengthwise along the bones, almost removing the eye of meat from the bones. Place the sage, thyme, and fennel in the cut. Tie the roast together again with string between the ribs.

4. Heat a large sauté pan and add the oil. Place the pork roast fat-side down in the hot pan and brown, being careful not to burn. Remove and set aside.

5. Lay the chopped onion, carrot, and celery in the bottom of a roasting pan and put the pork roast on top. Add 1 cup of water to the drippings in the sauté pan, bring to a boil, and pour over the roast.

6. Place the roast in a 275 degree oven and cook until the internal temperature reaches 145 degrees, about 2½ hours. Remove the pork from the pan and keep warm.

7. Transfer the contents of the roasting pan to a saucepan. Add the flour and cook for 5 minutes at medium heat. Place the roasting pan on the stove and deglaze it with the chicken stock. Pour this liquid into the saucepan and continue cooking.

8. Stir in the cider, bring to a boil and simmer another 10 minutes. Strain into a clean saucepan and check for seasoning.

Roasted Rosemary Potatoes, Cipollini Onions, and Carrots

12 small Yukon gold potatoes

2 Tbsp olive oil
2 Tbsp chopped rosemary
1 Tbsp minced garlic
1 Tbsp kosher salt
2 tsp ground pepper

12 Cipollini onions
6 large carrots

1. Rinse the potatoes but do not peel. Cut a small slice off the bottom of each potato so that it will lay flat. Make deep cuts every ¼" across the potato, but not through the bottom.

2. Add the olive oil, rosemary, garlic, salt, and pepper to a large bowl. Toss the potatoes in this mixture, working the seasoning into the cuts along the length of the potato. Place the potatoes on a foil-lined sheet pan and set aside.

3. For easy peeling, blanch the Cipollini onions in 2 quarts of boiling water for 1 minute, remove, and slip off the skins. Trim and peel the carrots and cut into large 2" pieces.

4. Toss the onions and the carrots in the olive oil mixture and add them to the potatoes on the sheet pan. Place in a 400 degree oven and roast for 40 minutes. Serve with the pork roast.

– Dessert –
Baked Mutsu Apples with Walnuts and Oatmeal

6 portions

7 large Mutsu apples (or other large cooking apple)
1 cup cold water
1 Tbsp lemon juice

4 Tbsp butter
½ cup dried cranberries
½ cup chopped walnuts
¼ cup old fashioned oatmeal
¼ cup brown sugar
1 tsp ground cinnamon
½ tsp salt

½ cup pure maple syrup
¼ cup dark rum
¼ cup apple cider

1. Combine the water and lemon juice in a deep bowl. Peel the apples, dip them in the lemon water, and remove. Cut the stem end from 6 of the apples, about ¾" down from the top. Hollow out these apples with a paring knife and a spoon, being careful to not cut through the bottom. Dip in lemon water again and set aside.

2. Peel, core, and dice the remaining apples. Heat a large sauté pan and add the butter. When it melts, add the diced apple, the cranberries, walnuts, oatmeal, brown sugar, cinnamon, and salt. Cook for 5 minutes at medium heat.

3. Place the 6 hollowed-out apples in a casserole and fill the cavities with the cooked mixture. Combine the maple syrup, rum, and cider and pour over the apples. Bake, uncovered, in a 400 degree oven for 30 minutes. Serve with vanilla ice cream or whipped cream if desired.

Stuffed Jack-B-Little Pumpkins

8 portions

8 Jack-B-Little pumpkins (about 3" in diameter)

2 Tbsp olive oil
1 large onion, peeled and chopped
1 Tbsp minced garlic
2 cups diced cheese pumpkin (or substitute butternut squash)
1 cup red lentils
2 plum tomatoes, diced
2 Tbsp tomato paste
2 cups vegetable stock

1 tsp ground cumin
1 tsp turmeric
2 tsp kosher salt
1 tsp ground pepper
⅛ tsp red pepper flakes
1 Tbsp grated ginger
1 can (15 oz.) chick peas, drained and rinsed

1 cup chopped peanuts
1 lime, zest and juice
¼ cup chopped cilantro

1. Scrub the pumpkins under cold water. Place them on a foil-lined sheet pan and spray lightly with no-stick. Roast in a 350 degree oven for 30 minutes, remove and cool.

2. Heat a large, shallow saucepan and add the oil. Add the onion and garlic and cook at low heat for 3 minutes. Stir in the pumpkin, lentils, tomatoes, and tomato paste. Continue cooking and add the vegetable stock.

3. Season with the cumin, turmeric, salt, pepper, and red pepper flakes. Bring to a boil, then reduce the heat and add the ginger and chick peas. Simmer until the lentils are cooked and the pumpkin is tender, about 20 minutes.

4. Add the peanuts, lime juice and zest, and the cilantro. Remove from the heat.

5. Cut the tops from the pumpkins about ¾" down from the top. Scoop out the seeds with a spoon and stuff the pumpkins with the filling. Place the extra filling in a small casserole. At service time, heat the stuffed pumpkins and the remaining filling in a 350 degree oven for 20 minutes.

Roasted Cauliflower with Pumpkin and Chickpeas

6 to 8 portions

1 medium-sized cheese pumpkin

1 head of cauliflower

¼ cup olive oil
1 large onion, peeled and sliced
1 Tbsp sliced garlic
2 tsp minced ginger
1 Tbsp curry powder
1 tsp turmeric
¼ tsp red pepper flakes
1 Tbsp kosher salt

2 cans (15 oz) chickpeas
¼ cup chopped cilantro

1. Cut the top off the pumpkin and split it in half. Scoop out the seeds with a large spoon and cut the pumpkin into 1" thick wedges. Peel the skin off with a paring knife and cut the pumpkin into 1" chunks. You should have about 8 cups of pumpkin.

2. Turn the cauliflower upside down, remove the leaves, and cut the core out with a stiff knife. Remove the florets with a knife, working from the bottom.

3. Heat a large sauté pan and add the oil. Add the sliced onions and cook for 3 minutes. Stir in the garlic, ginger, curry powder, turmeric, red pepper flakes, and salt. Continue cooking for another 3 minutes and place in a large bowl.

4. Toss the pumpkin and the cauliflower in this mixture, then transfer them to a foil-lined sheet pan. Place in a 400 degree oven until the vegetables are tender and brown, about 25 minutes.

5. Rinse the chickpeas and add them to the sheet pan with the vegetables. Roast for another 5 minutes and remove. Garnish with chopped cilantro and serve.

   Note: *This recipe goes very well with lamb shish kebab, grilled chicken breasts, or grilled shrimp.*

Spaghetti Squash with Pesto and Slow-Roasted Tomatoes

6 portions

8 plum tomatoes

2 Tbsp olive oil
1 Tbsp minced garlic
1 Tbsp fresh thyme
1 tsp kosher salt
1 tsp ground pepper

3 medium-sized spaghetti squash

Pesto
¼ cup pine nuts
2 cups coarsely chopped basil leaves
1 cup chopped flat leaf parsley
1 Tbsp minced garlic
½ cup olive oil
½ tsp kosher salt
½ tsp ground pepper
½ cup grated parmesan cheese

1. Trim the ends off the tomatoes and split them in half lengthwise. Line a sheet pan with foil and place the tomatoes on the pan cut side-up. Brush them with the oil and sprinkle with the garlic, thyme, salt, and pepper. Put them in a 250 degree oven for 3 hours.

2. Cut the ends off the spaghetti squash and split lengthwise. Scoop out the seeds with a spoon. Line a sheet pan with foil and spray it with no-stick. Place the squash cut side-down on the sheet pan and roast in a 350 degree oven for 45 minutes.

3. When cool enough to handle, scrape out the strands of spaghetti squash with a dinner fork into a bowl. They should resemble spaghetti.

4. For the pesto, heat a dry sauté pan and add the pine nuts. Toast them for 3 minutes and remove. Add the pine nuts to the bowl of a food processor along with the basil, parsley, and garlic.

5. Pulse until coarsely chopped and drizzle in the olive oil and add the salt and pepper. Transfer to a bowl and stir in the grated cheese.

6. At service time, chop 4 slow roasted tomatoes and add them to the spaghetti squash in the bowl. Add ¼ cup of the pesto to the bowl and toss the ingredients together.

7. Fill the empty squash shells with the mixture, garnish with the remaining tomatoes and heat in a 350 degree oven for 15 minutes. Alternatively, just place the squash mixture in a casserole with the tomatoes and heat in the oven. Serve in pasta bowls.

Butternut Squash Ravioli with Mushroom Sage Sauce

6 to 8 portions

1 large butternut squash

2 Tbsp butter
½ tsp allspice
½ tsp nutmeg
1 tsp ground cinnamon
½ cup grated parmesan cheese
1 tsp kosher salt
½ tsp ground pepper

Wonton wrappers
1 egg white
1 tsp kosher salt

For the Sauce
½ cup butter
12 fresh sage leaves

½ cup minced shallots
1 pkg. baby bella mushrooms, trimmed and sliced
1 pkg. shiitake mushrooms, trimmed and sliced

1 cup red wine
1 cup heavy cream
1 tsp kosher salt
½ tsp ground pepper

¼ cup chopped parsley

1. Trim the ends off the squash, split in half lengthwise, and scoop out the seeds with a spoon. Line a sheet pan with foil and spray with no-stick.

2. Place the squash cut side-down on the sheet pan and roast in a 350 degree oven for 45 minutes. Remove from the oven, cool briefly, and scoop out the flesh into a bowl. Mash the squash with a potato masher.

3. Mix in the butter, allspice, nutmeg, cinnamon, parmesan, salt, and pepper with a rubber spatula.

4. Place the Wonton wrappers in lines on a cutting board and brush lightly with the egg white. Place a tablespoon of the filling on a wrapper, then cover with another wrapper. Seal the edges with a fork and repeat until filling is used. For ease of handling, freeze the ravioli if you are not going to use them right away.

5. Bring 4 quarts of water to a boil in a pasta pot and add the salt. Drop the ravioli in the water a few at a time, being careful not to crowd. Cook for 4 minutes as they rise to the top. Remove the cooked ravioli with a slotted spoon and keep warm.

6. For the sauce, melt the butter in a large sauté pan and add the sage leaves. As they begin to crisp, remove them with tongs and place on a paper towel.

7. Add the shallots to the pan and cook for 3 minutes before adding the baby bella and shiitake mushrooms. Cook at medium heat until the mushrooms give up their moisture, about 10 minutes.

8. Add the wine and continue cooking for another 5 minutes. Stir in the cream and season with the salt and pepper.

9. Portion the warm ravioli into pasta bowls and spoon the sauce over them. Garnish with chopped parsley and the reserved sage leaves.

German Potato Dumplings (Kartoffelklöse)

24 dumplings

4 large russet potatoes

1 cup flour
1 cup farina (Cream of
    Wheat)
1 Tbsp kosher salt
1 tsp ground pepper
1 tsp ground nutmeg
4 eggs, beaten

1 French baguette

2 Tbsp butter
1 Tbsp kosher salt

1. Bring 2 quarts of water to a boil. Wash the potatoes and add to the boiling water. Simmer them in their skins until fully cooked, about 40 minutes.

2. Cool the potatoes briefly, then peel and cut into large chunks. Press them through a potato ricer into a large bowl. You should have about 8 cups of potato.

3. Whisk the flour, farina, salt, pepper, and nutmeg together and add to the potatoes. Stir in the beaten eggs with a wooden spoon to form a dough. Using your hands, form the dough into balls the size of a golf ball. You will end up with about 2 dozen.

4. Cut the baguette into ½" squares and place them on a foil-lined sheet pan. Roast in a 350 degree oven for 15 minutes. Reserve one third of the bread for croutons; place the rest in a food processor and process into bread crumbs.

5. Heat a large sauté pan, melt the butter, and add the bread crumbs. Sauté, stirring, until golden, about 3 minutes.

6. Bring 4 quarts of water to a boil in a large pot and add the salt. Take each dumpling in your hand and insert one of the croutons into the center, pressing with your fingers to seal the dough around it.

7. Drop the dumplings into the boiling water and let them rise to the surface and cook another minute before removing with a slotted spoon. Cook in batches and do not crowd the dumplings in the pot. As you remove them, roll them in the sautéed bread crumbs and keep warm.

Note: *Serve these dumplings with the following recipe for veal.*

Veal Medallions with Mushrooms and Cream

4 portions

1 lb veal cutlets
1 tsp kosher salt
½ tsp ground pepper
1 cup flour

2 Tbsp butter
12 sage leaves

2 Tbsp olive oil
½ cup chopped shallots
1 pkg. baby bella mushrooms, trimmed and sliced
1 pkg. shiitake mushrooms, trimmed and sliced
1 pkg. oyster mushrooms, trimmed and sliced

2 Tbsp flour
1 cup chicken stock
1 cup heavy cream
1 tsp kosher salt
½ tsp ground pepper
1 lemon, zest and juice

1. Cut the veal into 3" medallions and pound between two pieces of plastic film with a meat mallet or frying pan. Season the veal with the salt and pepper and dredge in the flour.

2. Melt the butter in a large sauté pan and add the sage leaves. Cook until the sage is crisp, remove it with tongs, and add the veal. Over high heat, brown the veal quickly on both sides and set aside, reserving the pan.

3. Add the oil to the pan and, when hot, add the shallots. Cook for 3 minutes and add the mushrooms. Continue to cook at medium heat until the mushrooms begin to brown and release their moisture.

4. Stir in the flour and continue cooking. Add the chicken stock, cream, salt, and pepper. Bring to a boil, then add the veal medallions, lemon zest and juice. Check for seasoning and serve with the German potato dumplings (previous recipe).

– Wine Notes –

When accompanied by the German potato dumplings, the wine choice should be a German Riesling. A Trocken Kabinett or Spatlese from the Phalz or Rheinhessen would work well. A dry Riesling from the North Fork would also be good.

The author with Veal Medallions and Potato Dumplings

— Unharvested —
By Robert Frost

A scent of ripeness from over a wall.
And come to leave the routine road
And look for what had made me stall,
There sure enough was an apple tree
That had eased itself of its summer load,
And of all but its trivial foliage free,
Now breathed as light as a lady's fan.
For there had been an apple fall
As complete as the apple had given man.
The ground was one circle of solid red.
May something go always Unharvested!
May much stay out of our stated plan,
Apples or something forgotten and left,
So smelling their sweetness would be no theft.

Butternut Squash Ravioli with Mushroom Sage Sauce

Individual Yankee Pot Roast of Beef

Individual Yankee Pot Roast of Beef

4 portions

2 lbs boneless beef chuck steak, 2" thick
1 tsp kosher salt
1 tsp ground pepper

16 small white onions

1 Tbsp canola oil

2 shallots, minced
1 carrot, peeled and diced
1 stalk celery, diced
3 cloves garlic, sliced
¼ cup flour
2 Tbsp tomato paste

2 cups chicken stock
1 cup water

1 bay leaf
3 sprigs thyme
6 parsley stems
4 sage leaves

Vegetables
1 pkg. baby bella mushrooms
2 Tbsp butter

3 carrots
2 parsnips
1 turnip
4 small potatoes
¼ cup chopped parsley

1. Cut the steak into 4 equal pieces. Tie a piece of string around each one to give them the look of a filet mignon. Season with the salt and pepper and let them come to room temperature.

2. Blanch the onions in 1 quart of boiling water for 1 minute. Rinse under cold water, peel, and set aside.

3. Heat a Dutch oven and add the oil. Over high heat, brown the steaks on both sides. Do not crowd. Remove and brown the pearl onions in the same pot. Remove and set aside.

4. Lower the heat in the Dutch oven and add the shallots, carrot, celery, and garlic. Cook briefly and add the flour to make a roux. Continue cooking and add the tomato paste.

5. After another 3 minutes add the chicken stock and water. Bring the sauce to a boil and arrange the meat in the pot in one layer. Lower the heat to a simmer.

6. Tie the bay leaf, thyme, parsley stems, and sage with a string to make a bouquet garni. Place this in the pot, cover, and put into a 325 degree oven for 45 minutes.

7. Trim the stems off the mushrooms, heat a sauté pan, and add the butter. Cook the mushrooms until they brown and release their moisture.

8. Peel the carrots, parsnips, and turnip. Cut them into 2" uniform pieces. Rinse the potatoes and cut them in half or quarters, peeling if desired.

9. Remove the Dutch oven from the oven and add the reserved onions, mushrooms, carrots, parsnips, turnip, and potatoes. Cover and return to the oven and cook at 325 degrees for another hour.

10. Remove again, skim any fat from the top, and check the meat for tenderness. Garnish with the chopped parsley and serve.

– Wine Notes –

The rich braised beef with the sauce requires a big red wine. A local meritage or Bordeaux blend would be very good, as would a California Cabernet Sauvignon.

Pork Schnitzel with Potato-Apple Pancakes and Chunky Applesauce

4 to 6 portions

Pork Schnitzel
1½ lbs pork cutlets
1 tsp kosher salt
½ tsp ground pepper

1 cup flour
1 egg
½ cup milk
2 cups plain breadcrumbs

2 Tbsp butter
1 Tbsp canola oil

Potato Apple Pancakes
2 large russet potatoes
2 large Mutsu apples (or other cooking apple)

2 eggs
2 Tbsp flour
1 tsp kosher salt
½ cup finely chopped green onions

¼ cup canola oil

Chunky Applesauce
3 large Mutsu apples (or other cooking apple)
½ cup brown sugar
1 tsp ground cinnamon
¼ tsp ground nutmeg
1/8 tsp ground cloves
1 lemon, zest and juice
½ tsp vanilla extract

1. Pound the pork cutlets between 2 pieces of plastic film with a meat mallet or frying pan. Season them with the salt and pepper and set aside.

2. Set up a breading station by putting the flour in a shallow pan, whisking the egg and milk together in a bowl, and placing the breadcrumbs in another shallow pan. Dredge the pork cutlets in the flour, then in the egg wash, and finally press them into the breadcrumbs. Place on a foil-lined sheet pan and set aside.

3. At service time, heat a large sauté pan and add the butter and oil. Cook the breaded pork on medium heat, browning each side for about 5 minutes. Place back on the sheet pan and hold in a warm oven.

4. For the pancakes, peel the potatoes and shred them into a bowl using the large holes of a box grater. Peel the apples and shred them into the bowl with the potatoes. Dump the grated potatoes and apples into a clean kitchen towel and twist to squeeze as much liquid out of them as possible.

5. Break the eggs into a large bowl and stir in the flour, salt, and green onions. Add the grated potatoes and apples and combine with a wooden spoon.

6. Heat a large sauté pan and add half of the oil. Using a ½-cup measure, portion out the potato mixture into the hot pan. Flatten the pancakes with a spatula and cook at medium heat until brown, then turn and brown the other side. Cook in small batches, adding more oil if necessary. Remove to a warm oven and hold for service.

7. For the applesauce, peel and core the apples and cut them into 1" chunks. Place them in a saucepan with the brown sugar, cinnamon, nutmeg, cloves, lemon zest and juice. Bring to a boil, cover, and simmer for 20 minutes. Add the vanilla and mash by hand with a potato masher.

8. Serve two pancakes on each plate with two pork cutlets. Serve the applesauce on the side. Alternatively, line a large platter with the pancakes and place the schnitzel on top.

Mixed Hearty Greens and Sausage Pie

4 to 6 portions

Deep Dish Pie Crust
2 cups flour
½ tsp salt
1/3 cup chilled shortening
1/3 cup chilled butter
½ cup ice water

Pie Filling
1 head kale
1 head collard greens
1 bag field spinach (10 oz.)

Italian sweet sausage, loose
2 Tbsp olive oil
1 large onion, peeled and chopped
1 Tbsp minced garlic

1 cup white wine

8 oz soft goat cheese
2 eggs, beaten
½ cup chopped basil
1 tsp kosher salt
1 tsp ground pepper

1. For the 10" pie crust, add the flour and salt to the bowl of a food processor and pulse to combine. Add the shortening and pulse a few times, then add the butter and pulse until mixture resembles coarse cornmeal.

2. Empty into a bowl and stir in the ice water with a fork to form a dough. Turn the dough out onto a floured surface and knead a few times with your hands. Flatten into a disc, wrap in plastic film, and refrigerate for 30 minutes.

3. Fill a sink with cold water, cut the stem ends off the greens, and wash them thoroughly in the sink. Lift out of the water and drain in a colander. Remove the leaves from the stems with a paring knife and cut the leaves into 2" pieces.

4. Spray a large sauté pan with no-stick and place on medium heat. Add the sausage and cook, breaking it apart with a fork as it browns. When cooked, transfer it to a large bowl. Add the olive oil to the same pan along with the onions and garlic. Cook for 3 minutes, then add to the sausage bowl.

5. Add the wine to the same sauté pan along with the greens. Turn up the heat, cover, and bring to a boil. Remove the cover and continue cooking until the greens are tender, about 5 minutes.

6. Dump the greens into a colander and press as much liquid out of them as you can. Add them to the bowl with the sausage and onions.

7. Combine the goat cheese, eggs, basil, salt, and pepper in a separate bowl. Roll out the pie dough and place it in a 10" deep pie pan.

8. Fold the cheese mixture into the greens and sausage mixture and pour into the pie shell. Bake in a 400 degree oven for 30 minutes, or until to top is brown and it is firm in the center. Let cool on a rack for 20 minutes before serving.

Duck Ragout Braised in Pinot Noir

8 portions

8 Long Island duck legs

Duck Stock
Bones from above legs
1 onion, peeled and chopped
1 carrot, chopped
1 stalk celery, chopped

6 stems parsley
3 sprigs thyme
1 bay leaf
1 leek, white part, sliced

Duck ragout
2 lbs duck pieces, skin-on

16 small white onions
16 mushroom caps

½ cup diced carrots
1 Tbsp minced garlic
¼ cup flour
2 cups pinot noir wine

2 cups duck stock
1 Tbsp kosher salt
1 tsp ground pepper

¼ cup chopped parsley

– Wine Notes –
A full-bodied Pinot Noir from Burgundy would be my first choice. A generic Bourgogne Rouge from a good producer or a more expensive Volnay from the Cote de Beaune.

1. Place the duck legs on a cutting board skin-side down. Trim any excess fat off the overhanging skin. Run the point of a stiff knife along the leg and thigh bone. Peel back the meat, cutting under the bones to separate them from the meat. Cut the meat into 2" pieces, leaving the skin on.

2. Place the bones in a roasting pan with the onions, carrot, and celery. Roast in a 425 degree oven for 30 minutes to brown the bones. Transfer the bones, vegetables, and drippings to a soup pot and just cover with cold water. Bring to a boil and skim off any impurities.

3. Tie the parsley stems, thyme, bay leaf, and sliced leek together with string to make a bouquet garni. Add this to the stock and turn down the heat to a simmer. Cook for 3 hours and strain. Chill overnight if possible, and remove solidified fat before using (if you can't chill overnight, skim the fat from the top before using).

4. Heat a Dutch oven and spray with no-stick. Brown the duck pieces skin-side down at high heat, being careful not to crowd and not to burn. Cook in batches, removing the duck and pouring off excess fat.

5. Blanch the onions for 1 minute in 1 quart of boiling water. Cool under cold water and peel. Brown the onions in a little duck fat in the Dutch oven and remove. Brown the mushroom caps in a little duck fat also and remove.

6. Add the carrots and garlic to the Dutch oven along with 2 tablespoons of the duck fat. Stir in the flour and continue cooking at medium heat. Stir in the pinot noir wine and bring it to a boil.

7. Add the duck stock and lower the heat. Add back the duck, onions, and mushrooms, season with the salt and pepper, cover, and place in a 325 degree oven until duck is tender, about 45 minutes.

8. Remove from the oven, skim any fat from the surface, and stir in the parsley. Check for seasoning and serve over wide noodles or rice.

Pork Schnitzel with Potato-Apple Pancakes

Mixed Hearty Greens and Sausage Pie

November

...The earth hath yielded up her fruits
To bless the farmer's labors,
And peace and plenty crown the lives
Of cheery friends and neighbors;
In fertile vales, on prairies broad,
In homes by lake and river,
Ten thousand thousand hearts unite
bless the Gracious Giver.

Thanksgiving for the harvest full,
The orchards' mellow treasures,
The purple grapes, the golden corn,
And all the joys and pleasures,
And bounties rich and manifold,
That make life worth the living—
For these, alike, the young and old,
Join in a glad thanksgiving ...

— from *Thanksgiving*
By Andrew Downing
(1838–1917)

The season for Peconic Bay scallops begins the first week of November and runs until March if the supply holds out. These treasures have been called "the pearls of the North Fork" and we all wait eagerly for the season to begin. The farmstands slow down during November, but are still stocked with all the hearty vegetables of late fall: turnips, rutabaga, cabbage, potatoes, leeks, onions, acorn squash, kale, and winter beets. It all builds up to Thanksgiving, when all of America cooks and gives thanks for our heritage.

Prime Meal 1
A North Fork Thanksgiving for a small gathering

Bay Scallop, Oyster, and Clam Soup

Roasted Individual Poussin Chickens with Holiday Side Dishes

Pear Tart Tatin

Recommended wine: *Sparkling wine and Pinot Noir*

Prime Meal 2
The Basics of A Traditional Thanksgiving

Roast Turkey, Sage and Chestnut Stuffing, and Cranberry Chutney

Pumpkin Chiffon Pie

Recommended wine: *Sparkling wine and Pinot Noir*

Selected Recipes
1. *Peconic Bay Scallop Seviche*
2. *Sautéed Bay Scallops with Potato Gnocchi*
3. *Peconic Bay Scallop Stew*
4. *Bay Scallop Gratin with Linguine*
5. *Cabbage, Kale, Radish, and Potato Gratin*
6. *Roasted Root and Tuber Vegetables*
7. *Duck Breast Roulades with Wild Rice Stuffing*
8. *Braised Chicken Thighs in Red Wine with Portabella, Baby Bella, Shiitake, Oyster, and Porcini Mushrooms*

PRIME MEAL 1
A North Fork Thanksgiving for a small gathering

– First Course –
Bay Scallop, Oyster and Clam Soup

4 portions

1 dozen littleneck clams
1 dozen oysters
4 Tbsp butter
2 leeks, white part, chopped
½ cup minced shallots
1 Tbsp minced garlic
1 cup chardonnay
¼ cup chopped parsley
½ lb bay scallops
2 cups heavy cream
½ tsp kosher salt
1 tsp ground pepper

1. Scrub the clams and oysters under cold water. Melt the butter in a large saucepan and add the leeks, shallots, and garlic. Cook at low heat, covered, for 5 minutes.

2. Add the chardonnay and parsley to the pan and increase the heat. Add the clams, cover, and cook at high heat. As the clams open, remove them with tongs and set aside.

3. When the clams are all removed, add the oysters to the pan, cover, and continue cooking until they just begin to open. Remove and set aside.

4. Lower the heat to a simmer and add the scallops and cream. Simmer until scallops are just cooked, about 3 minutes.

5. Remove the clams and oysters from their shells and add back to the soup. Add the salt and pepper and check for seasoning. Serve with oyster crackers.

– *Entree* –
Roasted Individual Poussin Chickens
with Holiday Vegetables, Gravy, and Cranberry Relish

4 portions

Stuffing

Stuffing

2 Tbsp butter
1 cup chopped onion
1 cup chopped celery
1 Tbsp minced garlic
2 Tbsp chopped sage

½ cup wild rice
2 cups chicken stock
½ cup brown rice

½ cup dried cranberries
½ cup chopped dried
  apricots
½ cup chopped walnuts
1 tsp kosher salt
½ tsp ground pepper
1 tsp dried sage

Poussin Chickens

Four 1-lb poussin chickens
(or two Cornish game hens)

1 cup chopped onion
½ cup chopped celery
½ cup chopped carrots
2 Tbsp melted butter
1 tsp smoked paprika
1 tsp kosher salt
½ tsp ground pepper

1. Heat a shallow saucepan and add the butter. Stir in the onion, celery, garlic, and sage. Cook at low heat until the vegetables soften, about 5 minutes.

2. Add the wild rice and chicken stock. Bring to a boil and simmer, covered, for 15 minutes. Stir in the brown rice, cover, and continue cooking for another 30 minutes, or until the rice is tender. If liquid remains, drain it off.

3. Remove the mixture from the stove and fold in the cranberries, apricots, and walnuts. Season with the salt, pepper, and dried sage. Check for seasoning.

Poussin Chickens*

4. Remove the giblets from the chickens and rinse under cold water. Trim off any excess neck bone and flap skin. Fill the cavities loosely with the rice stuffing and set the chickens on the cutting board, breast side-up.

5. Cut a piece of string about 18" long and hook it over the neck bone. Draw the string around the chicken, holding the wings and legs tight to the body and tie the string tightly.

6. Place the chopped onion, celery, and carrot in the bottom of a small roasting pan. Brush the chickens with the butter and season them with the paprika, salt, and pepper. Place them on top of the vegetables in the roasting pan and refrigerate while preparing the vegetables and gravy.

__Note:__ the poussin is a young chicken, about 4 weeks old and weighing 1 pound. The Cornish hen is similar, but weighs from 1½ to 2 pounds. If you use Cornish hens, one is enough for two people.

205

Holiday Vegetables

Carrots
1 bunch young carrots, stem on
1 Tbsp olive oil
2 Tbsp chopped dill
1 Tbsp honey
1 tsp kosher salt
½ tsp ground pepper

Cauliflower
½ head cauliflower, cut into
   florets
1 Tbsp olive oil
1 tsp ground cumin
½ tsp ground turmeric
Dash cayenne pepper
1 tsp kosher salt
½ tsp ground pepper

Fingerling Potatoes
1 lb fingerling potatoes
2 Tbsp olive oil
2 Tbsp chopped rosemary
1 tsp kosher salt
½ tsp ground pepper

Brussels Sprouts
1 quart Brussels sprouts
4 oz thinly sliced pancetta
2 cloves sliced garlic
1 tsp kosher salt
½ tsp ground pepper

Rutabaga
1 rutabaga (about 1 lb.)
2 tsp kosher salt
¼ cup milk
2 Tbsp butter
1 tsp kosher salt
½ tsp ground pepper
½ tsp ground nutmeg

Carrots, Cauliflower, and Fingerling Potatoes

1. For the carrots, trim the stems and peel. If small, leave them whole. If large, cut into 3" pieces. Combine the olive oil, dill, honey, salt, and pepper in a bowl and toss the carrots in it. Place them on a foil-lined sheet pan and set aside.

2. For the cauliflower, combine the olive oil, cumin, turmeric, cayenne, salt, and pepper in a bowl and toss the cauliflower in it. Transfer to the sheet pan with the carrots.

3. For the potatoes, rinse, but do not peel. Cut them in half if they are large. Combine the olive oil, rosemary, salt, and pepper in a bowl and toss the potatoes in it. Add to the sheet pan with the carrots and cauliflower.

Brussels Sprouts and Rutabaga

1. For the Brussels sprouts, trim the stems, remove the outer leaves, and cut the sprouts in half through the stem. Heat a large sauté pan, spray it with no-stick, and add the pancetta.

2. When the pancetta turns crisp, remove it and add the garlic and Brussels sprouts. Cook at medium-high heat until sprouts begin to brown, about 5 minutes. Chop the reserved pancetta and add it to the sprouts along with the salt and pepper. Transfer to a casserole dish and set aside.

3. For the rutabaga, peel and cut it into 2" pieces. Bring 1 quart of water to a boil in a saucepan and add the rutabaga and the salt. Simmer until tender, about 25 minutes.

4. In a separate small pan, add the milk, butter, salt, pepper, and nutmeg. Heat to a simmer. Drain the rutabaga, mash by hand with a potato masher, and stir in the milk mixture. Place in a casserole and set aside.

Gravy and Cranberry Relish

Gravy
2 cups chicken stock
2 Tbsp butter
3 Tbsp flour

Cranberry Relish
1 pkg. cranberries
1 navel orange
1 cup sugar

1. For the gravy, add the chicken stock to a saucepan and bring it to a simmer. In a separate small pan, melt the butter and stir in the flour to make a roux. Whisk the roux into the stock and simmer for 15 minutes to thicken. Stir in the reserved pan drippings when the chickens finish cooking.

2. For the relish, rinse the cranberries and place them in a bowl. Rinse the orange and trim off the ends, but do not peel. Cut the orange into small wedges and scrape out as many seeds as you can.

3. Add the orange wedges to the cranberries, and grind this mixture through the meat grinder attachment of your electric mixer. Stir in the sugar and refrigerate (if you don't have a meat grinder, pulse the mixture in your food processor).
   Note: *the gravy and relish may be prepared ahead of everything else.*

Cooking and Assembly

1. About 2 hours before the meal, heat an oven to 425 degrees. Place the roasting pan with the chickens on the top rack of the oven. Roast 15 minutes, then baste the chickens with the drippings and put the sheet pan of vegetables on the bottom rack.

2. Continue roasting for 30 minutes more, basting the chickens every 15 minutes. Insert a meat thermometer to check for doneness; it should read 165 degrees. The vegetables should be lightly browned and beginning to turn soft.

3. Remove the chickens and transfer them to a platter. Deglaze the roasting pan on top of the stove by adding 1 cup of water to the pan and stirring all the drippings over high heat for 5 minutes. Strain into a bowl and add to the above chicken gravy.

4. Arrange the roasted vegetables around the chickens on the platter. Serve the Brussels sprouts and rutabaga separately along with the gravy and cranberry relish.

> *– Wine Notes –*
> *To begin a holiday meal, sparkling wine is my favorite. One of our local Methode Champenoise, or a French Champagne, makes an excellent choice. For the main course, my personal preference is a Pinot Noir, such as a Gevrey Chambertin. If you like a lush, fruity wine, try a Valpolicella from Veneto, Italy.*

Roasted Poussin Chickens with Holiday Vegetables, Gravy and Cranberry relish

Pear Tart Tatin

– *Dessert* –
Pear Tart Tatin

8 portions

1⅓ cups flour
¼ cup confectioners sugar
½ tsp salt
4 oz (1 stick) cold butter
1 egg

5 ripe Bosc pears
1 lemon, zest and juice
2 Tbsp sugar

4 Tbsp butter
⅔ cup sugar
1 tsp ground nutmeg

1. Combine the flour, sugar, and salt in a food processor and pulse a few times. Dice the cold butter and pulse it into the flour mixture until it resembles coarse cornmeal. Add the egg and pulse it into the mixture until a dough forms.

2. Turn the dough out onto a floured surface and knead a few times with your hands. Flatten it into a disc, wrap in plastic film, and refrigerate for 30 minutes.

3. Peel the pears and cut them into 4 quarters, cutting through the stem. Remove the core with a paring knife and toss them into a bowl with the lemon zest and juice, and the sugar.

4. Melt the butter in a 10" cast iron skillet and sprinkle the sugar over it. Cook until the sugar melts, about 5 minutes, and remove from the heat. Fan the pears around the pan, slightly overlapping. Place the last 2 slices of pear in the center of the pan.

5. Put the pan back on medium heat and cook, uncovered, until a golden caramel color develops, about 25 minutes. Do not disturb the pears as they cook. Remove from the heat and sprinkle the nutmeg on top.

6. Roll out the dough a little larger than the skillet and place it on top of the pears, tucking in the excess dough inside the skillet. Place it in a 375 degree oven for 30 minutes. It should be golden brown on top and bubbling.

7. Remove from the oven and let cool on a rack for about 10 minutes. Cut around the edges with a paring knife. Place a large plate or serving platter upside-down tightly over the skillet. Using oven mitts, flip the skillet and plate over quickly. Let it cool to room temperature before serving.

PRIME MEAL II
The Basics of Thanksgiving

Roast Turkey

10 to 12 portions

1 Fresh Turkey, 12-15 lbs.

Brine for turkey
2 quarts vegetable stock
¾ cup kosher salt
½ cup brown sugar
1 Tbsp black pepper-
corns
1 Tbsp allspice berries
1 Tbsp chopped candied
ginger
2 quarts cold water
1 quart ice cubes

Cavity stuffing
1 sliced apple
½ onion, peeled and sliced
4 sprigs rosemary
6 sage leaves
1 cinnamon stick
2 Tbsp canola oil
2 cups chopped onion
1 cup chopped celery
1 cup chopped carrot

1. Remove the giblets and neck from the turkey along with any excess fat. Rinse the turkey under cold water and drain.

2. Add the vegetable stock, salt, sugar, peppercorns, allspice, and ginger to a large stock pot big enough to hold the turkey. Bring the mixture to a boil and remove from the stove. Add the cold water and the ice to cool down the brine. Place the turkey in the brine and refrigerate overnight.

3. Remove the turkey from the brine and dry it off with paper towels. Stuff the cavity with the apple, onion, rosemary, sage, and cinnamon. Cut off the wing tips and tie the wings and legs close to the body with string. Place the turkey, breast side-up, in a V-shaped poultry rack set in a roasting pan.

4. Brush the outside of the turkey with canola oil and place it in a 450 degree oven for 20 minutes. Remove from the oven and turn down the heat to 325 degrees.

5. Sprinkle the onions, celery, and carrots around the turkey in the roasting pan and place it back in the oven. Baste the turkey every 30 minutes and cook until the internal temperature reads 165 degrees, about 2½ hours.

6. Remove the turkey from the oven and transfer it to a sheet pan. Reserve the roasting pan for making gravy. Cover the turkey with foil and let rest 30 minutes before carving.

Note: *This recipe was adapted from a recipe by Alton Brown of the Food Network. After cooking turkey many ways in my long restaurant career, I think this brine method is the best.*

Turkey Gravy

2 tsp canola oil
Reserved turkey neck and giblets (no liver)
4 cups chicken stock

4 Tbsp butter
½ cup flour
2 tsp kosher salt
1 tsp ground pepper

1. Heat a large soup pot and add the oil. Add the turkey neck and giblets and cook over medium-high heat until they are brown, but not burnt. Add the commercial chicken stock along with 2 cups of water. Simmer for 2 hours while the turkey is cooking.

2. When you remove the turkey from the oven and transfer it to a sheet pan, scrape the vegetables and the drippings into the soup pot with the broth. Place the empty roasting pan on the stove and deglaze it with 1 cup of water. Add this to the broth. Strain the broth into a clean pot and skim the fat off the surface.

3. Melt the butter in a small pan and stir in the flour to make a roux. Let it cook for 3 minutes before whisking it into the broth. Let it come to a boil, turn down the heat, and add the salt and pepper. Taste for seasoning.

Sage and Chestnut Stuffing

1 loaf French bread
2 cups chicken stock

2 Tbsp butter
12 sage leaves
1 large onion, diced
2 cups celery, diced
¼ cup chopped parsley
8 oz cooked shelled chestnuts

1 tsp kosher salt
1 tsp ground pepper
1 Tbsp dried sage

1. Cut the bread into ½" cubes (about 8 cups) and place it in a large bowl. Heat the chicken stock and pour it over the bread.

2. Melt the butter in a large sauté pan and add the fresh sage leaves. When the sage begins to crisp, remove it with tongs and set aside. Add the onions, celery, and parsley to the pan and continue cooking at low heat. Chop the cooked chestnuts and add them to the pan.

3. Add this vegetable mixture to the soaking bread cubes in the bowl. Stir in the salt, pepper, and dried sage and transfer to a casserole. Cook, uncovered, in a 350 degree oven for 45 minutes. If it seems too dry, add a little more chicken stock.

Cranberry Chutney

1 pkg. (3 cups) fresh cranberries
1 cup dried cranberries
1½ cups sugar
1 Tbsp ground cinnamon
1 tsp ground ginger
¼ tsp ground cloves
½ cup water

1 cooking apple, peeled, cored, and chopped
½ cup chopped celery
½ cup chopped walnuts
¼ cup chopped shallots

1. Combine the cranberries, dried cranberries, sugar, cinnamon, ginger, cloves, and water in a saucepan. Bring to a boil and simmer, stirring, for 10 minutes or until cranberries begin to pop.

2. Add the apple, celery, walnuts, and shallots and continue cooking at low heat for another 10 minutes. Serve either warm or cold.

Pumpkin Chiffon Pie

12 to 16 portions

For the crust
2½ cups flour
½ tsp salt
1 cup chilled shortening
½ cup ice water

For the filling
1 fresh cheese pumpkin

2 Tbsp unflavored gelatin
1⅓ cups brown sugar
1 tsp ground nutmeg
1 tsp ground cinnamon
1 tsp kosher salt
¼ tsp ground ginger

6 egg yolks
1 cup milk

6 egg whites
¾ cup sugar
2 cups heavy cream

1. Place the flour and the salt in the bowl of a food processor and pulse to combine. Cut the chilled shortening into small pieces and pulse into the flour to resemble coarse cornmeal.

2. Empty the mixture into a bowl and stir in the ice water gently with a dinner fork to form a dough. Divide the dough into 2 balls and flatten them into discs on a floured surface. Wrap the discs in plastic film and refrigerate for 30 minutes.

3. Roll out the dough on a floured board and fit into two 9" pie pans. Flute the edge and poke holes all over with a dinner fork (or line with foil and fill with dried beans). Bake at 400 degrees until lightly browned, about 10 minutes, and remove.

4. Cut the top off the pumpkin. Scoop out the seeds, and cut it into wedges. Peel the wedges and cut them into 1" pieces.

5. Cook in a steamer pan (or boiling water) until tender, about 15 minutes, and drain. Measure out 4 cups of the pumpkin, and mash by hand with a potato masher.
   Note: *one medium cheese pumpkin will yield about 4 cooked cups.*

5. In a small bowl, whisk together the gelatin, brown sugar, nutmeg, cinnamon, salt, and ginger. Combine with the mashed pumpkin in a large saucepan.

6. Whisk the egg yolks and the milk together in a bowl and add them to the pumpkin. Bring this mixture gradually to a simmer over medium heat, stirring constantly. Do not boil. Cook about 15 minutes, remove, and cool.

7. Beat the egg whites in an electric mixer until soft peaks form and add the sugar. In a separate bowl, beat the heavy cream until stiff peaks form.

8. Fold the egg whites and the whipped cream into the cooled pumpkin mixture with a rubber spatula. Place the mixture into the cooked pie crusts and chill for 2 hours or more.

Peconic Bay Scallop Seviche

6 to 8 portions

1 lb very fresh Peconic Bay scallops
3 limes, zest and juice
½ cup minced red onion
¼ cup chopped cilantro
1 Tbsp minced jalapeno pepper
1 tsp minced garlic
½ tsp kosher salt
¼ tsp ground pepper

2 ripe avocados
Juice of one lime

1 bunch watercress
1 cup grape tomatoes
2 Tbsp chopped cilantro

1. Combine the 3 limes' juice, 1 tsp. of the zest, and the scallops in a bowl. Add the red onion, cilantro, jalapeno, garlic, salt, and pepper. Toss gently together and refrigerate for 2 hours before service (do not marinate overnight).

2. Cut the avocados in half, remove the pit, and score the flesh into ½" squares with a paring knife. Scoop out the squares with a spoon into a bowl and toss them with the lime juice.

3. Rinse the watercress, pat it dry with a paper towel, and remove the leaves (save some watercress for garnish). Rinse the grape tomatoes and cut them in half.

4. To assemble, place watercress leaves in the bottom of 6 to 8 martini glasses. Arrange the avocado on top of the watercress and place the marinated scallops on top of the avocado. Garnish with the tomatoes and reserved watercress. Sprinkle some of the marinade over all.

Sautéed Bay Scallops with Potato Gnocchi

4 portions

Gnocchi
1½ lbs russet potatoes
2 Tbsp grated parmesan cheese
1 egg, beaten
1 tsp kosher salt
¼ tsp ground nutmeg
1 cup flour

4 quarts water
1 Tbsp kosher salt

Scallops
1 lb Peconic Bay scallops
2 Tbsp butter
1 Tbsp olive oil
1 cup heavy cream
1 Tbsp lemon juice
¼ cup chopped parsley

1. Boil the potatoes in their skins until very tender, about 30 minutes. Cool just until you can handle them, peel, and cut into large chunks. Press them through a potato ricer into a large bowl (using a masher is OK, but do not leave lumps).

2. Add the parmesan cheese, egg, salt, nutmeg, and flour. Mix together with a wooden spoon, turn out onto a floured board, and knead into a dough with your hands (if too moist, add a little more flour).

3. Cut the dough into 6 equal pieces. Using your hands, roll each piece on a floured board into a rope about 1" thick. Cut these ropes into 1" pieces. Repeat until all the dough is used.

4. Holding a dinner fork in one hand, roll each piece over the back of the fork to make little grooves. As it rolls off the fork, press a hole in the underside with your little finger (see photo).

4. Bring the water to a boil in a large pasta pot and add the salt. Add the gnocchi to the boiling water in batches, cooking each batch until the gnocchi float, about 5 minutes. Remove and keep warm.

5. For the scallops, heat a large sauté pan and add the butter and olive oil. Add the scallops and cook quickly over high heat, tossing them to prevent burning.

6. Add the cream, lemon juice, and the gnocchi. Toss gently and bring to a simmer. Stir in the chopped parsley and check for seasoning. Serve in pasta bowls.

– Wine Notes –

Peconic Bay scallops in most recipes go very well with a Sauvignon Blanc wine. Because they are an East End treasure it would seem appropriate to drink a Long Island wine. For an Italian flavor, I would go with a Tocai Friulano or a Pinot Grigio from Friuli.

Peconic Bay Scallop Stew

4 portions

4 cups Yukon Gold potatoes,
    peeled and diced
1 celery root, peeled and diced
1½ cups heavy cream
1 Tbsp minced garlic
1 bay leaf
1 tsp dried thyme
1 tsp kosher salt
½ tsp ground pepper

1 lb Peconic Bay scallops
2 Tbsp butter
1 Tbsp olive oil

½ cup minced shallots
1 cup chardonnay

1. Set up a double boiler on the stove. Add the potatoes, celery root, cream, garlic, bay leaf, thyme, salt, and pepper. Cook, covered, for 45 minutes. When cooked, the potatoes should be very tender. Remove the bay leaf.

2. Heat a large sauté pan and add the butter and olive oil. Add the scallops, cover, and cook at medium heat for 3 minutes. The scallops will turn opaque and release some of their juices. Remove the scallops with a slotted spoon and set aside.

3. Add the shallots and the chardonnay to the pan and bring to a boil. Let the liquid reduce by half and add it to the potato mixture along with the scallops. Stir in the parsley, check for seasoning, and serve in pasta bowls.

— Root Cellar —
By Theodore Roethke

Nothing would sleep in that cellar, dank as a ditch,
Bulbs broke out of boxes hunting for chinks in the dark,
Shoots dangled and drooped,
Lolling obscenely from mildewed crates,
Hung down long yellow evil necks, like tropical snakes.
And what a congress of stinks!—
Roots ripe as old bait,
Pulpy stems, rank, silo-rich,
Leaf-mold, manure, lime, piled against slippery planks.
Nothing would give up life:
Even the dirt kept breathing a small breath.

Bay Scallop Gratin with Linguine

4 to 6 portions

1½ lbs Peconic Bay scallops
1 Tbsp minced garlic
2 Tbsp fresh thyme
1 lemon, zest and juice
1 tsp kosher salt
½ tsp ground pepper
¼ cup olive oil
½ cup panko crumbs

Sauce
2 Tbsp olive oil
1 red onion, peeled and
   chopped
1 Tbsp minced garlic
2 cups grape tomatoes,
   cut in half
½ cup white wine
½ cup chopped basil
1 tsp kosher salt
½ tsp ground pepper

1 head broccoli rabe
3 quarts water
1 pkg. linguine

1. Place the scallops in a bowl. Add the garlic, thyme, lemon zest and juice, salt, pepper, olive oil, and panko. Toss the scallops in the marinade and refrigerate while you prepare the pasta and sauce.

2. Heat a sauté pan and add the olive oil. Add the onion and cook until it is soft. Stir in the garlic and tomatoes and continue cooking. Add the wine and bring to a boil, letting it reduce and thicken. Remove from the heat and stir in the basil, salt, and pepper.

3. Rinse the broccoli rabe, trim off the lower stems, and chop coarsely. Bring the water to a boil in a pasta pot and add the linguine. When it is just cooked, add the broccoli rabe and bring back to a boil. Drain the whole mixture and combine with the sauce. Keep warm.

4. Remove the scallops from the refrigerator and place the entire contents on a foil-lined sheet pan. Heat your broiler and broil the scallops until beginning to brown, about 10 minutes. Divide the pasta mixture between 4-6 pasta bowls and place the scallops on top.

> **– *Wine Notes* –**
> This pasta dish with the garlic, tomatoes, and broccoli rabe would be good with a local stainless steel Chardonnay or an Italian Soave from Veneto or Gavi from the Piedmont.

Cabbage, Kale, Radish, and Potato Gratin

6 to 8 portions

3 strips bacon, diced
1 large onion, peeled and diced
4 red potatoes, skin-on, diced
1 bay leaf
1 Tbsp chopped rosemary
2 tsp kosher salt
1 tsp ground pepper

½ head cabbage, diced
1 bunch of kale, leaves removed and chopped
1 bunch radishes, trimmed and sliced
1 cup chicken stock
1 cup heavy cream

2 Tbsp butter
2 cups panko crumbs

1 Tbsp minced garlic
1 Tbsp Dijon mustard
1 tsp kosher salt
1 tsp ground pepper

1. Heat a large, shallow pan and add the bacon. Cook at medium heat until it renders its fat and begins to crisp. Add the onions and continue cooking for 3 minutes before adding the potatoes, bay leaf, rosemary, salt, and pepper. Cook another 5 minutes as potatoes begin to brown.

2. Add the cabbage, kale, and radishes along with the chicken stock. Cover and cook at medium heat for another 10 minutes. Stir in the cream and remove from the stove. Transfer to a large casserole, cover with foil, and bake in a 400 degree oven until potatoes are fully cooked, about 20 minutes.

3. Heat a sauté pan and add the butter. When it melts, add the panko crumbs. Cook until crumbs begin to brown, and remove.

4. Stir in the garlic, mustard, salt, and pepper. Remove the casserole from the oven, discard the foil, and sprinkle the crumb mixture on top. Bake, uncovered, another 10 minutes at 400 degrees.

Note: *This fall recipe is particularly good with baked ham or roast pork.*

Roasted Root and Tuber Vegetables

6 to 8 portions

3 medium-sized white or red
  potatoes, skin-on
1 small rutabaga
3 large carrots
2 large parsnips
2 turnips
2 orange beets (substitute red)
1 large sweet potato
1 head celery root
2 small Sunchokes (Jerusalem
  artichokes)
12 small white onions

¼ cup olive oil
1 Tbsp kosher salt
2 tsp ground pepper

2 Tbsp chopped fresh rosemary
8 cloves garlic, peeled and sliced

1. Wash, drain, and peel all vegetables (except potatoes). Cut all the vegetables in uniform-size pieces measuring about 2". They can be wedges, squares or rectangles, depending upon the vegetable.

2. Place the olive oil, salt, and pepper in a large bowl and add the vegetables. Toss them in the oil and place them on a foil-lined sheet pan. Do not crowd. Use two pans if necessary.

3. Place the vegetables in a 400 degree oven for 20 minutes and remove. Add the chopped rosemary and the sliced garlic, toss gently, and return to the 400 degree oven until all vegetables start to soften and brown, about 20 minutes.

Note: *This fall and winter recipe is particularly good with roasted or braised beef or lamb.*

Duck Breast Roulades with Wild Rice Stuffing

4 portions

2 lbs boneless duck breast (4 pieces)

1 Tbsp butter
½ cup chopped shallots
1 cup wild rice
3 cups chicken stock

3 carrots
2 Tbsp butter
12 sweet gherkins

2 Tbsp Dijon mustard
1 Tbsp kosher salt
1 tsp ground pepper

1 lb thinly-sliced bacon

1 Tbsp canola oil

1 cup chopped onion
½ cup chopped celery
½ cup chopped carrot

2 Tbsp flour
1 Tbsp tomato paste
2 cups red wine
¼ tsp ground allspice
¼ tsp ground cloves
½ tsp dried thyme

1. Remove the skin from the duck breasts and slice in half horizontally. You should have 8 cutlets. Place these between sheets of plastic film and pound into thin cutlets with a meat mallet or frying pan. Set aside and refrigerate.

2. Heat a saucepan and add the butter. Stir in the shallots and cook at low heat for 3 minutes. Add the wild rice and the chicken stock and bring to a boil. Simmer, covered, until rice is just tender, about 45 minutes.

3. Peel the carrots and cut them into uniform sticks, ¼" thick and 3" long. Heat a sauté pan, melt the butter, and add the carrot sticks. Cook until soft, about 5 minutes and set aside. Cut the sweet gherkins into thin strips.

4. Place the duck breast cutlets on a cutting board and spread a thin coating of the mustard on them. Sprinkle them with the salt and pepper and place 1 tablespoon of the cooked wild rice in the middle (reserve leftover wild rice in a warm place).

5. Arrange the cooked carrot strips and sweet gherkins on top of the wild rice. Roll up the roulades and wrap each one with 2 strips of bacon. Skewer each roulade with 2 toothpicks to hold them together.

6. Heat a large sauté pan and add the canola oil. Brown the roulades on each side until the bacon is cooked, about 5 minutes, and remove. Cook in batches if necessary to avoid crowding.

7. Pour off the excess fat, leaving a coating in the pan. Add the chopped onion, celery, and carrots to the drippings and cook until soft, about 3 minutes.

8. Stir in the flour and the tomato paste and continue cooking at medium heat. Add the red wine and bring the sauce to a boil. Reduce the heat and season with the allspice, cloves, and thyme.

9. Place the roulades in a casserole and pour the sauce over them. Cover with foil and cook in a 350 degree oven for 40 minutes. Remove the roulades from the casserole and take out the toothpicks. Place the roulades on a bed of the wild rice and garnish with a slice of sweet gherkin.

10. Skim any fat off the top of the sauce and serve on the side. Strain the sauce if desired.

– Wine Notes –
A Long Island reserve Merlot has the fruit, the structure, and the local heritage to fit this dish. A Tuscan Brunello di Montalcino would be a special occasion choice.

Braised Chicken Thighs in Red Wine
with Portabella, Baby Bella, Shiitake, Oyster,
and Porcini Mushrooms

4 portions

2 lbs chicken thighs, skin on, with the bone
2 Tbsp canola oil

1 oz dried porcini mushrooms

2 portabella mushroom caps
1 pkg. baby bella mushrooms (cremini)
1 pkg. shiitake mushrooms
1 pkg. oyster mushrooms

1 Tbsp canola oil

½ cup chopped shallots
1 Tbsp minced garlic
1 carrot, peeled and diced
1 stalk celery, diced
2 Tbsp flour
1 cup red wine

2 sprigs fresh thyme
1 bay leaf
1 tsp kosher salt
½ tsp ground pepper

2 Tbsp butter
¼ cup chopped parsley

– Wine Notes –
All those mushrooms and the wine-braised chicken require an earthy full-bodied red wine. A famous Rhône blend such as Chateauneuf du Pape or a Crozes Hermitage would be excellent.

1. Cut the chicken thighs in half along the bone. Remove the bone, leaving the skin on. You should end up with 8 pieces of chicken. Heat a saucepan and add the oil. Brown the bones at high heat and barely cover with water. Simmer this broth for 30 minutes or more.

2. Place the dried porcini mushrooms in a bowl and add 2 cups of hot tap water. Let sit for 30 minutes and drain, reserving the liquid. Chop the mushrooms and set aside.

3. Using a spoon, scrape the gills from the underside of the portabella caps. Cut the caps into 1" pieces and add to a large bowl. Trim the baby bellas, shiitakes, and oyster mushrooms and slice them into the bowl with the portabellas.

4. Heat a Dutch oven and add the oil. Brown the chicken thighs, skin-side down, at high heat. Turn, brown the other side, and remove.

5. Lower the heat and add the shallots, garlic, carrots, and celery. Cook for 5 minutes and add the flour. Continue cooking at medium heat and stir in the red wine.

6. Add ½ cup of the porcini liquid and ½ cup of the chicken broth to the wine mixture. Bring it back to a boil, add back the chicken, and season with the thyme, bay leaf, salt, and pepper. Cover and simmer at low heat for 30 minutes.

7. While the chicken is cooking, heat a large sauté pan and add the butter. Add the fresh mushrooms and cook at high heat for 5 minutes.

8. Add the chopped porcini mushrooms and continue cooking, tossing the mushrooms to prevent burning. When they have released their moisture and begin to brown, add them to the chicken in the Dutch oven. Stir in the parsley, check for seasoning and serve.

Note: *To add to the rich, earthy aroma and texture, serve this dish with wild rice.*

Duck Breast Roulades

Braised Chicken Thighs in Red Wine with Mushrooms

December

So now is come our joyful'st feast!
Let every man be jolly,
Eache roome with yvie leaves is drest,
And every post with holly.
Though some churls at our mirth repine,
Round your foreheads garlands twine,
Drown sorrow in a cup of wine,
And let us all be merry.
Now all our neighbours' chimnies smoke,
And Christmas blocks are burning;
Their ovens they with bak't meats choke,
And all their spits are turning.
Without the door let sorrow lie,
And if, for cold, it hap to die,
We'll bury't in a Christmas pye,
And evermore be merry ..."

— from *A Christmas Carol*
By George Wither (1588-1667)

December on the North Fork and all over the country is a time when friends, colleagues, and family gather to celebrate the holidays. At these celebrations we drink cocktails, wine, and other beverages, and enjoy hors d'oeuvres.

We need something that can stimulate the appetite with an array of flavor, texture, and appearance without filling us up. Made-from-scratch appetizers using fresh ingredients assembled at the last minute may be called canapés, tapas, antipasto, or hors d'oeuvres – but they are all small portions of savory foods that are often highly seasoned. While they are often a lot of work to prepare for such a small offering, they are very important because they are the guest's first taste of what is to come.

After all the celebrations, we get to the sumptuous holiday dinner that comes on or before Christmas and Hannukkah for most families. It is a time to show off our culinary skills and create a memorable meal for all.

Holiday Hors d'oeuvres
Shrimp Dumplings
Asian Spring Rolls
Vegetables a la Greque
Franks in a Blanket
Crab- and Bacon-Stuffed Mushrooms
Beet- and Goat Cheese-Stuffed Endive
Classic Shrimp Cocktail
Zucchini Rolls with Goat Cheese

Selected Recipes
1. *Individual Beef Pot Pies*
2. *Osso Buco with Risotto Milanese and Gremolata*
3. *Roast Capon with Gravy, Bread Stuffing, and Vegetables*

Prime Meal – Two North Fork Christmas Dinners

Holiday Dinner 1
A Seafood Tower – Shrimp, Oysters, Littleneck Clams and Snow Crab

Rack of Lamb, Red Potatoes, and Roasted Vegetables

Schwartzwalder Kirschtorte (Black Forest Cherry Cake)

Recommended wine: *A Bordeaux or Bordeaux Blend*

Holiday Dinner 2
Sautéed Crabcake Remoulade

Chateaubriand au Poivre with Port Wine Sauce

Raspberry Trifle

Recommended wine: *A Napa Valley Cabernet Sauvignon or a Bordeaux*

Shrimp Dumplings

12 portions

½ **lb** raw shrimp, peeled and deveined
½ **cup** water chestnuts
½ **cup** shiitake mushroom caps
½ **cup** green onions

1 egg, beaten
1 **Tbsp** soy sauce
1 **Tbsp** honey
2 **tsp** sesame oil
¼ **tsp** kosher salt
Dash Tabasco sauce

1 **pkg.** Wonton skins

1. Finely chop the shrimp and place in a bowl. Finely chop the water chestnuts, shiitake mushrooms, and the green onions. Add them to the shrimp.

2. Whisk together the egg, soy sauce, honey, sesame oil, salt, and Tabasco. Gently stir into the shrimp mixture.

3. Lay out the Wonton skins on a cutting board. Brush them lightly with water and spoon 2 tsp. of filling on each Wonton skin. Lift the edges up around the filling and press together to form a small bag, or purse, sealing the edges with your fingers.

4. Steam in a wicker steamer basket (or other steamer) for 15 minutes. Serve with dipping sauce (recipe below).

Dipping Sauce for Dumplings and Spring Rolls

¼ **cup** soy sauce
¼ **cup** rice wine vinegar
2 **Tbsp** lime juice
2 **Tbsp** Asian fish sauce
1 **tsp** sugar
1 **tsp** minced garlic
Dash Tabasco sauce
1 **Tbsp** sesame oil

Combine the soy sauce, vinegar, lime juice, fish sauce, sugar, garlic, Tabasco, and sesame oil in a small bowl. Serve with dumplings and spring rolls.

Asian Spring Rolls

12 portions

1 **bunch** baby bok choy
1 red bell pepper
1 **pkg.** shiitake mushrooms
6 radishes
1 **bunch** green onions

1 **pkg.** soba noodles (or vermicelli)

1. Wash and trim all vegetables. Cut the bok choy and the red pepper into thin julienne strips. Remove the stems from the mushrooms and cut into thin strips. Thinly slice the radishes and the green onions.

2. Cook the soba noodles in 2 quarts of boiling water for 2 minutes and drain.

1 pkg. Asian rice paper

½ cup chopped cilantro
2 oz shredded ginger
1 bunch fresh mint

3. Add 1 quart of hot tap water to a shallow pan. Dip each piece of rice paper in the hot water for 30 seconds and lay it on a piece of plastic film on top of a cutting board.

4. Arrange the vegetables in the center resting parallel to each other. Sprinkle with the cilantro and ginger. Spoon 1 tsp. of the dipping sauce on top and garnish with a mint leaf.

5. Fold in the ends of the rice paper and roll into a tight cylinder. At service time, cut the rolls in half on a slant and stand them up against each other on a tray.

Vegetables a la Greque

12 portions

½ cup extra virgin olive oil
1 cup white wine
2 lemons, zest and juice
1 Tbsp coriander seeds
4 bay leaves
1 Tbsp dried oregano
1 tsp fennel seeds
4 sprigs fresh thyme
12 whole black peppercorns
1 Tbsp kosher salt

4 carrots
12 small white onions
1 pkg. white mushrooms
1 bulb fresh fennel
½ lb green beans
1 red bell pepper
1 yellow bell pepper
1 jicama
½ cup chopped parsley
1 thinly sliced lemon

1. In a large soup pot, combine the olive oil, wine, lemons, coriander, bay leaves, oregano, fennel, thyme, peppercorns, and salt. Bring this mixture to a boil and shut off the heat.

2. Prepare the vegetables: cut the carrots into 2" sticks; peel the onions; remove the stems from the mushrooms; cut the fennel into 2" slices; trim the ends off the green beans; cut the peppers into strips; and cut the jicama into ¼" thick sticks (other vegetables can be used also).

3. Add the vegetables to the broth, cover, and simmer for 20 minutes. Transfer the vegetables and their broth to shallow pans and refrigerate overnight. To serve, remove the vegetables from the marinade, arrange them on a platter, and garnish with the chopped parsley and lemon slices.

– Wine Notes –

Sparkling wines are especially good with holiday parties where hors d'oeuvres are served. Prosecco from the Veneto in Italy is especially popular, but the growing number of quality sparkling wines on Long Island would be a good choice. Authentic Champagne from France is always well received.

Franks in a Blanket

12 portions

½ **lb** frozen puff pastry sheets
½ **cup** orange juice
2 Tbsp dry sherry
2 Tbsp brown sugar
1 Tbsp Dijon mustard
1 pkg. mini franks

1. Place a puff pastry sheet on a floured board. When it thaws, roll it out a little thinner, ending up with a rectangle.

2. Make a glaze by combining the orange juice, sherry, and brown sugar in a small saucepan. Cook until slightly thickened, then stir in the mustard.

3. Brush the puff pastry with the glaze. Lay a row of franks along the long side of the pastry end to end. Roll up the pastry over the row of franks and cut between each frank with a knife.

4. Seal the ends with your fingers and place them on a parchment-lined sheet pan. Repeat until the pastry is gone. At service time, bake in a 375 degree oven until brown, about 10 minutes.

Crab- and Bacon-Stuffed Mushrooms

12 portions

4 cups water
1 Tbsp lemon juice
1 lb large white mushrooms

3 strips bacon
½ **cup** diced onion
½ red bell pepper, finely diced
1 stalk celery, finely diced

8 oz lump crabmeat
Reserved bacon
½ **tsp** kosher salt
Dash cayenne pepper
½ **cup** panko crumbs
3 Tbsp mayonnaise
1 lemon, zest and juice
2 Tbsp minced chives

1. Bring the water to a boil and add the lemon juice. Remove the stems from the mushroom caps and brush any dirt off of them. Blanch them in the boiling water for 2 minutes and drain. Pat dry with paper towels.

2. Dice the bacon and sauté in a skillet until crisp. Remove with a slotted spoon and reserve. Add the onion, pepper, and celery to the bacon fat and cook until vegetables are soft.

3. Empty the crabmeat into a bowl, pick out any cartilage, and separate the crabmeat. Add the reserved bacon, salt, cayenne, panko crumbs, mayonnaise, and lemon zest and juice. Fold in the sautéed vegetables and the chives.

4. Check for seasoning and stuff the mushroom caps. At service time, place the stuffed mushrooms on a foil-lined sheet pan and heat in a 400 degree oven for 10 minutes.

Beet- and Goat Cheese-Stuffed Endive

1 bunch medium-sized beets
½ cup minced red onion
1 Tbsp prepared horseradish

3 Tbsp balsamic vinegar
1 tsp kosher salt
½ tsp ground pepper
¼ cup olive oil

2 heads Belgian endive
4 oz goat cheese

1. Trim the stems off the beets and scrub under cold water. Wrap loosely in foil, spray with no-stick, and place on a sheet pan. Roast in a 375 degree oven until tender, about 1 hour. Cool, peel, and dice. Place in a bowl with the red onion and the horseradish.

2. Combine the vinegar, salt, and pepper and whisk in the olive oil to make a dressing. Add to the beets and refrigerate.

3. Separate the leaves from the endive, rinse, and dry with paper towels. Spoon the beet relish into the Belgian endive and garnish with a small piece of goat cheese. Arrange on a platter to serve.

Classic Shrimp Cocktail

2 lbs jumbo shrimp (16-20), in the shell
2 quarts cold water
1 Tbsp pickling spice
2 bay leaves
1 Tbsp kosher salt
Reserved shrimp shells

Cocktail Sauce
½ cup catsup
½ cup chili sauce
2 Tbsp prepared horseradish
1 Tbsp Worcestershire sauce
2 Tbsp lemon juice
Dash kosher salt
Dash Tabasco sauce
Parsley sprigs
Lemon wedges

1. Peel and devein the shrimp, leaving the tails on. Reserve the shells.

2. Put the cold water into a saucepan and add the pickling spice, bay leaves, salt, and shrimp shells. Bring to a boil and simmer for 20 minutes.

3. Strain into another saucepan and bring to a boil. Add the peeled shrimp and bring back to a boil. Simmer for 2 more minutes and drain. Chill in an ice bath and refrigerate.

4. For the sauce, combine the catsup, chili sauce, horseradish, Worcestershire, lemon, salt, and Tabasco in a bowl and refrigerate. At service time, arrange shrimp on a platter with the sauce on the side. Garnish with parsley sprigs and lemon wedges.

Note: *Removing the shells first gives the cooking broth a little more flavor, but if you prefer a traditional look to the shrimp, cook them in their shells, then peel and devein.*

Zucchini Rolls with Goat Cheese

12 portions

8 oz fresh, soft, goat cheese
¼ cup minced red pepper
¼ cup minced green pepper
2 Tbsp minced green onion

1 lemon, zest and juice
½ tsp kosher salt
½ tsp ground pepper
Few drops Tabasco sauce
2 Tbsp finely sliced basil

3 medium zucchini
Pesto (see page 189)

1 pkg. baby arugula

1. Place the goat cheese in a bowl and allow it to come to room temperature. Stir in the red and green pepper and the green onion.

2. Add the lemon zest and juice, and season with the salt, pepper, and Tabasco. Fold in the basil.

3. Trim the ends off the zucchini, rinse, and cut lengthwise ribbons using a vegetable peeler (or a mandolin). Lay out each slice on a cutting board and coat it with fresh pesto.

4. Put 3 or 4 leaves of arugula on the pesto and spoon the goat cheese mixture on top. Roll up the zucchini ribbon, turn it on end, and run a toothpick through it to hold it together. Serve standing up on a platter.

Zucchini Rolls with Goat Cheese

Beet- and Goat Cheese-Stuffed Endive

Individual Beef Pot Pies

6 portions

3 lbs boneless beef
    chuck steak
4 strips bacon, diced

4 Tbsp butter
1 cup diced onion
½ cup diced celery
½ cup diced carrots
1 Tbsp minced garlic
¼ cup flour
1½ cups red wine
1½ cups beef stock

6 parsley stems
1 leek, white part, sliced
3 sprigs thyme
1 bay leaf

Vegetables
2 quarts water
2 tsp kosher salt
2 potatoes, peeled, 1" dice
3 turnips, peeled, cut in
    wedges
4 carrots, peeled, split, cut
in 1" pieces
1 pkg. frozen peas
¼ cup parsley
2 Tbsp sage leaves
2 Tbsp chopped rosemary
2 tsp kosher salt
1 tsp ground pepper

Pie crust
2½ cups flour
1 tsp salt
1 cup chilled shortening
½ cup ice water
1 egg
1 Tbsp water

1. Cut the chuck steak into square, 1" pieces, trimming off any fat and gristle. Heat a Dutch oven and add the bacon. When the bacon is crisp, remove and set aside. Turn up the heat and brown the beef in batches, being careful not to crowd. Set the beef aside with the bacon and lower the heat.

2. Add the butter to the Dutch oven along with the onion, celery, carrots, and garlic. Cook at medium heat for 3 minutes and stir in the flour to make a roux. Continue cooking and add the wine and the beef stock, bringing it back to a boil.

3. Tie together the parsley stems, leek, thyme, and bay leaf to make a bouquet garni, then add it to the sauce. Add back the beef and the bacon, cover, and place in a 300 degree oven until the meat is very tender, about 1½ hours.

4. While the meat cooks, prepare the vegetables. Bring the water to a boil in a soup pot and add the salt. Add the potatoes and carrots and cook for 5 minutes, then add the turnips and continue cooking for 3 minutes before adding the peas. Bring back to a boil and drain. Plunge the vegetables in an ice bath to cool, then drain.

5. Combine the parsley, sage, and rosemary in a small dish. set aside.

6. For the crust, add the flour and salt to the bowl of a food processor and pulse to combine. Cut the shortening into small pieces and pulse into the flour so that it resembles coarse cornmeal. Turn the mixture out into a bowl and stir in the ice water with a dinner fork. Form 2 balls of dough with your hands and flatten them into discs. Wrap in plastic film and refrigerate for 30 minutes.

Assembly

7. Add the blanched vegetables to the meat mixture and divide between 6 ceramic ramekins. Sprinkle the herb mixture on the beef along with the salt and pepper.

8. Roll out the dough on a floured surface and cut pieces to fit the ramekins. Lay these on top of the meat and poke a few holes to let out the steam. Combine the egg and water and brush it on the crust. Place the ramekins in a 400 degree oven until brown and bubbly, about 25 minutes.

Osso Buco with Risotto Milanese and Gremolata

6 portions

6 osso buco veal shanks, 2" thick
1 tsp kosher salt
1 tsp ground pepper
2 Tbsp olive oil
1 Tbsp butter
1½ cups white wine
2 Tbsp butter
1 large onion, peeled and finely diced
2 stalks celery, finely diced
2 carrots, peeled and finely diced
8 oz finely diced mushrooms
1 Tbsp minced garlic
1 can (28 oz.) whole tomatoes (San Marzano)
3 strips orange rind
1 Tbsp kosher salt
1 tsp ground pepper
Juice from tomatoes

1 quart chicken stock
Pinch saffron

2 Tbsp olive oil
1 onion, peeled and chopped
8 oz finely diced mushrooms
2 cups Arborio rice

1 cup white wine
3 Tbsp butter
1 cup grated parmesan cheese

1. Sprinkle the osso buco with the salt and pepper and allow to come to room temperature. Heat a large sauté pan and add the olive oil and butter. When very hot, add the veal and let it brown before turning. Do not crowd or let it burn, but keep the heat high enough to develop a rich brown color. Set the meat aside and lower the heat.

2. Deglaze the sauté pan by adding the wine, placing it back on the heat, and scraping the drippings with a wooden spoon. Strain this liquid into a bowl and set aside.

3. Heat a large saucepan and add the butter. Stir in the finely diced onion, celery, and carrots and cook at medium heat for 5 minutes. Continue cooking and add the mushrooms, then the garlic.

4. Strain the tomatoes, saving the juice. Chop the tomatoes and add them to the vegetables along with the orange strips, salt, and pepper. Cook another 5 minutes and add the reserved deglazing liquid and the tomato juice.

5. Arrange the osso buco in the pan with the vegetables in one layer. Bring to a boil, cover, and place in a 300 degree oven until the veal is very tender, about 1½ hours.

Risotto Milanese

1. Add the chicken stock to a saucepan, bring it to a boil, and shut it off. Add the saffron to the hot stock and set aside.

2. In another saucepan, heat the olive oil and add the onion and the mushrooms. Cook until and mushrooms give up their moisture, about 5 minutes. Add the Arborio rice and let it cook, stirring, for 3 minutes.

3. Add the wine and let it reduce to almost evaporated. Ladle in the chicken stock gradually, stirring with a wooden spoon and letting it reduce between batches. Continue until the rice becomes tender, about 25 minutes. When it is tender and creamy, stir in the butter and the grated cheese. Check for seasoning and serve with the osso buco.

Gremolata Garnish

3 cloves garlic, finely minced
Zest of **1** lemon
¼ cup chopped parsley

Combine the garlic, lemon zest, and parsley. Sprinkle over the osso buco at service time.

Note: *this recipe was adapted from a recipe of Guy Peusch, who was the chef at Stonewall's Restaurant for 10 years.*

Osso Buco Milanese

– Wine Notes –

This elegant, rich entrée requires an equally elegant and rich wine from Northern Italy. A Barbaresco or a Barolo would be my first choice. A Chianti Classico would be a less expensive alternative.

Roast Capon with Gravy, Bread Stuffing, and Vegetables

6 to 8 portions

8 lb fresh capon

4 oz unsalted butter
1 lemon, zest and juice
1 Tbsp fresh thyme leaves

6 sprigs fresh thyme
2 sprigs fresh rosemary
1 lemon, cut in half
2 tsp kosher salt
1 tsp ground pepper

6 cippolini onions, peeled
4 large carrots, peeled and
   cut into large pieces
2 stalks celery, chopped

Bread stuffing
½ loaf country white bread,
   cubed
½ loaf whole wheat sandwich bread, cubed

6 Tbsp butter
2 cups chopped onion
1 cup chopped celery
2 Tbsp chopped fresh sage
2 Tbsp fresh thyme leaves
1 tsp kosher salt
1 tsp ground pepper
2 eggs
3 cups chicken stock

1. Remove the giblets and excess fat from the capon and rinse under cold water. Dry with paper towels and place in a V-rack inside a roasting pan.

2. Soften the butter and stir in the lemon zest, juice, and thyme. Using your fingers, loosen the skin of the capon. Using a teaspoon, slip as much of the butter mixture as possible under the skin, then rub the outside of the capon to distribute the butter mixture.

3. Place the fresh thyme, rosemary, and lemon halves in the cavity, along with some of the salt and pepper. Tie the legs together with string and tie the wings close to the body with another string. Rub the remaining butter mixture on the outside of the capon and sprinkle with salt and pepper.

4. Place the capon in a 425 degree oven and roast for 30 minutes, basting once or twice. Remove from the oven and lower the heat to 325 degrees.

5. Add the cippolini onions, the carrots, and the celery to the drippings in the roasting pan. Remove the capon from the V-rack and place on top of the vegetables in the roasting pan. Put it back in the oven and continue cooking at low heat until the internal temperature reaches 165 degrees, about 2 hours.

6. For the stuffing, place the bread cubes on a foil-lined sheet pan and toast in a 325 degree oven for 30 minutes, then transfer to a large bowl.

7. Melt the butter in a saute pan and add the onions and celery. Cook at medium heat until the onions soften, then add the sage, thyme, salt, and pepper. In a separate bowl, whisk together the eggs and chicken stock.

8. Add both the onion mixture and the egg mixture to the bread cubes and transfer to a shallow casserole. Cover with foil and cook in the 325 degree oven for 30 minutes, then remove the foil and continue cooking for another 30 minutes.

9. Remove the capon from the oven, place in a clean pan, cover loosely with foil, and let rest for 30 minutes. Remove the onions and carrots from the pan and keep warm.

10. Place the roasting pan on the stove and add 2 cups of water. Over high heat, deglaze the pan by scraping all the drippings loose with a wooden spoon. After about 3 minutes, strain this liquid into a bowl and set aside.

For the gravy
2 cups chicken stock
3 tbsp butter
¼ cup flour

11. For the gravy, heat the chicken stock in a saucepan. In a separate small pan, melt the butter and stir in the flour to make a roux. Cook for 3 minutes at low heat, and whisk into the chicken stock. Whisk in the reserved pan drippings and bring to a boil. Check for seasoning and keep warm.

12. Carve the capon at the table as you would a turkey, or cut it apart in the kitchen. Serve with the stuffing, gravy, and vegetables.

PRIME MEAL 1

– *First Course* –
A Seafood Tower of Chilled Shrimp, Oysters, Littleneck Clams, and Snow Crab Claws

6 portions

12 jumbo shrimp, in their
    shells
1 Tbsp pickling spice
1 tsp kosher salt
12 oysters on the half shell
12 littleneck clams on the
    half shell
6 snow crab claws,
    thawed

½ cup Champagne vinegar
¼ cup minced shallots
1 tsp cracked black pepper

¼ cup grated fresh horse-
    radish
2 Tbsp chili sauce
½ cup catsup
Few drops Tabasco
1 Tbsp lemon juice
½ tsp kosher salt

Lemon wedges
Parsley sprigs

1. Place 1 quart of cold water in a saucepan and add the pickling spice and salt. Bring to a boil and add the shrimp. Bring back to a boil, cook for 2 minutes and drain. Cool the shrimp under cold water, peel, and devein, leaving the tails on.

2. Shuck the oysters and clams (or have your fish market shuck them) and chill. Thaw the crab claws in the refrigerator.

3. Make a Champagne mignonette by combining the vinegar, shallots, and pepper in a small bowl and refrigerate.

4. Make the cocktail sauce by combining the horseradish, chili sauce, catsup, Tabasco, lemon juice, and salt in another small bowl and refrigerate.

5. At service time, arrange all of the seafood in a "tower" in the center of the table or arrange on 6 individual plates. Garnish with lemon wedges and sprigs of parsley.

– *Wine Notes* –
The raw shellfish needs a crisp, light bodied, white wine. Local North Fork Chenin Blanc, Albarino, and Sauvignon Blanc along with our sparkling wines would be good. A French village Chablis would be my foreign choice.

– Entrée –
Herb-Crusted Rack of Lamb with Red Potatoes, Roasted Vegetables and Mint Sauce

6 portions

1 American rack of lamb (7 rib bones)
½ cup olive oil
2 heads of garlic
3 sprigs thyme
3 sprigs rosemary
1 Tbsp thyme leaves
1 Tbsp rosemary leaves
2 Tbsp mint leaves
¼ cup panko crumbs
2 Tbsp kosher salt
1 Tbsp ground pepper

Vegetables and potatoes
6 medium-sized red potatoes
1 bunch carrots, stems on
½ lb string beans
2 leeks, white part, split in half
3 small artichokes, split in half, outer leaves and choke removed
1 bulb fennel, sliced in ¼" thick slice

1. Trim some of the fat off of the cap covering the rack of lamb. Score the remaining fat with the point of a knife into a cross-hatched pattern.

2. Pour the olive oil into a small casserole. Cut off the tops of the garlic heads and place them in the oil along with the sprigs of thyme and rosemary. Cover the casserole with foil and cook in a 350 degree oven for 45 minutes. Remove, discard the herbs, and squeeze the garlic out of its skin.

3. Add the cooked garlic to a small bowl along with the thyme, rosemary, and mint. Mash them all together, and stir in 1 tablespoon of the seasoned oil and the panko crumbs.

4. Combine the salt and pepper in another small bowl. Rub the panko mixture over the rack of lamb and sprinkle with some of the salt and pepper. Place the rack of lamb on a small foil-lined sheet pan.

5. Place the remainder of the seasoned oil in a large bowl. Cut deep slits in the red potatoes across the potato and almost through the bottom. Toss them in the oil and place on another small foil-lined sheet pan. Sprinkle with some of the salt and pepper.

6. Roast the rack of lamb and the potatoes at 350 degrees for about 45 minutes. The internal temperature of the lamb should reach 125 degrees. Remove and let rest under a foil tent for 20 minutes before carving. The potatoes should be fully cooked.

7. Trim and peel the carrots, leaving them whole if they are small. Trim the green beans, rinse the leeks, and trim the artichokes and fennel. Toss all of the vegetables in the seasoned oil, place on another foil-lined sheet pan, and sprinkle with the rest of the salt and pepper.

8. Increase the oven temperature to 425 degrees and roast the vegetables for 25 minutes, or until they are soft and beginning to brown.

9. At service time, carve the lamb through the rib bones and serve with the potatoes and vegetables. Serve with the mint sauce on the side.

Mint Sauce

1 cup mint leaves, coarsely
   chopped
¼ cup boiling water
2 Tbsp white wine vinegar
2 Tbsp sugar
¼ tsp kosher salt
⅛ tsp ground pepper

Place the mint leaves in a bowl and pour the boiling water over them. Add the vinegar, sugar, salt, and pepper and let steep for 20 minutes before serving.

– Wine Notes –

This classic roast lamb recipe would be the time to uncork a Bordeaux from the Medoc. A local choice would be a reserve Merlot with a little age on it.

Schwarzwalder Kirschtorte
(Black Forest Cherry Cake)

8-10 portions

For the Base

⅔ cup flour
1 Tbsp cocoa
½ tsp baking powder
¼ cup sugar
1 egg white
3 Tbsp cold butter
1 tsp Kirschwasser (cherry brandy)

Sour Cherry Filling

One 15 oz. can sour pitted cherries in juice
1 Tbsp cornstarch
1 Tbsp cold water
1 Tbsp Kirschwasser

Sponge Cake

⅔ cup flour
1 tsp cinnamon
2 tsp cornstarch
1 tsp cocoa
½ tsp baking powder
4 egg yolks
¼ cup hot water
⅓ cup sugar
4 egg whites
¼ cup sugar
½ tsp vanilla extract

Frosting

3 cups heavy cream
½ cup confectioners sugar
½ tsp vanilla extract

1. Whisk together the flour, cocoa, baking powder, and sugar in a large bowl. Stir in 1 unbeaten egg white.

2. Chop the cold butter into small pieces and cut it into the flour mixture as you would for a pie crust. Turn out onto a floured board, knead into a ball, and flatten into a disc. Wrap in plastic film and refrigerate for 30 minutes.

3. Preheat the oven to 350 degrees. Spray the bottom of a 10" springform pan with no-stick. Roll out the chilled dough on a floured surface, then place it on the bottom of the springform pan. Bake at 350 degrees for 12 minutes and remove. When slightly cool, remove the sides from the springform pan and slide the base onto a cake stand. Sprinkle with Kirschwasser.

4. Strain the can of cherries into a bowl, saving the juice. Heat a small saucepan and add ½ cup of the juice. Dissolve the cornstarch in the water and add to the juice. Bring to a boil, and when thickened, remove from the heat and add back the cherries. Add the Kirschwasser and refrigerate.

5. For the sponge cake, whisk together the flour, cinnamon, cornstarch, cocoa, and baking powder. Beat the egg yolks, hot water, and sugar at high speed with an electric mixer until the volume doubles, about 5 minutes.

6. In another bowl beat the egg whites until soft peaks form. Add the sugar and vanilla at low speed. Fold the egg whites and yolks together in a large bowl and gently fold in the dry ingredients.

7. Spray the springform pan with no-stick, place the cake batter in it, and bake at 350 degrees for 30 minutes. Cool on a rack for a few minutes, then remove sides of the pan and cool.

8. Whip the cream at high speed with an electric mixer until soft peaks form, and add the confectioners sugar and vanilla.

Assembly
2 Tbsp Kirschwasser
¾ cup cherry preserves
½ cup cherry preserves
4 oz bar German (or other)
    dark chocolate

9. Place the cake stand in front of you with the base on it. Spread the cherry preserves on the base. Cut the sponge cake in half horizontally with a bread knife. Place one half on the jam-coated base and sprinkle with Kirschwasser.

10. Add 2 cups of the whipped cream to the cherry filling and spread onto the cake layer. Cover this with the other half of the cake. Sprinkle more Kirschwasser on this layer and coat with whipped cream. Cover the sides with whipped cream and smooth it all with a spatula.

11. Place the remaining whipped cream in a pastry bag with a star tube and pipe out 16 stars on top of the cake. Place a Maraschino cherry on each star. With a vegetable peeler, make shavings from the chocolate bar onto a piece of waxed paper, and refrigerate before garnishing the cake.

Note: *This recipe was given to me by Hildegard Bahrdt, a German woman who works at my daughter's winery in Bockenheim, Germany. The recipe was passed down from her mother and is well worth the sometimes complex recipe. I have adapted the recipe to readily available American ingredients and measurements.*

PRIME MEAL 11

– First Course –
Sautéed Crabcakes with Remoulade Sauce

8 portions

1 lb jumbo lump crabmeat, fresh or pasteurized
1 egg
¼ cup mayonnaise
1 tsp minced garlic
1½ tsp dry mustard
2 minced green onions
½ tsp kosher salt
¼ tsp ground pepper
1 tsp Worcestershire sauce
Dash Tabasco sauce
½ cup panko crumbs

1 cup panko crumbs
¼ cup canola oil

1. Empty the crabmeat into a bowl, gently separate the meat, and pick out any cartilage.

2. Beat the egg in a bowl and add the mayonnaise, garlic, mustard, onion, salt, pepper, Worcestershire, and Tabasco. Gently fold the crab into the mayonnaise mixture along with the ½ cup of panko.

3. Mold the crab mixture into 8 crabcakes with your hands, squeezing gently so that it just holds together. Refrigerate until service time.

4. At service time, dip the crabcakes into the panko crumbs, covering both sides. Heat a large sauté pan and add half the oil. Cook the crabcakes at medium heat until golden and heated through, about 3 minutes per side. Cook in batches, adding more oil when necessary. Do not crowd.

Remoulade Sauce

½ cup mayonnaise
1 tsp capers, minced
½ tsp Dijon mustard
1 tsp minced garlic
2 sweet gherkin pickles, chopped
¼ tsp Tabasco sauce
1 lemon, zest and juice
2 Tbsp chopped parsley
½ tsp kosher salt
¼ tsp ground pepper

Combine the mayonnaise, capers, mustard, garlic, pickles, Tabasco, lemon zest and juice, parsley, salt, and pepper in a bowl and refrigerate. Serve on the side with the crabcakes.

– Wine Notes –
The dense, rich crab in this recipe needs to be matched by one of the excellent barrel-fermented Chardonnays from Long Island. From France, a white Burgundy or a Champagne would work fine.

– Entrée –
Chateaubriand au Poivre with Port Wine Sauce

8 portions

2½ lbs trimmed center
cut beef tenderloin
1 Tbsp kosher salt

Brown Stock
2 lbs veal marrow bones
1 chopped onion
2 chopped carrots
2 stalks celery, chopped

1 leek, white part, sliced
lengthwise
6 parsley stems
1 bay leaf
3 sprigs thyme
12 black peppercorns

1. Sprinkle the meat all over with the salt and refrigerate on a rack overnight (this is called a dry brine).

2. Place the veal bones in a small roasting pan and cook in a 425 degree oven for 30 minutes. Add the onions, carrots, and celery, and roast another 20 minutes.

3. Remove the bones and vegetables from the oven and transfer to a soup pot. Place the roasting pan on the stove and deglaze with 1 cup of water. Add this to the soup pot, along with enough water to cover the bones. Bring the stock to a boil, skim off any impurities, and simmer.

4. Tie the leek, parsley stems, bay leaf, and thyme together to make a bouquet garni. Add to the simmering stock along with the peppercorns. Continue simmering at low heat for 4 hours.

5. Strain and refrigerate overnight. The next day, remove the solidified fat from the top of the stock and pour the stock into a saucepan. Bring it to a boil and let it reduce to about 2 cups.

   Note: *Making a stock in this way may seem like too much trouble, but it will create a base for a magnificent sauce. You can eliminate this step and use commercial beef stock in the following sauce recipe, but it will not be the same.*

Cooking the Meat and Finishing the Sauce

1 Tbsp olive oil
2 Tbsp cracked peppercorns
1 cup chopped onion
½ cup chopped carrots
½ cup chopped celery

1. Let the meat come to room temperature, and rub off any excess salt with a paper towel. Brush it with the olive oil and coat it with the cracked peppercorns. Place the onion, carrots, and celery in a small roasting pan and put the meat on top of the vegetables.

Continued...

2 Tbsp butter
3 Tbsp flour
¼ cup minced shallots
¼ cup brandy
1 sprig rosemary

1 cup port wine
2 cups brown stock
   (from above)

2. Preheat the oven to 425 degrees, place the meat in the oven, and roast for 30 minutes. The internal temperature should read 100 degrees. Remove the meat to a platter and cover loosely with foil. Put the platter in a warm place and let rest for 20 minutes before serving.

3. Put the roasting pan on the stove and deglaze with 1 cup of water at high heat. Strain the drippings into a bowl and set aside.

4. Melt the butter in a saucepan and stir in the flour to make a roux. Add the shallots and continue cooking for 3 minutes. Stir in the brandy and rosemary.

5. As the brandy reduces, add the port wine, the brown stock, and the reserved drippings from the roast. Simmer the sauce for 20 minutes, remove the rosemary, and check for seasoning.

6. At service time, cut the chateaubriand into thick slices and serve with the sauce on the side.

Suggested Accompaniments for Chateaubriand

Sautéed Mushroom Caps

8 large mushroom caps
1 Tbsp butter

Heat a large sauté pan, add the butter, and cook the mushrooms until golden brown, and remove.

Roasted Tomatoes

8 small whole tomatoes
2 Tbsp panko crumbs
1 Tbsp Worcestershire sauce
1 tsp minced garlic
2 Tbsp olive oil

Cut the tops off the tomatoes and make a thin slice off the bottom so that they stand upright. Sprinkle with the panko, Worcestershire, garlic, and olive oil. Roast in a 425 degree oven for 15 minutes.

Roasted New Potatoes

8 small potatoes, skin-on
1 Tbsp chopped rosemary
1 tsp kosher salt
½ tsp ground pepper
1 Tbsp olive oil

For the potatoes, cut them in half (unless very small) and place them in a bowl with the rosemary, salt, pepper, and olive oil. Toss them in the seasoning and transfer to a foil-lined sheet pan. Roast in a 425 degree oven until tender, about 25 minutes.

Haricot Vert
(Green beans)

1 lb haricot vert
salt and pepper

For the haricot vert, trim the ends and cook in a steamer just before service and season with salt and pepper.

Arrange all the vegetables on the platter with the meat and serve.

– Wine Notes –
This is a big, festive meal, with a rich sauce. I would choose a Napa Valley Cabernet Sauvignon, a reserve Malbec, or a local Meritage blend.

– Dessert –
Raspberry Trifle

8 portions

Pound cake
½ **lb** butter
2 cups sugar
5 eggs

3 cups flour
½ **tsp** baking powder
½ **tsp** baking soda
1 tsp salt
¾ **cup** buttermilk
1 tsp vanilla extract

Trifle
½ **cup** sugar
¼ **cup** water
¼ **cup** lemon juice
2 Tbsp raspberry liqueur

1 cup raspberry jam
2 Tbsp raspberry liqueur
4 cups raspberries

2 cups heavy cream
2 Tbsp confectioners
 sugar

1 cup raspberries

1. For the pound cake, cream the butter and sugar for 5 minutes in an electric mixer, using the paddle attachment at medium speed. Beat in the eggs one at a time.

2. Whisk the flour, baking powder, baking soda, and salt together in a bowl. Combine the buttermilk and vanilla in another bowl.

3. With the mixer on low speed, add the flour mixture and the buttermilk mixture alternately, beginning and ending with the flour.

4. Spray 2 loaf pans with no-stick and divide the batter between them. Bake in a 350 degree oven for 55 minutes, or until a skewer comes out clean. Remove the cakes from the oven, cool slightly, and turn out onto a rack to cool. Wrap in plastic film and refrigerate.

5. To make the trifle, make a syrup by bringing the sugar, water, lemon juice, and raspberry liqueur to a boil. Remove from the heat and cool.

6. Combine the raspberry jam, and the raspberry liqueur in a bowl and carefully fold in the fresh raspberries and set aside.

7. Whip the cream in an electric mixer until soft peaks form and add the confectioners sugar.

8. To assemble the trifle, slice the chilled pound cake into ¾" thick slices. Cut the slices in half to make squares. Fill the bottom of a trifle dish with pound cake and brush with the syrup (or fill individual glasses).

9. Spread the raspberry mixture over this and then a layer of whipped cream. Repeat with two more layers and garnish the top with fresh raspberries. Chill for 2 hours before serving.

Note: *this pound cake recipe was adapted from Ina Garten and the trifle was adapted from Martha Stewart.*

Raspberry Trifle

POEM PERMISSIONS

PHOTO CREDITS

Katharine Schroeder

Page 31:   Pickled vegetables
Page 33:   Deviled eggs and caviar
Page 147: Crabmeat-stuffed beefsteak tomatoes
Page 186: Baked Mutsu Apples
Page 214: Peconic Bay scallop seviche
Page 249: Raspberry Trifle

Jay Webster

Page 162: Chowder Contest
Page 170: Chowder Contest trophy

Randee Daddona

Page 122: Family and friends eating lobster stew
Page 122: Plate of lobster stew

Sharron Russell

Back cover photo

All other photographs by John Ross

INDEX